MODERNIST FICTION, COSMOPOLITANISM, AND THE POLITICS OF COMMUNITY

In *Modernist Fiction, Cosmopolitanism, and the Politics of Community*, Jessica Berman argues that the fiction of Henry James, Marcel Proust, Virginia Woolf, and Gertrude Stein engages directly with early twentieth-century transformations of community and cosmopolitanism. Although these modernist writers develop radically different models for social organization, their writings return again and again to issues of commonality, shared voice, and exchange of experience, particularly in relation to dominant discourses of gender and nationality. The writings of James, Proust, Woolf, and Stein not only inscribe early-twentieth century anxieties about race, ethnicity, nationality and gender, but confront them with demands for modern, cosmopolitan versions of community. This study seeks to revise theories of community and cosmopolitanism in light of their construction in narrative, and in particular it seeks to reveal the ways that modernist fiction can provide meaningful alternative models of community.

JESSICA BERMAN is Assistant Professor of English and Women's Studies at the University of Maryland, Baltimore County. She has published articles on Virginia Woolf and Henry James. She was the organizer of the Tenth Annual Conference on Virginia Woolf: Virginia Woolf Out of Bounds.

MODERNIST FICTION, COSMOPOLITANISM, AND THE POLITICS OF COMMUNITY

JESSICA BERMAN

University of Maryland, Baltimore County

CAMBRIDGE
UNIVERSITY PRESS

PUBLISHED BY THE PRESS SYNDICATE OF THE UNIVERSITY OF CAMBRIDGE
The Pitt Building, Trumpington Street, Cambridge, United Kingdom

CAMBRIDGE UNIVERSITY PRESS
The Edinburgh Building, Cambridge CB2 2RU, UK
40 West 20th Street, New York NY 10011–4211, USA
10 Stamford Road, Oakleigh, VIC 3166, Australia
Ruiz de Alarcón 13, 28014 Madrid, Spain
Dock House, The Waterfront, Cape Town 8001, South Africa

http://www.cambridge.org

First published 2001

Printed in the United Kingdom at the University Press, Cambridge

Typeface Baskerville 11/12.5pt   *System* Poltype® [VN]

A catalogue record for this book is available from the British Library

Library of Congress Cataloguing in Publication data
Berman, Jessica Schifs
Modernist fiction, cosmopolitanism, and the politics of community / Jessica Berman.
p. cm.
Includes bibliographical references and index.
ISBN 0 521 80589 9
1. American fiction – 20th century – History and criticism.   2. Modernism (Literature) –
United States.   3. James, Henry, 1843–1916 – Political and social views.   4. Proust, Marcel,
1871–1922 – Political and social views.   5. Woolf, Virginia, 1882–1941 – Political and social
views.   6. Stein, Gertrude, 1874–1946 – Political and social views.   7. Politics and literature –
History – 20th century.   8. Literature and society – History – 20th century.
9. Internationalism in literature.   10. Community life in literature.   11. Modernism (Literature)

PS374.M535 B47 2001
813'.5209112 – dc21   00-067491

ISBN 0 521 80589 9

For Michael, Emma, and Aaron, of course

Contents

Acknowledgments

During the years of writing this book I have incurred many debts. I wish to acknowledge the generous support of the Mrs. Giles Whiting Foundation in the early stages of this project, the DRIF fund of the University of Maryland, Baltimore County, for a faculty summer stipend in its latter stages. I also thank the Chairs of the English Department of the University of Maryland, Baltimore County, Ken Baldwin and James McKusick, for the support that made completion of this book possible.

I also gratefully acknowledge the support of my colleagues in the English department at UMBC: Suzy Anger, Leeds Barroll, Raphael Falco, Joan Korenman, Lucille McCarthy, James McCusick, and Lena Cowen Orlin, whose mentoring in the hallways and via e-mail was both generous and invaluable. I am also deeply indebted to the members of the Women's Studies Co-ordinating Committee and to Rebecca Boehling, Marjoleine Kars, Joan Korenman, and Carole McCann in particular for being my intellectual community over the past five years. Thanks to Ed Ahearn for suggestions along the way and to George Levine for generously sharing his knowledge at the late stages and to Mark Hussey, Karen Levenback, and Vara Neverow for their encouragement of all things Woolfian.

This book owes its genesis to a remarkable series of teachers. First, I am grateful to Tony Arenella, Lindsey Chesbrough, and Judy Codding, whose efforts to create a participatory democracy and a "Just Community School" at the Scarsdale Alternative School taught me the personal and political importance of community. I thank Natalie Zemon Davis, whose spark propelled me towards history and academia, and Wayne Booth and Harry Harootunian, who shared both their example and their learning. I also have the privilege of expressing my deep gratitude to Françoise Meltzer, mentor and friend, who showed me how it's done.

Finally, there would be no book without the support of Louis and Katherine Fernandez, Katherine Salhus, and especially my parents,

Benjamin and Ellyn Schifs Berman. To Emma and Aaron and, always and forever, Michael, I am profoundly grateful.

My thanks also go to Ray Ryan at Cambridge University Press for believing in this project and to Rachel De Wachter, Leigh Mueller, and Hazel Barnes for seeing it through.

Portions of this book have appeared previously in print. An earlier version of part of Chapter 2 appeared as "Feminizing the Nation: Woman as Cultural Icon in Late James," *Henry James Review* 17 (1996): 58–76. An earlier version of part of Chapter 4 appeared as "Reading Beyond the Subject: Virginia Woolf's Constructions of Community," in Helen Wussow, ed., *New Essays on Virginia Woolf* (Dallas: Contemporary Research Press, 1995), 50–82. I am grateful to the publisher for permission to reprint "Of Oceans and Opposition: The Action of *The Waves*," from Merry Pawlowski, ed., *Virginia Woolf and Fascism* (London: Palgrave, 2001). For permission to reprint selections from the novels, diaries, and essays of Virginia Woolf, I thank The Society of Authors.

Excerpts from *The Waves*, copyright 1931 by Harcourt, Inc., and renewed 1959 by Leonard Woolf, and from *Orlando*, copyright 1928 by Virginia Woolf and renewed 1956 by Leonard Woolf, reprinted by permission of Harcourt, Inc. Excerpt from *The Essays of Virginia Woolf*, Volume II by Andrew McNellie, copyright © 1987 by Quentin Bell and Angelica Garnett, and from *The Letters of Virginia Woolf*, volume IV: *1929–1931*, copyright © 1978 by Quentin Bell and Angelica Garnett, reprinted by permission of Harcourt, Inc.

CHAPTER I

Cosmopolitan Communities

Most novels are in some sense knowable communities.
Raymond Williams, *The Country and the City*, 165

Is there a poetics of the "interstitial" community?
Homi K. Bhabha, *The Location of Culture*, 231

The political is the place where community as such is brought into play.
Jean-Luc Nancy, *The Inoperative Community*, xxxviii[1]

Walter Benjamin tells us in his celebrated essay, "The Storyteller," that, in the period after the First World War, "a process that had been going on for a long time" began to become apparent. "It is as if something inalienable to us ... were taken from us," he writes, "the ability to exchange experiences." This ability to exchange experiences is the storyteller's art. It is, for Benjamin, an art that is based not only on the possibility of imagining a community of listeners but also on the relevance of experiences of the past. In the First World War, "A generation that had gone to school on a horse-drawn streetcar now stood under the open sky in a countryside in which nothing remained unchanged but the clouds."[2] None of the past experiences of that generation prepared them to stand in that changed countryside; none helped them translate it into a story they could tell.

Speaking of a much earlier stage in this same process, Raymond Williams writes: "The growth of towns and especially of cities and a metropolis; the increasing division and complexity of labour; the altered and critical relations between and within social classes: in changes like these any assumption of a knowable community – a whole community, wholly knowable – became harder and harder to sustain." The question of the knowable community here, for Williams, is not simply a question of the object of scrutiny, of the complexity of the community-present as compared with the seemingly simpler community of the past.

Rather, it is a matter of shared perspective, "of what is desired and what needs to be known."[3] In the nineteenth century, for Williams, it is "a matter of consciousness" and of "continuing as well as day-to-day experience."[4] In the twentieth century, however, the connection of these two realms is seen to disappear. Social experience becomes fragmentary; the only community available seems to be the "community of speech."[5]

Both Benjamin and Williams imagine community as the crucial link between speaker and listener and thus as the underlying condition of storytelling. Both Benjamin and Williams also imagine community as the realm in which narrative and history coincide, the realm in which past experiences in common make possible a shared linguistic meaning. And both see, in twentieth-century Europe, the problem of the loss of this realm of the knowable, a loss which becomes for them a key experience of the narratives of modernism.

Fragmentation seems inevitable and intrinsic to modernist narrative. We recognize fragmented voices and fragmented identities as hallmarks of what has been called "high modernist" writing, whether we speak of their resolution into alternate patterns of meaning or dissolution in the crisis of the subject.[6] The transition from social to narrative form is often made to hinge upon this very issue. As Michael Levenson sees it, for example, "The dislocation of the self within society is recapitulated within modernist forms" which nonetheless present "the nostalgic longing for a whole self." In this model the community is either fully absent, or significantly present as a looming, oppressive force. The effort of modernist fiction then becomes the "effort to wrest an image of an autonomous subjectivity from intractable communal norms."[7]

In Williams's late essay, "When Was Modernism?" modernist fiction becomes associated with the institutionalization and restriction of its texts, a hurdle to be overcome on the way to a future community. Once again community as a possible subject of concern within the canon of European modernist fiction disappears. It becomes for Williams a problem of the post-modern and its potential, a problem of finding a new way back to the question of community: "We must search out and counterpose an alternative tradition taken from the neglected works left in the wide margin of the century, a tradition which may address itself ... to a modern *future* in which community may be imagined again."[8]

On the other hand, this book begins with the premise that in much high modernist fiction we can already see community being imagined over and over again. The demise of the knowable community, the

explosion of shared experiences of the past, the disruption of the meaning of old stories and of the possibility of new communicable experience,
become not only reflected but contested in the works of writers such as
Henry James, Marcel Proust, Virginia Woolf, and Gertrude Stein.
These writers engage directly with early twentieth-century historical
and political transformations of community, transformations that occasioned on the one hand an almost desperate effort to recoup community
in the form of nationalism and fascism, and on the other hand an
insistence on deepening cosmopolitanism. Although James, Proust,
Woolf, and Stein develop radically different models for social organization, their narratives consistently place the notion of community at
their core. Their writings return again and again to issues of commonality, shared voice, and exchange of experience, especially in relation to
dominant discourses of gender and nationality.

Yet the threat of totalitarian models of national community, whether
in the form of nativism, anti-Semitism, immigration restriction, proto-
fascism, or unmodified patriarchal dominance, looms large in the first
three decades of the century. It is in response to this threat that, I will
claim, community becomes linked to a cosmopolitan perspective in a
manner that revises and enriches both terms. The often-remarked
cosmopolitanism of these writers, then, seems less and less like personal
pique and more and more like creative opposition that leaves an
instructive social legacy in its wake. While these writers were not all
radical or even progressive, especially in their real-world politics, the
writings of James, Proust, Woolf, and Stein not only inscribe early
twentieth-century anxieties about race, ethnicity, and gender, but confront them with demands for modern, cosmopolitan versions of community.

This book thus takes on a dual project: first, to revise the theory of
community in order to insist that it respond to the narrative construction of that term, and in particular to the ways that modernist fiction can
provide meaningful alternative models of community. Homi Bhabha
and others have claimed that nationality must be seen as a narrative
process. So then, I argue, must community. Communities come into
being to a large extent in the kinds of stories of connection we have been
told or are able to tell about ourselves, the stories that Benjamin insists
are transformed by modernity. Before beginning the adjudication of
rights and responsibilities, or the espousal of shared public values, we
move in a realm of being-in-common that rests upon the border between "I" and "we," a border that may not necessarily coincide with the

political boundaries that surround us. In imagining this liminal zone as something other than simple statehood, the story of community comes into being. It is precisely this connection between narrative and the reconstruction of community that has not been addressed by either theoreticians of community or literary critics, and which I see as forcefully emerging within the modernist fiction in question.

Second, this book seeks to revise our reading of modernist fiction in order to expand our understanding of what is still too often derogatively termed "international modernism," and to demonstrate modernism's historical and political engagement with the dual question of community and cosmopolitanism.[9] This revisionary work has already been well begun on writers like Joyce, who lend themselves especially well to the concerns of post-colonial critics, but it has yet to be sufficiently undertaken with regard to writers who are less obviously enmeshed in the problems of empire – those in question here.[10] To that end, after this introduction each chapter begins with a section devoted to an historical field where questions of nationality and affiliation emerge. Rather than attempt to demonstrate the historical "cause" of the texts in question, this material highlights the broader discursive terrain in which they arise, and serves as a vehicle for what Susan Stanford Friedman has recently termed "cultural parataxis," the use of key juxtapositions in order to highlight the cultural ramifications of modernist texts.[11]

Chapter 2 first explores the development of the notion of the cosmopolitan within the American popular press at the end of the nineteenth century, especially as it comes to be connected to ideas about femininity in such magazines as *Cosmopolitan* and *Harper's Bazar*. From this vantage point, Henry James's late international fiction and his late commentaries on feminine voice and manners come to exemplify the paradoxical relationship among cosmopolitanism, nativism, and notions of the ideal woman within modernist discourse about America.

Chapter 3 begins by examining Proust's *A la recherche du temps perdu* in light of the radical French Zionist thought of Bernard Lazare, which has been so crucial to the political theory of Hannah Arendt. Lazare's category of "conscious pariahdom" speaks not only to political questions of Jewish identity but also to narrative questions about identity and community. By reading *A la recherche du temps perdu* against Lazare's thought, this chapter demonstrates how Proust's seemingly idiosyncratic fascinations with both parvenu and pariah, with hidden perversion and open voyeurism, may be seen as key terms in a coherent politics of marginality.

Chapter 4 first examines the connection between the model of community embodied in the British Women's Co-operative Guild and that found in Virginia Woolf's writing. This sense of relation she calls a "mosaic," implying by her use of that term not only a version of the psychologically decentered self as we commonly read it in modernist fiction, but also a model of a fractured yet coherent political life, one directly engaged with many of the same concerns as the Guild women. By reading *Orlando* and *The Waves* within the terms of this model and within the context of the British political crisis of 1929–31, Chapter 4 further demonstrates the anti-fascist, feminist model of community that arises in those novels. *The Waves* ultimately presents us with an alternative model of both community and action, one which serves as a countercurrent, marking and resisting the gathering of political force.

Finally, Chapter 5 begins by reading Gertrude Stein's narratives *The Making of Americans* and *Ida* within the context of American cultural geography at the turn of the twentieth century. It argues that Stein's writings ask us to read her focus on wandering literally, as expressions of the importance of geography, (dis)placement, and movement within the construction of subjectivity. The second half of this chapter connects this topographical model of identity to the grammatical reworkings of subjectivity in Stein's later prose. Stein's radical narratives may be seen not only to reconstruct the subject as nomadic and polyvocal, but also to challenge the dichotomy between community and cosmopolitanism implied by nationalism. It is in this sense that Stein's narratives become important to the contemporary discussion of social affiliation, especially in their constant return to the question of America. It is also in this sense that they raise the question of feminist nomadism as Rosi Braidotti describes it, and of feminist ethics as elaborated in the writings of Luce Irigaray and Tina Chanter.

This book is an interdisciplinary effort that seeks to bring politics, history, and geography to bear on the narrative construction of community. It seeks to further the discussion of the social contexts of modernist fiction in such books as Michael Tratner's *Modernism and Mass Politics* and James English's *Comic Transactions* not only through its attention to extra-literary discourse, but also through its emphasis on gender politics.[12] Far too frequently the issue of gender seems to slip out of sight, disappearing in an attempt to reach a more universal model of community. On the contrary, this book claims, the question of gender often becomes the pole around which spheres of community spin and collide, governing both their possibility and their politics.

Current political theory on community seems caught between the effort to argue universally and the recognition that real-world communities emerge primarily through local and specific commonalities. While aware of the difficulty of legislating for any particular common good, such as the golden rule, current new communitarian writings still promote specific liberal maxims (such as "strong rights presume strong responsibilities" and "the pursuit of self-interest can be balanced by a commitment to the community") and place them within the context of contemporary (usually North American) politics.[13] Meant to be an intervention in the multicultural drift away from the common values of a liberal democracy, communitarian thought clings to the political notion of the autonomous self that engages in communicative action and consensus-building as a second-order function of its consent to live in society.[14] Communitarians thus often consider gender and ethnic differences as part of a social experience appended to a core identity and privilege the public realm as the locus of political community. There is no recognition that community might grow even within the private sphere, as a part of identity-building itself, emerging from an imagined set of contingent relations between subjects who always already exist both in common and separately. Nor does communitarian theory fully account for the fluctuation of community belonging, where one day a community of women may command allegiance while the next day the conflicting demands of an ethnic or neighborhood group may be most compelling.

In much the same way, discourse-based theories of community, like Habermas's, present a utopian version of affiliation in the public sphere, where moments of communication serve to represent a clear set of shared values, rather than acting as crucial but contingent performances of the community itself.[15] It is in this sense, as this book will argue, that the modernist narratives in question here become instructive, highlighting not only the variety of responses that may be described as "community" but also the range of discursive versions of those communities that are distinctly not predicated on direct communicative speech or the transparency of the intention of the speaker. In fact, the common presumption within the modernist fiction in question here, that discourse is fraught not only with difficulty but also with the constant making and un-making of human inter-connections, provides the means by which these narratives will construct radically modern versions of community. It is in their transposition of this question of community from the domain of public citizenship and the state to a

liminal zone where community is both intimate and political, both local
and worldly, that these narratives will prompt a reassessment of the
relationship between community and cosmopolitanism. As Edward
Said suggests, "the formal dislocations and displacements of modernist
culture" as well as its encyclopedic forms, its juxtapositions, and its
ironic modes, emerge in part as a consequence of empire and thus from
the pressure of the world on previously self-enclosed communities.[16]
The response, I would argue, will be neither a simple retreat, nor an
attempt to shore up the traditional community (or its presumptive heir,
the imperial nation-state), but a re-engagement with the very relationship between community and world.

The relationship between community and world, however, enters
very little into the current discussion about community, particularly in
North America, which turns on the possibility of constructing public
versions of affiliation within a specific rights-based social system. The
liberal thought of John Rawls[17] remains the focus of debate for a wide
group of thinkers such as Michael Sandel, Amy Gutmann, and Iris
Marion Young, and thus limits their ability to see community as a
challenge to the punctual self at the center of Rawls's system and to the
nation state at its periphery.[18] Those more focused on sociological
critique, such as Amitai Etzioni, founder of the Communitarian
Network and editor of the journal *Responsive Community*, confine
themselves instead to American current affairs.[19] But current affairs
in Etzioni's version seem to have no relation to either a concrete
past or an intellectual history. Community for Etzioni seems to exist
primarily in the realm of the debate about the so-called "welfare
state" of the 1960s, and has little to say about its conceptual under-
pinnings.

But community as a term of debate within sociological and political
theory has a history far longer than the welfare state. Community has
often been seen as the mediating link between the subject and its
possibility for socially significant action as well as, for theoreticians from
J. S. Mill and Ernst Renan to Benedict Anderson, the key precursor to
national identity. Yet, in the nineteenth century, community was not
easily equated with the state; rather, *Gemeinschaft* was often seen to be in
conflict with *Gesellschaft* politics, its forms of affiliation an antidote to
alienating social organizations. For Marx, in *The German Ideology* and *The
Grundrisse*, ancient and medieval communities represent the historical
locus of the conflict between co-operative and antagonistic social forms,
already tainted by the family, its division of labor, and its claims of
ownership.[20] The emerging disjunction between civil society and the

state is already present in his early analysis of these forms of community, as is the estrangement of the people from the social power that ought to inhere in their affiliation. Still, in rescuing the possibility of community from the family or from the debilitating conditions of the division of labor, Marx will remain able to see community as the means by which the worker becomes world-historical, outside of the bounds of the state. As he puts it in *The Civil War in France*, the "commune, which breaks the modern State power, has been mistaken for a reproduction of the mediaeval Communes," but is instead a "new historical creation," one which is itself both the new realm of social relations and its first act.[21]

This transformative power is absent from much of the social scientific writing on community at the end of the nineteenth century. Writing in the 1880s Ferdinand Tönnies draws a nostalgic distinction between the small, rural community of the past, as characterized by inherent solidarity and unity of purpose, and contemporary society, which lacks all potential to create true bonds among its members. Tönnies's *Gemeinschaft* draws from a model of the family where bonds are indissoluble and relationships natural, and is firmly based in what we might call a "community of proximity," one which grows out of shared territory, blood ties, and constant interaction among its members, rather than shared values or interests. Even friendship, which for Tönnies is independent of kinship and neighborhood, relies on the face-to-face. "Spiritual friendship," he writes, "forms a kind of invisible scene or meeting which has to be kept alive by artistic intuition and creative will."[22] However, according to Tönnies, in the modern period of *Gesellschaft*, when no face-to-face community exists, even art becomes incapable of creating community.

On the other hand, Durkheim rejects this assumption that there can be no real solidarity or *Gemeinschaft* in modern industrial society. In the preface to the second (1902) edition of *The Division of Labor in Society*, he describes the secondary groups or corporations that will replace the communities of proximity as still to come, waiting in the wings much like Marx's commune of the future. For Durkheim they will constitute "the well-spring of all moral activity."[23] This is, however, still to come – Durkheim considers his contemporary world to be without "a whole system of organs necessary to social life (la vie commune)."[24] And, in *Le Suicide*,[25] Durkheim further retreats from his optimism about modern, "organic" society, calling for new communal relationships to counteract its tendency towards debilitating *anomie*.

For most twentieth-century social scientists, community remains the term for pre-industrial and not modern forms of affiliation, and thus for them is only obliquely relevant to twentieth-century social life or the modern nation-state. From Max Weber to Robert Redfield, whose influential study, *The Little Community*, appropriates the term for anthropological use, the same kind of nostalgia that pervades Tönnies's work is distinctly evident. Redfield, for example, defines the kind of "small community" he studies among the Mayan Indians of the Yucatán, as characterized by four qualities: "distinctiveness, smallness, homogeneity, and all-providing self-sufficiency." Although new versions of small communities may still be found within the modern city, Redfield argues that these qualities diminish as societies move towards urbanization. He describes urban societies in a distinctly negative light, calling them not only heterogeneous but also based in "impersonal institutions [and] what has been called atomization of the external world."[26] For Redfield, community is certainly not recuperated by the modern nation-state.

Thus it is somewhat anomalous for Benedict Anderson to depict the nation-as-imagined-community in terms of a continuous rise in the period from the beginnings of "print-capitalism" to the twentieth century.[27] Or, what becomes clear is that Anderson relies on a political tradition in many ways distinct from theoretical elaborations of community *per se*. While community may be necessary to late nineteenth- and twentieth-century European ideas of nationality, nationality is not necessary to ideas of community and it is a failure of Anderson's work to see it as such.[28] However, what Anderson makes clear is the historical conjunction of these terms within European discourse of nationality from Mill and Renan on, and the degree to which modern notions of the nation-state depend upon these conjunctions. Thus in the late nineteenth century the idea of community becomes appropriated by the need to imagine the nation as "the clearly expressed desire to continue a common life" rather than some more concrete combination of language, race, and history.[29]

Yet, within the American pragmatic thought of George Herbert Mead and John Dewey we find a means of imagining community and its relationship to public structures of belonging as both potentially modern and transformative, one which Anderson notably avoids. For both Mead and Dewey, community is reconceived as a central category of experience, one which cannot be relegated to a pre-industrial past, completely distinguished from any conception of the (social) self, or appropriated by the national idea. Their pragmatic thought thus imagines the self as always implicated within circles of affiliation while those circles are conceived as contingent and overlapping. In this manner, Mead and Dewey may be said to present, in the early to mid years of the twentieth century, what is often mis-understood to be a post-modern condition, that of incomplete and relational selves seen in fluctuating political association. In fact, it will be the argument of this book that, in much the same manner and in response to many of the same historical pressures, modernist fiction will also often pre-figure this dimension of what we too easily term "post-modern thought." Thus, in this sense, both the pragmatic inscription of a relational self and the modernist narration of community serve to challenge the absolute division between modern and post-modern culture, especially as it concerns models of social organization and political life.

Writing in 1913, Mead argues that the self cannot exist in consciousness as a subject but only as an object of memory and observation – a claim that resonates deeply with the narrative construction of self in Proust and Woolf, among others. The individual only comes to perceive his/her existence in a social context, as that "me" who is acted upon by others and is remembered to have interacted with the social world: "The self which consciously stands over against other selves thus becomes an object, an other to himself, through the very fact that he hears himself talk, and replies."[30] For Mead, the subject is constituted by its experience within society, and is inconceivable, both metaphysically and politically speaking, without it. The most glaring error, he claims, in liberal political theory is the idea of the individual in a state of nature, or "the common assumption ... that we can conceive of the individual citizen existing before the community."[31]

Dewey makes this paradox of a socially constituted self more political, conceiving of the public realm as a "Great Community," itself comprised of an infinity of overlapping smaller communities or associations.[32] For Dewey, there can be no meaningful discussion of individuals and their relation to society, because neither term exists without the other. When we say "I think" we "accept and affirm a responsibility" that is always already social and political. We make clear that "the self as a centered organization of energy identifies itself ... with a belief or sentiment of independent and external origination."[33] When in later political writings Dewey emphasizes the development of the individual within community as a focus of education, therefore, he in no way conceives of the former as taking priority over the latter.

But in Dewey's critique of American democracy, national structures ultimately command more attention than the "domestic, economic, religious, ... artistic or educational" associations which he claims structure the moral life of citizens.[34] The private sphere of association never fully emerges as political and the Great Community comes to resemble national models of imagined community. It is in its indebtedness to this pragmatic tradition that the current communitarian thought of Michael Walzer and Charles Taylor, for example, derives both its assumptions about the social embeddedness of the liberal citizen and its focus on the national public sphere.[35] Walzer's *Spheres of Justice* addresses the question of group membership by referring constantly to the national community as "the community," as though there can be no other with significant claims on citizenship or the construction of justice.[36] The possibility of inscribing differences, or of accounting for citizens' overlapping loyalties or contingent affiliations, recedes. Equally inaccessible is the means by which we might begin to instantiate any recognition of group identities or rights within this system, if the community that is the basis for justice is always already the national community.

On the other hand, Charles Taylor's "politics of recognition" is grounded in a dialogic notion of identity whereby self-understanding is constructed and perpetuated in common with others. It thus incorporates the private community into its attempt at the universal. "My discovering my own identity doesn't mean that I work it out in isolation, but that I negotiate it through dialogue, partly overt, partly internal, with others... My own identity crucially depends on my dialogical relations with others."[37] Yet, despite his insistence that this dialogical construction of identity is ongoing throughout life (and therefore provides both the basis and the need for a politics of recognition of and by others), Taylor seems to want to limit our community identities to those that may be expressed as externally coherent and stable wholes. This is apparent in his discussion of our embedded identities: "Consider what we mean by *identity*. It is who we are, 'where we're coming from.' As such it is the background against which our tastes and desires and opinions and aspirations make sense."[38] Of course some aspects of this background will shift over time – yet, for Taylor background is static enough to be given a name, to be assumed worthy and accorded respect as an entity in its own right. In this sense when Taylor writes of the politics of recognition it is mainly for established cultural groups already active within the public sphere and seemingly unified in perspective, needs, and "worth," such as the French speakers in Quebec.

It might be said that Taylor's cultural groups are as much a myth as the notion of the monologic, "punctual" self of the Enlightenment that he himself debunks.[39] His "politics of recognition," while admirable, thus falls short of reimagining community as a mediating link between the dialogic self and the nation, or as the entrance into politics within both public and private spheres.[40] Surely the model of the politics of recognition falters when it does not account for differences *within* publicly recognized groupings or for the provisional quality of those groupings, whether in terms of their relationship to self-identity or simply as social entities in their own right. Because of this mode of identifying groups in need of public recognition, Taylor also seems unable to account for the myriad of differences within the so-called dominant culture.[41] Instead, Taylor's focus on cultural groupings as coherent political players in the public sphere demonstrates that he conceives of the state as a "social union of social unions,"[42] as Rawls puts it, only one where recognition of this fact is conceived of as a good rather than just a means.

This restriction of the political community to the question of the public sphere, and to a potential consensus among competing group claims, rests upon what we might call a utopian bent within pragmatic thought. For Dewey, for Walzer, even for Richard Rorty, the consensus of opinion will expand with the expansion of the democratic conversation; the liberal community can hope, through reform, to mediate its differences and internal contradictions. As Chantal Mouffe puts it, "like his hero John Dewey, Rorty's understanding of social conflict is limited because he is unable to come to terms with the implications of value pluralism and accept that the conflict between fundamental values can never be resolved."[43] Thus Rorty's faith in the American national project rests on his assumption of a public conversation good enough to extend social justice to all, without needing to raise questions about the metaphysics of the self, the nature of difference, the possibility of communication or the inter-relation of the public and private spheres. In this last sense particularly he shares Habermas's utopian view of the capaciousness of public conversation and the autonomy of an idealized public sphere. This idealized public sphere, both for Habermas and for Rorty, must presume, as its starting point, the possibility of a shared conception of "we," yet neither thinker accounts for the metaphysics that makes that "we" possible.[44]

On the other hand, feminist thought, like other marginalized discourse, cannot afford to idealize the public sphere or its construction of belonging, even when it still wants to posit its possibility. The internal fissures within a seemingly stable political "we," the hazards of the universal, and the importance of politics outside of the public sphere are all key assumptions across a wide range of contemporary feminist theory. When, for example, Iris Marion Young or Seyla Benhabib attempt a re-working of the problem of community along feminist lines, the self and its wealth of connections is seen not only to limit social consensus but also to do so in a positive fashion. Thus Young critiques the "ideal of community" as represented within universalized communitarian theory as expressing a "desire for the fusion of subjects with one another which in practice operates to exclude those with whom the group does not identify ... [while it] denies and represses ... the fact that the polity cannot be thought of as a unity in which all participants share a common experience and common values."[45] Fusion is precisely what is refused by Young's model of the city as social paradigm or Benhabib's version of a narratively constructed, embedded democratic citizen.[46] Even when these feminist theorists aspire to universalizable paradigms of justice, therefore, they predicate them on the assumption of an infinite variety of private sphere affiliations that are themselves always political.

Benhabib revises the Habermasian notion of the communicative function of the public sphere in order to distinguish between the search for substantive consensus and the process of demonstrating willingness to seek understanding with the other. In other words, for Benhabib, the public sphere is the place where we demonstrate our cultivation of what Hannah Arendt terms "enlarged thinking" – our ability to reverse perspectives and reason from the other's point of view. This is a processual morality. As she puts it, "it is less significant that 'we' discover 'the' general interest, but more significant that collective decisions be reached through procedures which are radically open and fair to all."[47] In fact it is in the everyday "ethical relationships in which we are always already immersed" that Benhabib finds the source for public ethics.[48] Yet she insists nonetheless on public conversation as the crucial component in what she considers a revised "interactive universalism." She thus recapitulates the failing of the Habermasian model to account for a self as not only narratively constructed but always already social, even prior to entrance into conversation. She therefore also ignores the extent to which the narratives of self are implicated in the conversations of community – in other words to which the "web of stories" (to borrow an Arendtian phrase which Benhabib employs) that makes up our shared world always overlaps, borrows from, and revises the web of stories we call our selves.

It is in this arena that Jean-Luc Nancy's theory of community has much to offer, both to the contemporary political discussion of justice and to our understanding of the variety of possible modes of construing community in the early years of the twentieth century during the height of what we call "high modernism." Drawing from the Heideggerian notion of being-in-the-world, Nancy describes community as an essential condition of being, one which engages radically separate subjects in what he calls the process of "compearance." There is no doubt, in Nancy's work, about the possibility of being-together – but the blind faith that distinctly separate citizens will "somehow" discover their interactive potential that we see in both liberal consensus theory, and even the most revised of Habermasian models, is gone. At the same time by positing what he calls an "inoperative community" ("la communauté désoeuvrée"), Nancy also avoids the problem of substantive consensus about particular political ends that pervades so much new communitarian writing. He claims that "thinking of community as essence – is in effect the closure of the political. Such a thinking constitutes closure because it assigns to community a *common* being, whereas community is a matter of something quite different, namely, of existence inasmuch as it is *in* common, but without letting itself be absorbed into a common substance."[49] Community thus becomes not only processual in Benhabib's sense but integral to the experience of being itself. In the recognition of oneself as both embedded in a realm of association and bodily finite at the same time one comes to know both community and its limit.

Of course, as we have seen, this sense of an embedded or relational self was also present in pragmatic thought in the first half of the twentieth century. Yet what is different here is that Nancy positions community within a realm of play that not only supplants the categories of self and other, but never resolves into an entity that has an identity or performs tasks.[50] Community for Nancy is precisely the opposite, that which resists, that which undoes these kinds of groups because they falsely present community as an entity secondary to existence which is predicated on the free joining of separate subjects. The nation can never qualify as a community in this model; Dewey's notion of the "Great Community" is seen to be limited precisely because it consolidates into a separate entity what is by definition a condition of being.

It is for this reason that Nancy Fraser and others have taken Nancy's theory to be a retreat from the practical domain of politics.[51] Yet by refusing the community as such – whether in the form of the nation or the party – Nancy also extends its range far beyond the consensual public sphere. Political community thus becomes open to the varieties of "being-in-common" that are often relegated to the margins of the national discussion and to the kinds of voices, such as those often present within fictional narratives, that seem to speak outside of politics in general. Political community may thus also be seen to apply to narrative performances of community that never seek to enter mainstream political life or engage in legislative action – in other words, to the kind of political communities that are created by the modernist fiction in question in this book.

Further, Chantal Mouffe makes clear how this abstract exploration of community is immediately relevant to real world politics. Though community may not exist to perform *a* work, or reach a consensus, it nonetheless can articulate shared political perspectives when they arise, and insist upon the need for common (though contingent and fluctuating) political identities. This in no way implies a return to an established consensus, which must always resist the infinite plurality of social voices and the many spheres of affiliation within which Mouffe understands human subjects to move. "In order to impede the closure of the democratic space, it is vital," she claims, "to abandon any reference to the possibility of consensus that, because it would be grounded on justice or on rationality, could not be destabilized. To believe in the possibility of such a consensus, even when it is conceived as an 'infinite task' is to postulate that harmony and reconciliation should be the goal of a democratic society."[52] Such harmony and reconciliation is precisely that which is impossible and that which silences the very plural voices which it is supposed to protect. It is the version of community that leads towards uniformity and totalitarian nationalism. It is the kind of community that in a variety of ways the narratives in question in this book will contest.

This kind of consensus also raises for Mouffe the question of social and political borders and the concern that any "we" also always announces a "they," an enemy.[53] Though she does not say so, Mouffe thus also connects the radical democratic perspective to the possibility of a new cosmopolitanism, one that relies on the contingency of borders to open the community to a wider network of differences. The gap widens between the theory of community and that of nationality, between a politics of connection and that of the modern nation-state. Radical community begins to figure as an antidote to the consolidation of social identity rather than its reason for being, and comes to demand a cosmopolitan perspective as a function of its very refusal of universality.

This notion of cosmopolitanism as a function or outgrowth of a radical deconstructive community looks distinctly different from traditional Kantian versions.[54] Martha Nussbaum's revised Kantian cosmopolitanism is important in that, as will this book, it recognizes the ethical and political claims of literature as formative of and inseparable from real world relations.[55] Nussbaum places human identity within a series of concentric circles, beginning from self, then moving out through family to neighbors, local groups, fellow countrymen – to which she adds the categories of "ethnic, linguistic, historical, professional, gender, or sexual identities" – and finally humanity as a whole. Thus we are both local and universal at once.[56] But a concentric set of circles still presumes not only a core self at the center, but the coincidence of the sets of affiliation that make up our social identities. Social divergences or antagonisms, between cultural groups, or simply between past and present versions of ourselves, are unilaterally swept away (where?). Provisional communities, such as those created out of limited performances of gender identities or life roles, disappear. Location becomes an obstacle to the universal, at best only a coloring of one of the rings of our existence – and never the kind of ubiquitous concern with geography that we will find in such cosmopolitan writers as Gertrude Stein.

On the other hand cosmopolitanism as a corollary of the kind of community both Nancy and Mouffe posit retains space for the local context of identity because it refuses the category of the universal. If the community creates itself as a recognition of both affiliation and its limits at once, and as both bordered and always subject to dispersal, then it will not lend itself easily to the reified boundaries of the nation-state. Rather than a series of concentric rings situated around the (universal) human subject, what we might call a "cosmopolitan community" would imagine, as the matrix of both self and community, overlapping webs of relation, some clearly woven out of local affiliations. Cosmopolitan communities then might in a sense be rooted,[57] might arise out of what Homi Bhabha refers to as the locations of culture and allow for what Arjun Appadurai calls the crucial sense of the locality "as a structure of feeling, a property of social life, and an ideology of situated community," while still in a very crucial sense remaining un-bordered.[58] If, as Bruce Robbins contends, "instead of an ideal of detachment, actually existing cosmopolitanism is a reality of (re)attachment, multiple attachment, or attachment at a distance,"[59] then the communities commanding such attachment may be described as cosmopolitan communities.

When Bhabha writes of the cosmopolitan condition, he alludes to a process of motion, the traveling culture *à la* James Clifford, that enacts a series of "interconnected cosmopolitanisms" in the "ways people leave home and return."[60] The itinerant and iterative "I" of Bhabha's cosmopolitan citizen is not simply a migrant remaking her/himself in the movement between cultures or in the dissolution of the essential self into "an endlessly fragmented subject in process." Rather it is a self that comes into being in the moment between these two locations, in the moment of translation that occupies the interstices: "In the process of cultural translation there opens up a 'space-in-between,' an interstitial temporality . . . I want to try to occupy this hybrid, in between space . . . [with] the subject of a 'translational' rather than 'concentric' cosmopolitanism."[61] Thus translation functions as a metaphor for the liminal zone between the punctual and the fragmented self, between the self and its communities of affiliation, both past and present, as well as between the loyalties and allegiances demanded by those communities, both large and small.

Yet, the idea of translation also serves more directly to indicate the discursive nature of the movement between community and cosmopolitanism. Imagining the relationship between a radical deconstructive community and an itinerant cosmopolitanism means imagining the embedded self as engaged with writing her/himself into two stories at once. The nation, as Bhabha elsewhere claims, is not simply created in narration, but comes into being in the intersection of the performative and the pedagogical in the ongoing discourses of nationality.[62] The current performance of the national story requires (though is often impeded by) the exigencies of the ongoing national narrative. At the same time, we might add, this narrative mechanism itself must be seen as conditioned by both the discourses of community which it might contain and overlap and the other national narratives in circulation around it.

At the same time as we recognize national, communal, and cosmopolitan narratives as always already implicated in each other, we must also see them as particular discourses, spoken from a particular location at a specific moment in time. There can be no question of translation if we do not first speak a particular language; there can be no question of the intersection of current performance and past narratives of nationality, if we cannot tell the stories to begin with. The notion of the nomadic, or the migrant, self implies one without ideal origins, or one unified locus of social belonging. Yet each time that it begins again, the iterative "I" created in the narrative of this migrancy still arises in a particular place at a particular time.[63] Precisely because they arise from the notion of the self as always already embedded in social and discursive formations, these narratives of community, nation, and cosmos remain bound to, if not limited by, questions of location and history.

This brings us once again to the question of post-modern theory and its relationship to modernist texts. On the one hand we may be tempted to echo Calinescu's claim that post-modernism is the most "quizzical" of modernity's faces, "not a new name for a new 'reality,' or 'mental structure,' or 'world view,' but a perspective from which one can ask certain questions about modernity."[64] Increasingly persuasive claims have been made about the many stylistic and thematic continuities between the modern and the post-modern.[65] But it seems pointless to wedge all varieties of contemporary thought and experience into the category "modern" just as it seems illogical to claim that writers who consciously called their work "modern" – as did Woolf in her essay "Modern Fiction" – or who grouped themselves with others whom we have long understood to have shared aims, were really just post-modernists in disguise.[66] More persuasive is Paul Gilroy's claim that "much of what is identified as postmodern may have been foreshadowed, or prefigured in the lineaments of modernity itself."[67] Thus, the use of post-modern theoretical perspectives here is two-fold: to help illuminate previously hidden "lineaments" in modernist writing and to demonstrate the continuing relevance of some of its dimensions, even within significantly changed and still changing cultural milieux.

The question of location and history also returns us to Benjamin, to the parable of the storyteller with which this chapter began, and to the double sense of distance that intervenes between us and the storytellers of previous eras. Benjamin calls our attention to the scene of community and its relationship to time. The opening paragraphs of "The Storyteller" vacillate back and forth between metaphors of time and place weaving an intricate interconnection between them even as Benjamin describes our increasing remoteness from that scene. The storyteller "is by no means a present force,"[68] meaning that he is not available to the world after the First World War. Yet the problem is immediately one of distance conceived physically ("Entfernung"). The alien landscape, in which home is unrecognizable, is what silences him – the storyteller must be able to combine "the lore of faraway places . . . with the lore of the past, as it best reveals itself to natives of a place,"[69] and that is impossible if the lore of the past no longer seems to have any connection to the place of the present.[70] The result is that the storyteller has no experiences that are communicable; he can imagine no community where the narrative juxtaposition of the familiar with the modern makes sense. A new modern means of imagining community as well as a new means of communicating about the past and its relationship to the present, both near and far, becomes necessary.

In other words, for Benjamin, the specific events of the First World War irrevocably alter the place in which the story of community can be narrated, thereby also altering the way that we, removed yet again from the scene of face-to-face narration, tell that story. Community therefore emerges not only as something that is both expressed and perpetuated in narratives, but also something historically contingent, and concerned with its contingency, subject to variation in material circumstances as well as to reconceptualization in the minds of the people. In both its new manifestations and its old, it is also something inherently linked to the experience of geographical distance, for it operates in translating the experience of the faraway into a story that can be told in the here and now. What happens for Benjamin in the world after the First World War is that the past is like the faraway present, equally in need of translation.

This emphasis on the common situation of both the community's past and the other of its present returns us again to the notion of the cosmopolitan. The only way for the community to create itself anew is to retell both its own stories and those of other places, and to recognize in them their common relationship to their own past and to the lives of others. At the same time, the process of translation for Benjamin clearly demands more than recognition of commonality. For in translating one seeks not to represent in one's own language the ideas of another but to expand one's own language so as to be able to speak the other's thoughts.[71] Bhabha's notion of cosmopolitanism as translation thus finds its roots not only in the post-colonial situation of migrancy, but in the earlier Benjaminian account of modernity and its relation to storytelling. Modern narratives of community arise in the movement and translation of foreign experience (whether of the past or of a geographically distant place) into common experience and the concomitant and never-ending movement back towards the foreign experience that this process entails.

In different ways, in the writings of Henry James, Marcel Proust, Virginia Woolf, and Gertrude Stein, community is constantly created, re-worked, and perpetuated in tension with historical discourses of social identity and nationality and with the sound of other voices of experience echoing around and within those discourses. Community, in the writings this book will consider, is always seen as historically contingent, a story that must be begun again because of the disruption in shared experience that for these writers characterizes the opening decades of the century, but also because it must always be begun again, a matter of writing being-in-common and its limit, of narrating its constant interruption, and of inscribing the echo of other communities in the discord of the familiar. The tensions between pedagogical models and contemporary enunciations of community thus emerge in these texts as struggles with history, with the question of social identity, and with the tendency of the twentieth-century state to equate all community life with national life, and all allegiances as matters of the public realm.[72] The tension also emerges in these texts in the willingness to announce the community as both local and international, private and public at once. Thus the different notions of community created by James, Proust, Woolf, and Stein call into question many of the cultural assumptions that privilege the public realm and society at large as the one, unified locus of social belonging.

At the same time, within their experimental prose the texts in question often push towards community as that which is enacted in the interstices of narrative form, or in its grammar and figures. Whether in the way that, in *The Making of Americans*, Stein's pronouns wander, sometimes invoking a singular identity and sometimes a whole classification of beings in the word "she," or in the way that, in *The Waves*, Woolf's language dissolves boundaries, so that the very sentences run rapidly in alliterative streams, deftly avoiding the intervening sounds,[73] these novels insist on new forms of social interconnection. These formal inscriptions rarely represent a community conceived of as a whole, united under some banner or other, ready, as Nancy puts it, to perform some sort of work. Instead what is important about the social constructions in the texts in question is precisely the way in which the gathering of identity always remains partial and fleeting, and the modernist style employed by these writers serves constantly to endorse and to perform this fact.

The formal emphasis on partial or incomplete perspectives may indeed be what separates these modernist texts from their realist equivalents – at least so far as the construction of community is concerned. One of the characteristics of nineteenth-century realist fiction may be described as its insistence that we have been presented with a coherent and complete version of events from a perspective that we too are invited to share. As Elizabeth Ermarth puts it, "The genial consensus of realistic narration implies a unity in human experience which assures us that we all inhabit the same world and that the same meanings are available to everyone. Disagreement is only an accident of position."[74] There is a presumed (if perhaps "provisional"[75]) wholeness to the English community of a novel like *Middlemarch* and a presumed effort to extend the sphere of its influence. If, as Benedict Anderson has made clear, the nation as imagined community is "conceived in language,"[76] and, as Timothy Brennan points out, "the rise of European nationalism coincided especially with one form of literature – the novel,"[77] then we must consider realism's construction of narrative consensus as implicated in the imagining of the imperial nation-state.[78]

The modernist rejection of a communal moral perspective on a self-complete and linguistically well-ordered world, on the other hand, might be seen to imply a wholesale rejection of the politics linked to realism and consensus. But this is an argument that is clearly difficult to support across the broad spectrum of modernist writing. Presuming a specific politics from a generic narrative form is suspect – somewhat like presuming that free verse is always written about freedom. In this sense those who want to draw broad connections from a large body of texts to a specific political ideology often stray too far.[79] Forms lend themselves to a variety of political purposes. As the varying political positions among the authors in this study show, fragmented perspectives or experimental styles do not always coincide with the shattering of real-world political verities.

Yet in the rejection of narrative consensus there remain clear implications for reading the political engagement of modernist fiction as well as for recasting the idea of the political community with which we began. Without claiming that we can derive a specific political doctrine from a certain textual mode, we can nonetheless recognize the possibilities it makes available and the social assumptions that, in concert with other thematic and discursive elements, a particular text enables.[80] Thus if a text insists on the partialness of perspective, as Henry James's late novels increasingly do, we can understand its form to be undermining realistic consensus and to be questioning the self-complete communal perspective, thus making room for a mode of social organization outside of those available within the realist paradigm. It need not necessarily, however, insist on the opposite of consensus, that is, on the privacy of vision or the impossibility of establishing commonality. Rather, narrative form in late James may be seen to enact another, different version of commonality, one where limited perspectives begin the very movement towards community. In *The Ambassadors,* for example, community is partially constructed in the play between the several incomplete perspectives evoked by the text and the common recognition of the limitation of their interconnection, rather than in their (or our) shared consensus. This formal construction of community not only challenges dominant nineteenth-century versions of the term but also directly contests the notion of community as a matter of the public realm, and as constituted by an ideal form of communication, both transparent and complete.

Thus modernist fiction enacts notions of community that may be seen to undermine political versions of established consensus or the blind universality that lurks behind a Rawlsian veil of ignorance. In that sense it begins the unworking necessary for a less presumptive mode of politics, one which decenters belonging and challenges commonplace notions of the universal political subject. This challenge emerges most clearly within the domain of gender, where these texts most clearly present the masculine assumptions so often contained within the construction of universal political citizenship and natural community. When Woolf famously contends that as a woman she has no country, she is not simply proclaiming her cosmopolitan sympathies but also clearly remarking on her exclusion from the very idea of the citizen.[81] The universal citizen, no matter how theorized, remains tainted by its historical gender and racial construction. And, I would argue, the philosophical notion of the universal subject and therefore of universal conceptions of rights, responsibilities, democracy, or community, cannot be separated from this history. They are grounded in a white masculinist version of consensus, one which may be seen to be tied to the rise of the modern nation-state as well as to realism's narrative consensus.

Yet the effort to re-create the universal position as a new basis for political community continues. Feminists in the journal *differences* propose new versions of universalism, though now based in "interactive universalism, a universalism aimed at establishing some community of values based on a notion of dialogue rather than consensus."[82] As Seyla Benhabib claims in *Situating the Self,* "a post-Enlightenment defense of universalism, without metaphysical props and historical conceits, is still viable. Such universalism would be interactive not legislative, cognizant of gender difference not gender blind, contextually sensitive and not situation indifferent."[83] While one must invoke notions of community (as spheres of communication or as local spheres of limited consensus) in order to defend a post-modern universalism, this universalism still works contrary to the idea of cosmopolitan narrative communities. It must defend a stable notion of dialogue, as though the positions enunciated could be separated and opposed, placed into common allegiance, or simply enlisted in an ongoing conversation. In other words the notion of public speech is here not sufficiently complicated, nor is the question of interlocking discourses within the narratives in question sufficiently addressed. These insufficiencies are precisely what modernist narratives demonstrate to us, for it is immediately apparent how hard it would be to discern the interactive component of "interactive universalism" if it were to stem from a fragmented or self-undermining text. How the public conversation might then proceed would be equally unclear.

Furthermore, despite the appeal of achieving consensus on some small set of shared values, or even on the very notion of participating in a common endeavor itself, such universalism belies the difficulty of delimiting that shared domain. In this sense the difference of woman raises the question of the differences that have been drawn between public and private spheres, between public and private realms of identity and affiliation. Where public and private are clearly drawn, women and unworking communities would both traditionally belong to the private sphere, while interactive universalism clearly belongs in the public arena, meant to be a means of bringing women into the conversation. If we want to complicate those divisions between spheres, as Nancy Fraser, Seyla Benhabib, and Drucilla Cornell all want to do, then the public conversation must also go private, which might mean, in a discursive sense, hermetic, non-transparent, and often non-referential. This kind of "private" discourse would lie outside Benhabib's scene of interaction, though not necessarily outside the realm of community. Here again, the question of modernist textuality becomes instructive. Any attempt to situate Gertrude Stein's surrealist love lyrics within a universal interactive politics, for example, seems immediately absurd.

Drucilla Cornell has recently approached this problem by appealing to the process of translation – that very process evoked by Benjamin in "The Storyteller" – in order to re-cast what she calls "the moral reminder of the universal":[84]

The task that cultural difference sets for us is the articulation of universality through a difficult labor of translation; the terms made to stand for one another are transformed in the process and the movement of that unanticipated transformation establishes the universal as that which is yet to be achieved and which, in order to resist domestication, may never be fully or finally achievable.[85]

Her version of universality, therefore, becomes less a question of consensus about the freedom, equality, and independence of human citizens than the process of speaking about these ideals between cultures, genders, and statuses. Yet, she makes clear that this process can only begin after the hierarchy of these positions and the specific historical construction of what it means to be "men" have been dismantled. Thus while Cornell's model is appealing in its ability to circumvent the question of difference and to make an appeal to universalism via a "reciprocal relativism"[86] of genders and cultures, it is still utopian in its vision. The difficulty of avoiding the historical construction of "men" remains; the universal cannot escape so easily the use that has been made of it.

Thus I want to argue that the feminist question of difference immediately evokes the challenge that community poses to the very category of the universal, and ought not be recuperated within it.[87] Benhabib's dialogue as a new model for public speech inadequately addresses the question of the position of the speakers and the problem of transparent discourse. At the same time, Cornell presumes the possibility of translating conversations about freedom and equality without also translating the limiting cultural histories lurking within those conversations. If instead we presume, as does Chantal Mouffe, that even this level of harmony implies an outside, an enemy left at its fringes, beyond the rules of the conversation, then we risk recapitulating the failings of the liberal communitarians. Community, as situated within a political world predicated on the need for constant translation between and among individual speakers and the discourses of provisional communities, and on the impossibility not only of consensus but also of discursive harmony, might, on the other hand, open itself to a new cosmopolitanism.

It will be clear that in emphasizing the role of female difference in the rewriting of community I am not advocating the kind of community that has been called an "ethics of care," nor am I using the figure of the "web" as a particularly feminine affiliative dynamic, however compelling that figure may be.[88] For one, this would oppose community to "masculinist" principles of justice in a manner that places justice beyond the reach of the conversation, just where I do not want it to go.[89] Second, though valuable on many levels, these perspectives often recreate gender as a universal category, as suspect as any other. It will be clear from the writing in question that such universal gender categories are precisely what the authors I study often call into question, especially when they broach the role of the homosexual.

Indeed, the constructions of community in these narratives often work to examine, critique or undermine the myth of Woman and its surrounding gendered categories, as well as the construction of the homo/heterosexual opposition.[90] The question of what defines a woman's voice will come to be identified in Henry James's writings with the feminized construction of late nineteenth-century American cosmopolitanism, whereas in Proust's writings the question more often hinges on communities that belie heterosexual identities. In order to posit in Proust's work a pariah community that is marked by Jewishness and/or homosexuality, I rely on a notion of community constructed out of the shattering of the illusion of the exemplary, in several different social domains. The pariah homosexuality that emerges in Proust is never a community as such – yet it offers the most compelling scene of shared, if often hidden, experience that is present in the novel.

Nor am I greatly concerned here with the many real-world communities which to a greater or lesser extent claim the loyalties of these writers. Modernism, it must be clear, was a cultural mode especially given to manifestos.[91] These manifestos seek to create, challenge or defend not only particular modes or perspectives but also communities of artists who share those perspectives. Thus when Woolf in "Character in Fiction" divides writers into two camps – the Edwardians (Wells, Bennett, and Galsworthy) and the Georgians (Forster, Lawrence, Strachey, Joyce) – she does so not only to combat the view of character seen in novels by the Edwardians, but also to align herself with character as it emerges in the work of the Georgians. Yet how many among Forster, Lawrence, Strachey, and Joyce would create Mrs. Brown in the corner of her railway carriage just as Woolf presents her to us, the source not only of modern fiction but also of "life itself"?[92] Woolf's sense of commonality with these writers, I would argue, is more about how we should read her own work than about how we should read Lawrence. The artistic community she creates for herself provides an imagined context for readership, rather than a real-world bond in the creation of a common project. Thus the manifesto may be thought of as another version of the narrative enactment of community, which ought not be bound by the real-world relationship (or lack thereof) among artists.

Further, because I argue that community is performed in its narratives and is not derived from an originary position or outside source, I restrict myself to those narratives. Thus while the James family, or

Bloomsbury, or Stein's salon all make fascinating study, they rarely concern me here. I include these "real-world" communities as part of the conditions of authorship of these novels, but not as the benchmark by which to judge them. In this sense too, I would claim, I avoid limiting the possibilities of community enacted in these novels to the political positions espoused by their authors.

But any study concerned with what I'm calling "high modernism" must come to terms with the fact that these writers generally perceived themselves and their art as part of "high culture." If we are to examine these texts in relationship to each other and to their cultural situation, we must accommodate this self-understanding. As Andreas Huyssen long ago made clear, the divide, or at least the appearance of the divide, between high and low culture is a key feature of "high modernism," both in the way it perceived itself and in the way that it was canonized in the period after the Second World War. Yet as Huyssen claims, "modernism's insistence on the autonomy of the art work, its obsessive hostility to mass culture, its radical separation from the culture of everyday life, and its programmatic distance from political, economic, and social concerns was always challenged as soon as it arose."[93] It is this challenge which I explore here, without negating the elitism that also often permeates these texts.[94]

Huyssen's discussion of the relationship between a masculinist version of high modernism and an excluded, feminized mass culture, however, points to another means of entering the debate. Seen through the filter of gender, the authors in question here hardly seem such unambiguous members of the club. In all the works examined in this study, culture is either at risk of becoming, or has already become, feminized. Huyssen claims that what is at issue in this exclusionary dichotomy is not the subversive gender subtext of these works, but rather the "universalizing account of modernism that has been able to hold sway for so long."[95] Yet another reason for examining James, Proust, Woolf, and Stein is to see how gender constructs in these authors' works serve to undercut both that universalizing account and the dichotomies (male/female; high culture/low culture; public/private; individual/community; nation/cosmos) that help sustain it. In this sense community serves here as a means not an end. Because it is both a component of one of these dichotomies and a participant in all of them, it provides a particularly good lens through which to re-examine our assumptions about the categories of modernist fiction.[96]

In another way Houston Baker's discussion of the alternative modernism of the Harlem Renaissance and Paul Gilroy's notion of the Black Atlantic, among others, also challenge us to specify not only what version of modernism we are discussing but also what social and cultural perspective it elaborates. They require us to reject the blind universalism often implied by our definitions of modernism as well as to challenge the pretensions to universality often found within them.[97] Further, while cosmopolitanism in these texts may often look like a gesture towards simple universality, espoused by writers within the intellectual cadres of Bloomsbury or the Left Bank who were privileged enough to feel themselves to exist without boundaries, it frequently hides an intense effort to specify the location and limitation of that cosmopolitanism. In other words, the world does not simply occupy the outermost circle of a concentric cosmopolitan perspective; the local community colors, shapes, and constrains the ways the world can be imagined. The most engaged of these modernist texts often espouse what K. Anthony Appiah has called a "rooted cosmopolitanism," one which is as implicated in the question of belonging as in universal detachment. As Stein famously remarked, "there's no point of roots if you can't take them with you."[98] In the modernist texts here discussed, the question both of roots and of where you take them is always at stake.

Thus modernist fiction becomes immersed in the politics of connection, in the performance of affiliation already on the brink of dispersal. This performance often creates radically new forms of cosmopolitan communities. It always engages with the inadequacies of dominant categories of affiliation, especially regarding gender and nationality. Seen in this context, modernist fiction challenges our ability to restrict social identity to civic consensus or the public politics of recognition, and becomes an instructive narrative model of how we can begin to imagine community anew.

CHAPTER 2

Henry James

"THE HISTORY OF THE VOICE": *COSMOPOLITAN*'S AMERICA

> The world is my country and all mankind are my countrymen!
>
> Masthead, *Cosmopolitan*, 1886

> Internationalism is on the increase... The creation of an international language would undoubtedly result in immense advantages to trade, commerce and labor, and to literature its service would be infinite.
>
> Maltus Questell Holyoake, "A Cosmopolitan Language," *Cosmopolitan* 14.1 (Nov. 1892): 19

> We don't want to fight, but by Jingo, if we do,
> We've got the ships, we've got the men,
> We've got the money, too!
>
> British popular song, *c.* 1876

Launched in the publishing euphoria that gripped the nation in the 1880s and 1890s, as new printing machinery and new trademark law revolutionized the industry,[1] *Cosmopolitan* exemplified an America newly enamored of worldly perspectives. Emblazoned on its cover for 1886, beneath its world-embracing slogan, was a picture of the newly completed Statue of Liberty, beckoning its readers into its pages as though into the bosom of the nation. On the cover of the magazine the statue stood not only for America's still open door, but for the magazine's vision of itself as various in its perspective and far-reaching in its content.[2] Its advertisements for 1887, the coming year, promised: "The Finest American Stories; Powerful Stories from the Russian; Brilliant Stories from the French; Beautiful Stories from the German; Striking Stories from the Dutch and Italian." Whereas the *Century* proclaimed it

"The world is my country and all mankind are my countrymen!" Masthead
Cosmopolitan, 1886. Reproduced by permission of the collections of the Library of
Congress.

was a "National Magazine" and that it would both restrict its use of foreign stories and appeal to "the broadest patriotism,"[3] readers of *Cosmopolitan* were enticed with the prospect of "Travels and Adventures to every country of the World: Strange Peoples! Queer Beliefs! Wonderful Scenery!"

Like the *Cosmopolitan* magazine that is its legacy, the original *Cosmopolitan* was, in part, directed at women, the main readers of general interest periodicals in the period.[4] It had no aspirations to be a new *Atlantic Monthly*, promising "No long and tedious articles ever published." Nor, however, did it seek to enter the ranks of the women's weeklies that catered to the practical interests of homemakers. As a monthly magazine, priced just below the level of the well-established *Century* and *Harper's*, *Cosmopolitan* called itself a family publication, providing a broad range of general-interest fiction, travel writings and social commentary that was meant to appeal to both men and women. Its success betokens the power of the mix;[5] its attitudes about America represent the immensely popular perspective, in the last decades of the nineteenth century, that the nation could be both open to travel and resolute in its national pride.

Yet the mix did not remain so simple or so easy to sustain over the course of the 1890s. The problem of creating a cosmopolitan nation, if we may call the vision of *Cosmopolitan* precisely that, runs afoul of both the Spanish–American War and the inward turn of American journalism in the 1890s, ending in the perpetual muckraking that marks the magazine in the early twentieth century. Once bought by Hearst, the magazine is international in title only. While it becomes a center for the new "sensationalist and quasi-socialist" journalism, its forays into foreign diplomacy, as well as into new roles for women, are well over.[6]

Thus the history of the magazine marks the possibilities and limitations of American cosmopolitanism in this period. It represents the wanderlust and desire for exotica that also fuels the expansion of worldwide exploration, the establishment of journals such as *National Geographic* (1888), and the fervor over the Chicago World Columbian Exhibition in 1892. It demonstrates the increasing interest in regional "social problems,"[7] including both the condition of African-Americans in the South and the lifestyles of European immigrants in the northern cities. It also displays the obsession with the international status of American womanhood, from articles on American "beauties" both at home and abroad, to Olive Shreiner's celebrated 1899 article on "The Woman Question."[8] Yet over the course of the period, in the pages of the magazine, wanderlust becomes tainted with expansionism, and the national begins to takes precedence over the worldly. "Race," always a frequent, if loosely employed, term, begins to take on new power,[9] coupled with newly racialized attention to women as progenitors and protectors of a new American people. While *Cosmopolitan* still means "having the whole world as one's country," it becomes newly suspect as a justification for open immigration and for the mongrelization of America. The Statue of Liberty, so prominent in *Cosmopolitan*'s early issues, disappears from its later pages, its symbol no longer a clear and guiding light into the promise of American identity.

It is not a surprise then to find women at the heart of the matter, and not simply because they are among the primary readership of the magazine. In a period characterized by contemporaries as "the Era of Woman"[10] and by current critics as that of the "feminization of America,"[11] women represented the potential of the nation, as well as its failings. As much as the pages of *Cosmopolitan* attest to the appeal of the ideal feminine virtues of grace, dignity, gentleness, and charm coupled with physical loveliness, they become the means by which thorny issues about race and nationality are broached. By raising new standards of beauty for a new and evolving American race, *Cosmopolitan* writers evoke the very question that will later drive the debate on immigration restriction.[12] And in discussing the fact that women who marry abroad are often accused of rejecting democracy,[13] the magazine raises the problem of communal identity and loyalty for those who insist on cosmopolitan lives. The question of ideal cosmopolitanism, in the first years of this magazine, hinges on the paired virtues of community and worldliness as evidenced in the body, attitude, and especially the voices of its women.

It is in this light that the history of feminized cosmopolitanism, as constructed in the pages of *Cosmopolitan* magazine, will also coincide with the development of cosmopolitanism in the later writings of Henry James. While in the 1890s already long an ex-patriot, James continues to respond to and participate in the development of American culture, especially in relation to its national self-conception. While it may be said that his literary life centers on London and Paris in this period, James's presence is felt often in the pages of *Cosmopolitan* magazine, whether in the common invocation of Daisy Miller within the portraits of Americans abroad, or in references by others, like William Dean Howells, who edits the magazine in 1892. James himself appears directly, contributing both short stories and biographical sketches in the 1890s and even showing up as the first author pictured in an article celebrating "The Making of an Illustrated Magazine."[14]

But it is in its struggle to perpetuate cosmopolitanism as an enlightened national identity, tied not only to the proliferation of perspectives but also to their specific unification in feminine language and behavior, that the magazine's cosmopolitanism coincides with the version present in James's late writings. Even as, in the United States, the term becomes challenged by the expanding dogmas of nationalism and of "race improvement," the possibility of defending it becomes ever more tied to the problem of women and their speech. These are precisely the constellation of concerns that lurk in many of James's stories from the 1890s on, in his late international novels, and in his 1905–6 essays on the *Speech and Manners of American Women*. While we cannot say that James, who thrived in the cosmopolitan literary circles of London and Paris, and flirted in the 1890s with Paul Bourget's version of the "cosmopolis," was engaged *solely* with the American context, his particular emphasis on female language and behavior, and on the community identity they betray, nonetheless brands him as particularly American. James's cosmopolitanism, this chapter will argue, arises from a complex interplay of ideas about community and cosmopolitanism which are in circulation both in Europe and in the United States from the 1890s through the first years of the twentieth century. The late international writings thus may be seen as crucial entries in a discursive battle over the meaning and possibility of cosmopolitanism, which hinges, particularly in the United States, on the insistently paradoxical relationship among cosmopolitanism, nativism, and notions of the ideal woman.

The tension between the local and the universal inhabits the history of the term "cosmopolitan" from its beginnings in Western thought, and re-emerges again and again in its successive incarnations. In Western political thought the notion begins out of the conception of the *polis* as a small civic unit where community arises from the face-to-face relations of family and friends,[15] yet which remains in need of civil associations beyond the local. For Aristotle the *polis* seems to bridge the gap between a political entity with abstract concern for justice, both natural and practical, and the more immediate necessity of friendship, in other words between civil society and community: "Friendship also seems to be the bond that holds communities together... Between friends there is no need for justice, but people who are just still need the quality of friendship."[16] Community is thus a supplement of justice, and, as such, determines the loyalty of citizens first and foremost to their families and associations, and then to the *polis* to which those associations belong.[17]

Smallness is therefore crucial in both the *Ethics* and the *Politics*. Aristotle writes at a time when Alexander and others were already dreaming of a wider state, and this is reflected in the glimmers of cosmopolitanism to be found in the *Ethics*.[18] While Aristotle nowhere directly sanctions Alexander's strategies of conquest and maintains from the outset that there can be no universal justice, both his *Politics* and his *Ethics* demonstrate his cognizance of the importance of the realm beyond the *polis*, and thus of the dual demands of both community and cosmopolitanism.

The development of a specific philosophy of the cosmopolis as a single community, however, dates from the writings of the Stoics. The *Republic* of Zeno, to follow Plutarch's commentary on it,

> may be summed up in this one main principle: that all the inhabitants of this world of ours should not live differentiated by their respective rules of justice in separate cities and communities, but that we should consider all men to be of one community and one polity, and that we should have a common life and an order common to us all.[19]

According to the Stoics, the demands of civic duty compel man to act in the realm of the world at large. The unity of all men as rational beings within the universe, and as common citizens of the mortal realm, demands that the universe function as if it were a "single polity."[20] Thus the distinction between community and cosmopolis is presumed to have fallen away as the cosmopolis is seen to subsume and supplant the community.

This conflation of terms also lurks behind Seneca's phrase "the whole world is my country," which has become the modern mantra of cosmopolitan thought.[21] With the influence of Seneca on early modern and modern Europe we see how this emphasis on the cosmos as community enters eighteenth- and nineteenth-century notions of cosmopolitanism. Yet we can easily see the tension between the local and the universal re-emerge. In the thought of the French *philosophes* the *esprit cosmopolite* becomes a universal humanism, where the rights of man extend beyond national borders and where the European community exerts claims that go beyond the duties of the citizen. The concern for republicanism also focuses on more local concerns; Montesquieu's *esprit géneral* develops out of the national past and local customs and manners.[22] For Kant, cosmopolitanism appears as a specific antidote to the rule of despots, and the "barbaric freedom of established states."[23]

In the 1784 essay, "The Idea for a Universal History from a Cosmopolitan Point of View," Kant states, "The greatest Problem for the human race, to the solution of which Nature drives man, is the achievement of a universal civic society which administers law among men."[24] In the 1795 essay, "Perpetual Peace," his concern with the forms of local as well as international government are made explicit.[25] Kant there claims that standing armies ought to be abolished, that national debt ought not to be contracted in such a way as to cause friction among states, and that the civil constitution of every state should be republican, recognizing the need for international law based not only on moral imperative but on political shifts in Europe, shifts which have made clear that the new European community demands cosmopolitanism:[26] "Since the narrower or wider community of the peoples of the earth has developed so far that a violation of rights in one place is felt throughout the world, the idea of a law of world citizenship is no high-flown or exaggerated notion."[27] Thus for Kant the categorical imperative enters the realm of pragmatic politics through the connection between community and cosmopolitanism.

Yet Kant is able to make these cosmopolitan claims without relinquishing his support for the idea of the state. This essay thus represents a moment in which the tension between nationhood and universal citizenship seems resolvable. For Kant, there is little difficulty in asserting that the moral can pertain to the local community, the state, *and* the cosmopolis. As Pheng Cheah points out, "Kant's cosmopolitanism signifies a turning point ... at which the 'political' becomes, by moral necessity, 'cosmopolitical.'"[28]

In this sense Kant's cosmopolitan perspective may be called prenational.[29] However, the Napoleonic wars effectively put an end to this stage in Europe. Benedict Anderson dates the age of new nationalisms generally to the period between 1776 and 1838. Yet it is clear that the nature of national claims changes in the post-Napoleonic period when what he calls "popular linguistic-nationalism" emerges.[30] E. J. Hobsbawm puts the systematic development of the modern nation-state even later, beginning in about 1830.[31] By the time Marx writes at mid-century, however, the nation clearly holds sway and the cosmopolitan "ideal" has become the cosmopolitan menace, one linked to the rise of an international bourgeoisie and the concomitant exploitation of national work forces: "The bourgeoisie has through its exploitation of the world market given a cosmopolitan character to production and consumption in every country."[32] The term "cosmopolitan" is no longer available, as it was to Kant and his predecessors, without regard to the solidified boundaries of capitalist, trading nation-states, and it is this transition that indelibly marks invocations of cosmopolitanism in Europe and the United States in the second half of the nineteenth century.

The term "cosmopolitan" becomes almost exclusively pejorative in British usage in the first half of the nineteenth century and almost always opposed to national identity and local community. It is perhaps not surprising to find Coleridge, already in 1809 writing in the *Friend*, about a "false philosophy that would persuade ... that cosmopolitanism is nobler than nationality." Carlyle too condemns "a certain attenuated cosmopolitanism [that] had taken place of the old home feeling." MacCaulay, that symbol of Great Britain's imperial attitude towards India, decries, in his history of England, the "cosmopolitan indifference to constitutions and religions which is often observable in persons whose life has been passed in vagrant diplomacy." In 1848, not only Marx, but also J. S. Mill remarks upon the fact that "capital is becoming more and more cosmopolitan."[33] In British usage the definition becomes pejorative precisely at the time that the conception of the modern nation-state is becoming increasingly dominant.[34]

If we turn to the American voice of Emerson, however, a clear difference in tone emerges. We may see Emerson seek to resolve the dualism between the local and the universal without recourse to the particular structures of state government. Emerson's Kantianism is evident in "Politics," where he claims that "an abstract of the codes of nations would be a transcript of the common conscience." Cosmopolitanism flows inevitably from this idealism: "Governments have their origin in the moral identity of men. Reason for one is seen to be reason for another, and for every other."[35] Yet these are also the grounds by which Emerson argues for the withering of the state, which for him ought eventually to become unnecessary. If "my right and wrong is their right and wrong"[36] then there will be commonality sufficient to unite wise men (and perhaps women). Thus when, in 1844 in the "Letter to a Young American," Emerson writes that "the legislation of this country should become more catholic and cosmopolitan than that of any other,"[37] he is employing the term "cosmopolitan" in what we may take to be a distinctly American sense – neither like Kant advocating a league of nations nor like Coleridge privileging nationality.

In Emerson's description of the new man we can also hear the particular expansiveness of ninteenth-century American political thought become wedded to this cosmopolitanism, as he calls for "men who are at home in every latitude and longitude, men of universal politics, who are interested in things in proportion to their truth and magnitude."[38] This is indeed an enlarged view of the world, one in which the particular vigor and adventurousness of Americans will lead towards a newly refreshed cosmopolitanism. Cosmopolitanism in this context seems to grow directly out of the strength of individual men, almost bypassing the community entirely, and in this manner the tension between local and universal appears to be resolved.

Yet clearly Emerson's thought also rests firmly on its particular understanding of the American identity and its relationship to the world. One might say then that his universalism is grounded in the United States, much as Montesquieu's was grounded in France. Until it is virtually eclipsed by nationalist sentiment in the last years of the nineteenth century, this essentially paradoxical cosmopolitan sensibility lurks within much American social discourse, emerging not only in the appeal to universal humanism which surrounds the new discourses of social reform in the 1890s,[39] but also in the popular press discussions about American achievements in science, technology, and world exploration.

In his recent collection of essays, Bruce Robbins writes of new, contemporary versions of "cosmopolitics" as "situated" in and developing out of particular transnational experiences rather than loyalty to a singular universal cosmos.[40] In this sense they oppose themselves to what they posit as the old universal cosmopolitanism, dreamed as an ahistorical unity of all peoples. Still, although it may be said that Western cosmopolitan thought often lays claim to that dream, and thus opens itself to the criticisms of those like Coleridge and Carlyle, it is also clear that it was always constrained by and indebted to very particular and located experiences of identity and belonging. If, as Martha Nussbaum reminds us, the tradition of cosmopolitan thought imagines loyalties as concentric circles with the local at the heart of the universal,[41] that model does not account for the ways in which the notion of the universal may remain contained within, or at least constrained by, particular experiences of the local. Yet this is precisely what we see in the development of cosmopolitanism in Western thought in general and in the United States in the second half of the nineteenth century in particular, where notions of community and cosmos seem bound up with an increasingly national pressure.

This odd combination may be symbolized within American culture by the opposition between the extraordinary boom in new American magazines that emerged from every section of the rapidly expanding country in the post-Civil-War period (their number growing from 700 to 1,200 in the five years from 1865 to 1870),[42] their insistence on the strength and primacy of American ways of life,[43] and the continued reliance of these magazines on travelogs, international perspectives, and literature by European writers.[44] The illustrations in the new magazines represent these very same cosmopolitan contradictions: magazines like *Harper's Weekly* pictured homesteading in the West, and those like *Leslie's Illustrated* began documenting scandalous conditions in the cities of the East, but many of the illustrations and especially the advertisements that flooded their pages were exotic or even anthropological, fueling a rapacious interest in America's assimilation of the world. Even when they depicted the slaughter of the buffalo in the West or the status of the freed slave in the South, American magazines of the post-War period treated these topics of national concern as though they were vehicles for safe, though compelling, armchair travel.

Thus if we see cosmopolitanism here figured as a positive quality in the mid to late nineteenth century, it is because it has undergone an American transformation, one which marries Emersonian idealism with the practical national push that will characterize the gilded age.[45] There is an enormous explosion in the use of the term in the United States in the 1890s, and more specifically around 1892. When we encounter the term in the 1890s, for example in the title of William Gilpin's *The Cosmopolitan Railway: Compacting and Fusing Together All The World's Continents*, in John Brisbane Walker's proposal for a "Cosmopolitan University," in the series of articles about a fictional reform club called the "Cosmopolis City Club,"[46] or simply on the masthead of *Cosmopolitan* Magazine itself – we see the use of "cosmopolitan" as an adjective attached to modern practical enterprises, with specific constituencies and worldly goals. While *Cosmopolitan*'s masthead invokes the claim that the "world is my country," the articles that follow make it clear that one is not meant thereby to question one's American loyalty or citizenship. The use here is figurative or cultural, and not specifically political.

Nor do we encounter elsewhere even the derogatory use, common in Great Britain at the time, of "cosmopolitan vagrancy," applied in the realm of diplomacy, or "cosmopolitan homelessness," applied in the realm of cultural identity. American popular use of the term in this period is almost exclusively positive, practical, and seemingly unthreatening to the expanding national consciousness. Women still take their daughters to Europe to travel, but it is less likely to be as a matter of finishing their education, which increasingly they can do at home. By all means take them to Europe to enjoy the scenery, as an article in the *Ladies Home Journal* exhorts, but "Give them first the benefit of the very best and most thorough educational facilities in America; and bear in mind, too ... that more Europeans are sending their children to America for education than you are aware."[47] The cosmopolitan has become a subspecies of the national, or, at best, a way of enlarging its scope, rather than a threat to its very existence.

But can we still call this perspective "cosmopolitan"? What separates this national expansiveness, then, from rapacious imperialism? Certainly the problem of the international movement of capital, raised by both Marx and Mill at mid-century, forces us to consider to what extent the term "cosmopolitan," when attached to post-Civil-War American culture, simply becomes a cover for the expansion of American national and commercial interests. For those women who are called "cosmopolitan" when they marry the princes and dukes of Europe, the pecuniary aspect of what has been termed "gilded prostitution" again throws into doubt any more expansive notion of the term.[48]

By the end of the Spanish–American War cosmopolitanism clearly has been elided into expansionism. In the late 1880s and early 1890s, however, the possibility that cosmopolitanism might be an ideal fueled but not besmirched by national strength was still not only conceivable but enticing. Well before she came to be coupled with Emma Lazarus's famous poem, the Statue of Liberty herself may be seen as a physical symbol of the connection of this cosmopolitan possibility to ideal images of women. While under the leadership of John Brisbane Walker from 1888 to 1905, *Cosmopolitan* represents a remarkable experiment in this ideal, one where articles on the principles of evolution, or the necessity of a cosmopolitan language, nestle side by side with treatises on "The Romance of Gloves." It marks both the rise of the cosmopolitan attitude and its extension from what Thomas Peyser calls a utopian sentiment[49] into a practical, if soon to be eclipsed, approach to American identity. The predominance of woman as a topic in its pages makes clear that cosmopolitanism is here conceived as a matter of feminine virtue and stewardship, not simply a corollary of the commercial connections of the international marketplace.[50]

In the period in 1892 when William Dean Howells edits the magazine, as indeed for most of the 1890s, *Cosmopolitan* marks the convergence of American *belles lettres* and the popular press under the aegis of this ideal.[51] Brander Matthews contributes an essay on "Books about German and French Literature" as well as a piece on the "Literary Independence of the United States."[52] Travelogs on Berlin, Japan, and Monte Carlo, essays on duck shooting in Australia and on "Lent Among the Mahometans" appear side by side with descriptions of life "In Our Cotton Belt" and in our "Great Cities." Jacob Riis writes about hospitals while George Washington Cable discusses "Education for the Common People of the South," all of which makes even the coverage of the World Columbian Exhibition seem limited in comparison.[53] Always concerned, under Walker's ownership, with advances in technology and transportation, *Cosmopolitan* also printed in these volumes articles on "The Great Railway Systems of the United States" as well as discussions of electricity, aerial navigation, and the construction of the airplane. The implication, of course, is that what is new is cosmopolitan and that the magazine will be a harbinger of the new.

Claims about female cultivation as the height of American national pride also abound throughout *Cosmopolitan*, as indeed throughout America in the years after the Civil War. The pairing of the terms of "woman" and "nation" extends from common nineteenth-century formulations of a feminized America. The image of the American West as a female frontier, or of the American spirit as promulgated by feminine civic virtue, dominated the consolidation of Americanness in the last half of the nineteenth century. A popular song from 1865, for example, places the nation in the bodies of its young girls, claiming that 'In the eyes, lips, and cheeks of our maidens / Ever flourish the Red, White and Blue.'[54] And as Annette Kolodny has put it, Americans assumed an "essential femininity of the terrain" that would nurture and protect the nation.[55]

This ideal version of female presence and utterance owes much to what has been called the cult of true womanhood.[56] The "cult" both observed and prescribed specific behavior for women in the enactment of domestic life.[57] But the nineteenth-century domestic woman always played a role as nurturer of the citizenship of the nation.[58] This way of thinking about women, as Nina Baym points out, also pushed beyond the domestic front, validating women's roles as teachers and sometimes as writers, as well as providing a rationale for their education.[59] The elevated status of woman as both ideal citizen and creator of the citizens of the future made woman "a participant in history and crucially blurred the supposedly sacrosanct boundaries between the private and the public."[60] It was just this aspect of the nineteenth-century conception of womanhood that would eventually open the way for women to extend the domestic sphere into the arena of public life or, as Paula Baker puts it, to expand "the profession of motherhood to include all of society, an argument that stressed the beneficial results that an application of feminine qualities had on society."[61]

This transition is easily seen in the pages of the family magazines of the 1890s where article after article debates such concerns as "Marriage Rates of College Women," "Notes on the Health of Women Students," the life of "Women Clerks in New York," the variety of "Avocations Open to Women," as well as timeless questions like "When Lady, When Woman?"[62] Whereas *Harper's Bazar* of 1888 ran an article by a bemused T. W. Higginson chronicling "The Invasion of Women," ten years later, in 1898, the corresponding piece is about the power of "The Sisterhood of Women," and proclaims that "no matter how much they may have lacked in the past, the women of today, especially those in business and professional life, are no longer strangers to the sentiment of fellowship: the countless women's organizations prove the case."[63] The question of the fellowship of both white and black American women, within newly expanded spheres of movement, becomes a pivotal question in the early to mid 1890s, just at the time when cosmopolitanism as an ideal is becoming revised, expanded, and ultimately attacked.

Thus we see the importance of the commentaries in these magazines on the Americanness of women or the relationship between American women and their European counterparts. Not only is the status of the nation and its domestic ideology at stake but also its assumption that the American woman or girl will demonstrate the height of American leisured cultivation as she takes her place in the world. If middle-class white women join clubs or work, then they will no longer be the national pride, and the red, white, and blue bloom of their figures may well disappear. If upper-class girls receive their education at Vassar or Radcliffe, and if European women begin to come to be schooled in America, rather than the other way around, then cosmopolitan knowledge of German or French, or understanding of European manners, ceases to be an important female commodity. Yet popular discourse in the 1890s still attributes these charms to American gentlewomen, and insists on the woman as repository of the paired virtues of community and cosmopolitanism. The conflict gives rise to a contest for women's culture that is also a contest about the value and possibility of cosmopolitanism.

The exhortations to women during the Spanish–American War

make this contest particularly clear. While many of the family magazines publish articles pushing for international arbitration or diplomatic
solutions before the sinking of the Maine, by March 1898 most have
reached acceptance of the necessity for war. More significantly, most
are urging women to join the fight, at least so far as to join the Red Cross
and help with relief efforts.[64] An article by a female MD claims that
women need to participate in the national struggle: "We may not have
arrived at the fighting line, that supposed qualification for citizenship;
but we surely have proved ourselves qualified as workers rather than
weepers. But where and how can we work?"[65] The link between
women's nursing and women's citizenship becomes clearly established;
the national identity presupposes a national duty which the women
readily take up. Yet the very pledge of the Red Cross to which all these
willing women "fighters" swear allegiance places this national identity
in a broader context. It reads in part, "I promise that I shall act as a true
sister to every human being, independent of nationality, creed, or
sex."[66] We can be sure the new male soldiers were not asked to pledge
any sort of universal brotherhood on their induction into the army. The
civic role of women forces them to be both national and cosmopolitan at
once.

During the Cuba crisis the conflict between these perspectives becomes a question of voice in a manner that highlights feminine speech as
the key to American cosmopolitanism. The emergence of the term
"Jingo" to refer to an immoderate, male patriot who expresses himself
with abandon, also implies its converse, the temperate feminine or
feminized voice of conciliation. Nearly every article of the many that
employ the newly popular term after its introduction by Charles William Eliot in 1895 uses it in a specifically gendered context, one which
implies not only masculine martial aggression but also its corresponding
verbal assault. As William Safire defines it, Jingoism is not only "national cockiness" but also the "bellicose remarks" that go with it. The term is
from its initial American use inherently linked to Theodore Roosevelt
and his willingness to speak off the cuff. [67] Though many men certainly
argue against Jingoism as against the war with Spain, the (unpopular)
public position of conciliation and diplomacy, as demonstrated in calm
reasoned speech and temperate tones, becomes identified with women,
and the idea of a feminized America.

What an odd paradox the justification of unbridled patriotism in the
form of the Jingo becomes! The country needs him, the reader learns, in
order not to be silenced by cosmopolitan sympathy: "The thing that is

just now most indispensable to the comfort of American families is a resident Jingo who thoroughly approves of the war. Every household should have one – in a cage if necessary – and encourage him to have a free expression of his views."[68] Such men tell women what they are so prone to forget, that this war is America's duty to the world, and they say it forcefully over and over again:

We are so averse to injuring any one that we sympathize with the enemy as the people who are likely to suffer most, and forget the suffering which Spain has brought upon others in our concern for what she is likely to undergo. That is why we need our resident Jingoes to keep the other side of the question continually before us.[69]

Whenever the Jingo appears, so does the issue of forceful versus conciliatory speech. The public patriotic posture in 1898 demands forceful masculine reiteration and derides both the feminine art of subtle persuasion and international sisterhood.

But of course the female art of verbal conciliation and gentle persuasiveness remains a publicly proclaimed virtue throughout the 1890s and well into the twentieth century. An 1894 article entitled "Have Women Found New Weapons?" proclaims that the new education will not be enough, that women ought cleave to their old skills: "Coaxing and smiling and tact and dress, and all charming accomplishments were never more necessary." And if the author concedes that women and men may increasingly be found in the same public arenas, women ought nonetheless stick to the abilities that have served them well in domestic battles, for "No man can coax as a woman can coax – and that with very few words indeed. An adept in the art can get, not the half, but the whole of the man's kingdom, if she mixes some charm with some discrimination and the proper amount of flattery." Still the most important feminine tool, according to this perspective, is silence: "Of course the tongue is a weapon, but not so sharp a weapon as silence."[70] Despite the growing pleas for women's patriotic activity in 1898, this common endorsement of moderation in speech continues.

Since the question of the national conversation, as Seyla Benhabib might put it, is the question of the national community itself, as well as the means for achieving its ethical and political perspective, this overt participation of women in public discourse signals a crucial and disorienting shift. In order to contain the threat of woman's new-found public voice, her speech must be assigned a specific part of the conversation and a clearer moral role in the development of the nation, which demands her adherence to particular codes of language and deportment. As Caroline Field Levander has aptly put it, the "persistent imagining of women's 'natural' linguistic difference, . . . reveals, not its inevitability, but rather its constructed, strategic, and crucial role in the dramatic social transformation that the nation underwent in the nineteenth century."[71]

We can also see the question of the literary marketplace bound up with the question of women's public speech, the feminization of American politics, and the possibility of cosmopolitanism in the 1890s. Richard Ohmann describes the last fifteen years of the nineteenth century as the inaugural moment of national mass culture and the modern magazine as one of its primary vehicles.[72] After the panic of 1893, prices for both weeklies and monthlies drop considerably and the modern practice of funding the magazine primarily through advertising dollars is born. The magazines thereafter become like stores; what they offer are the household accoutrements for upwardly mobile middle-class life and the cultural capital for what Ohmann calls "socially correct participation" in the national scene.[73] Thus the familiar ads from the period that depict women bicycling and playing tennis, women using modern stoves and modern typewriters, appropriate those objects and behaviors for the domain of female life and then insist that they fit within common female paradigms. That the gentle-woman who bicycles can still be (and still *ought* to be) white, elegant, and pure if she uses Ivory or Pears soap, is often the slogan. That she must purchase these products in order to be able to do so is usually the message.

The marketing of middle-class life is not only restricted to the advertisement of objects in the pages at the back of these popular monthlies and weeklies. Marketability pervades the editorial pages as well, providing voices, positions, and cultural experiences which, as Ohmann makes clear, re-inforce the desired social position of their audience.[74] The magazines often represent a very concerted effort to provide cultural material across a well-defined spectrum of interests and activities that are taken to be the key components of American life. Thus we may read *Cosmopolitan*'s recurring columns on technology, scientific progress, exploration, regional life, and health care, as well as on the new woman and her life style, as the means of marketing self-image, status, and national identity to the *Cosmopolitan* reader. The wide-ranging and up-to-date perspective becomes precisely what *Cosmopolitan* sells to its readers, and what makes them secure in their own habits of life. The potentially revolutionary female voices it presents, such as Olive Shreiner's on "The Woman Question," thus become commodified.

Like the latest fashions from Paris, the successes of the recent Opera Season, or the progress of the railroad, they function as cultural capital for the well-read. Woman's consumption of these perspectives, then, fits within her growing role as purchaser of household goods and services. The New Woman and her voice become a good buy: an important and up-to-date topic for social conversation rather than a disruption of conventional discourse.

Henry James's *Bostonians* already presents the question of women's public speech in the mid 1880s as one of marketability and commodification. [75] Ransom appears sympathetic to Verena at the end of the second book precisely when he admits that he can't find a market for his ideas. Her movement towards him is one of commiseration about the fickleness of editors.[76] Of course his declaration of love and proposal of marriage come only in the wake of his having an article accepted for publication, an event that makes possible the reversal of the final chapters. Verena's speech becomes supplanted by Ransom's articles in the *Rational Review*, an exchange that seems finally to be, if not fair or even, then ultimately meaningless. The problem is the corruption inherent in the marketing of speech for public consumption, whether on the stage or in some equally suspect literary venue. The impossibility of happiness clearly announced in the final lines of the novel is a corollary of the entanglement of both public and domestic speech within the corrupting domain of consumption. When Basil demands that Verena speak only to him on the platform of their dining-room table (379) he does not prevent her loss of self within the commercial realm of public performance, but simply transplants it back into the home.

This contest in *The Bostonians* seems to exist within a distinctly national frame of reference. Hardly a word in the novel gestures outside of its American context and indeed James claimed it to be an attempt to "do" America.[77] Thus we might be tempted to read the question of the commodification of speech, and of female speech in particular, here, as part of a critique of America. On the other hand, in much of James's short fiction of the 1890s and the first years of the twentieth century, the issue of literary production becomes more specifically linked to the cosmopolitan question. The term "cosmopolitan" does not appear with any regularity in James's fiction, except in the period around 1892.[78] When it does show up – in "Greville Fane," or in "Collaboration," for example – it is a term connected to the problems of cultural creation and the marketplace, usually presented as inhabiting all the cultural centers of Europe and the United States. Thus cosmopolitanism works in these texts as a corrective to the "international problem" in James's earlier work.[79] James abandons the conflict between an "innocent, parochial" America and the more "sophisticated, cosmopolitan Europe"[80] and instead focuses on the question of publication itself, and the degree to which it both necessitates and precludes a cosmopolitan perspective. The resulting conflict as presented in these stories makes the dilemma of the cosmopolitan a synonym for, or at least a corollary of, the problem of the American literary marketplace.[81]

The difference in James's cosmopolitanism of the 1890s may be seen still more clearly if we look back to his classic description of the cosmopolite in the 1878 piece "Occasional Paris." It is this text that has been used by Edel and others to describe James's cosmopolitan sympathies.[82] Yet in "Occasional Paris" James writes of the "baleful spirit of the cosmopolite" and argues as though he were a cosmopolite more by default than by preference: "To be a cosmopolite is not, I think, an ideal; the ideal should be to be a concentrated patriot. Being a cosmopolite is an accident, but one must make the best of it."[83] Accidental cosmopolitanism arrives through a constant need to compare and a concomitant unwillingness to choose sides, not at all like the purposeful version we see in the 1890s' stories. It is a refusal of the very question of loyalty (though not of national identity) and a habit of perspective not of action, as it will later be. It is, most especially, a traveler's cosmopolitanism this essay presents to us in 1878, a consequence of the ebb and flow of the young James's social and literary affinities, rather than a distinct philosophy of life.[84]

On the other hand, by the 1890s James has conceived of the cosmopolitan as more than an accident. He has shaped it as a motive at least equal to "concentrated patriotism" and, more than that, he has proposed it as a mode of living made possible by the attainment of a certain honesty of tone. His stories come to represent this mode as a means beyond the vagaries of national codes of decency or decorum and beyond the market-driven forces of immoderate or trumped-up speech. Story after story from the period between 1892 and 1898 returns to the scene of artistic production, whether of an opera as in "Collaboration," or of a series of popular fictions as in "Greville Fane," or of a profile of a celebrated author as in "Sir Dominick Ferrand" (first published as "Jersey Villas" in Howells's *Cosmopolitan* of 1892) and "John Delavoy" (first published in the European journal *Cosmopolis*).[85] In these stories, the question of publication raises the related question of restriction of subject matter, and the restriction of subject matter becomes a question of literary parochialism. In both "Sir Dominick Ferrand" and "John Delavoy" magazine editors reject work based upon a vague sense of public taste or decency, while the author is shown to have little connection with the marketplace.

Adeline Tintner describes the concern with decency in James's stories of the 1890s as representative of his distance from the cosmopolitan fiction being written primarily in France and Italy at the time. European cosmopolitan fiction often presents as a theme the corruption of the young, and its basis in a general social dissatisfaction.[86] The question of the hidden love affair is particularly crucial; hidden liaisons mark both the center of interest and often the center of retribution in the novels of cosmopolitan writers such as Paul Bourget and Gabriele D'Annunzio. For James, such affairs are anathema to fiction; as he claims in a letter to Bourget, novels ought to focus on "the stuff of human contact" rather than on its biological urges.[87] Thus James rejects the degree to which French novels of the time revolve around the unmasking or unraveling of these hidden liaisons, and the degree to which, in writers like Bourget, this event is used to signal the moral failings of the main characters.

This last point is especially crucial when we come to examine James's cosmopolitanism in the 1890s, for it makes clear that his distaste for sexual explicitness as a component of cosmopolitan fiction is not simply a result of a certain Anglo-Saxon rectitude. Rather, he finds the imposition of moral standards *antithetical* to the very cosmopolitanism that he is creating, and he thematizes this conflict again and again in the 1890s. The lessons of both "Sir Dominick Ferrand" and "John Delavoy" (as well as several of the stories from the following decade, such as "The Velvet Glove" [1902] and "The Story in It" [1909]) are, after all, that local codes of decency and market-driven sensibilities drastically *curtail* the possibilities of art. James seems to recognize the circular logic that drives the European cosmopolitan stories. In much French fiction of the 1890s, the affair becomes the focus of meaning and attention in the story, at the same time as its inevitability represents the bankruptcy of dominant cultural norms. Thus the cosmopolitan story depends on a moral situation seen as deplorable and yet its premise insists on the desirability of that very situation. This circularity also translates into the terms of the marketplace, where the salacious content of cosmopolitan French fiction produces sales that themselves contribute to the degeneration of culture which the stories had originally seemed to bemoan.

To be sure, cosmopolitanism as it is re-emerging in Europe in the 1880s and 1890s often contains within it the same kind of concern with national identity that we have seen in the United States. As Julia Prewitt Brown puts it, for Oscar Wilde, "the ethnic element is essential to any authentic cosmopolitanism."[88] Wilde, writing in "The Critic as Artist," sees nationality itself as dependent on contact with the foreign. Creativity grows from heredity and the weight of local experience as much as out of the condition of being purposefully uprooted.[89] Wilde often presented himself as above all ties to places. His infamous remark to James[90] – "You care for places? The world is my home"[91] – demonstrates this position. Yet, as Brown makes clear, Wilde did care for places, creating deep contacts with the cultures he encountered. In "The Critic as Artist," the question of the English tradition is ubiquitous, and the movement towards the worldly begins with a profound understanding of Shakespeare and his relation to Elizabethan England. Only after "know[ing] the materials that were at Shakespeare's disposal . . and the conditions of theatric presentation in the sixteenth and seventeenth century" can the critic "learn Shakespeare's true position in the history of European drama and the drama of the world."[92]

Thus in a certain sense, as Wilde makes clear, one may claim that 1890s cosmopolitanism, in both Europe and the United States contains within itself a nascent critique of the condition of rootlessness. Crass cosmopolitanism, or rootlessness, respects no ties or traditions; Wilde's cosmopolitanism (like James's) rests upon deep encounters with each culture that is met. Yet, in French cosmopolitan fiction it is increasingly the rootlessness that emerges victorious, as characters not only involve themselves in hidden love affairs but also construct their lives around a variety of lies and falsehoods seen to be inherent to their cosmopolitan condition. For example, in Bourget's 1893 novel *Cosmopolis*, one of the key texts of 1890s cosmopolitanism, worldliness ultimately devolves into race-based nationalism, as characters who are thrown together in Rome come in the end to display their various national proclivities. Still, in this novel the passion of the cosmopolitan condition lies in encountering people from other places who are intensely and intriguingly different.[93] In the later work of Bourget, however, this aspect of cosmopolitanism will develop into a virulently racist nationalism. By 1918, and the novel *Némésis*, the cosmopolitan becomes a Barresian *déraciné*, a figure at the heart of moral decadence and social decay.

As Tintner points out, it is no surprise that the cosmopolitan heroine/ menace of *Némésis* is an American girl named Daisy. We know that Bourget admired James, dedicating his 1885 novel *Cruel Enigma* to him, that James and Bourget were in close contact in the period surrounding

the writing of *Cosmopolis*, that James stayed with Bourget at his house in
1892 for a period of a few weeks,[94] and that they had a spirited
correspondence throughout the 1890s, in which James often criticized
Bourget's writing. James discusses Bourget at some length in essays from
1888 and 1899 and often mentions him in his notebooks and letters in
between. Tintner also claims that Bourget was deeply influenced by
James's work, often creating his fiction as a sort of elaboration or
commentary on that of James. To describe an American Daisy at the
core of degenerate cosmopolitan life must have been a deliberate attempt to beat James at his own game, or at least to show that Daisy, in
her decadent disregard for the traditions of Europe, was far from being a
simple *naif*.

Still, what is significant in this context is the return to woman as the
embodiment of cosmopolitanism, even if here figured negatively. Bourget's Daisy lies, has an affair, has an abortion, and is ultimately blown up
by a bomb, all seemingly in order to demonstrate the corruption of her
heritage (part Jewish, part Russian and the daughter of an American
millionaire). Yet there are male characters in Bourget's novel who are
also bereft of meaningful roots. That Daisy's behavior becomes the
center of disapprobation in the novel thus points to a particularly
gendered perspective, one which intimates that it is through women that
the corruption of cosmopolitanism takes place. The novel thus brings to
the fore the gender subtext within much of the earlier European cosmopolitan fiction – that the threat of degeneracy arises from the corrupt
cosmopolitan woman. Bourget implies that without disreputable
women even the most cosmopolitan men, living from hotel to hotel in
the centers of Europe, would not be subject to such corruption.

Further, Bourget often creates Daisy's corruption as a question of
voice. The matter of the abortion is broached in a chapter entitled
"Enigma" in which her lover, Hughes, demands to know what has
happened as the result of her pregnancy. Rather than reply, Daisy
exerts her power through silence.[95] In the succeeding pages Daisy lies,
claiming never to have been pregnant in the first place, and only a
hundred pages later delivers what is referred to as "the word from the
enigma" and the truth about her abortion. Her crime, the novel makes
clear, lies less in her choice of an abortion, and more in her aggressive
refusals to speak the truth.

Thus, in *Némésis*, the question of Daisy's voice is part and parcel of the
falsity and misplaced aggression pandemic to the cosmopolitan woman
within the French and Italian fiction of the time. Her verbal lies are

directly connected to the lying condition of all those cosmopolitan heroines who engage in clandestine affairs. Her speech marks woman as a danger and a threat to the social order. On the other hand, James's stories from the 1890s, in their insistence on cosmopolitan harmony and conciliation especially *as a result of* female speech, seem clearly opposed to this construction of female voice, and committed to perpetuating what we have seen is a distinctly American focus on woman's cosmopolitan potential. James clearly rejects Bourget's rampant nationalism, and his linked critique of women, in favor of a more American cosmopolitanism that is ultimately rooted in potential feminine harmony.

In the stories "Collaboration" and "Greville Fane," both published in September 1892, "cosmopolitan" comes to mean a significant benevolence in tone, or a coming to common terms after lively discussion. In "Collaboration," which Tintner claims is James's direct response to Bourget's *Cosmopolis*, the entire story is set within an American artist's studio in Paris which is described in these very terms. The studio is celebrated for its ability to draw artists and admirers and to encourage them to linger in conversation:

There are discussions of course and differences – sometimes even a violent circulation of sense and sound; but I have a consciousness that beauty flourishes and that harmonies prevail in the end . . . the place is really a chamber of justice, a temple of reconciliation: we understand each other if we only sit up late enough . . . My studio in short is the theatre of a cosmopolite drama. (234–5)

Cosmopolitanism here is linked both to the discord of conversational differences and to the accord that prevails in the end. The cosmopolite creates harmony out of the cacophony of these sounds.

This emphasis on the harmonizing tones of the cosmopolitan scene carries over directly into the plot of this story in which a German musician and French poet attempt to collaborate on an opera. The scene of their accidentally coming together is of course the narrator's studio, which resounds with "the reverberation of mighty music and great ideas, with the echoes of [the] 'universe'" (249). The possibility of collaboration is figured throughout as the ultimate musical harmony, one which elevates the artists above the particular ground on which they stand (249). But the engagement of Vendemer, the poet, to a French girl who lost her father in the 1870 war with Germany, presents an element of discord which provides the drama of the story. That Vendemer loves international artistic collaboration more than he loves his fiancée emerges as the triumph of the cosmopolitan over both family and *patrie*. In the end even the fiancée, who rejects her suitor over this collaboration, succumbs to the harmonies it produces, for the story ends with her at the piano, playing "with infinite expression," and from memory, the notes of the German composer.

Thus the woman of the tale is shown at first to be the obstacle to a higher cosmopolitan understanding which she finally attains through the literal acquisition of harmony. The matter of tone here is specific, yet no less socially significant because of that fact. The fiancée risks losing all when she advances her argument without amendment; she becomes enlightened when she modulates her tone.

The very same figure is employed, albeit in vastly different circumstances, in "Greville Fane," where the subject of the story is a kindly woman writer of popular melodramas about the aristocracy. The narrator tells us from the outset that "she was not a woman of genius . . . She could invent stories by the yard, but she couldn't write a page of English" (220). Her style is the problem, one further distinguished by its subordination to the passionate plots of her fiction. Still, the narrator explains in an almost sarcastic aside, "her types, her illustrations, her tone were nothing if not cosmopolitan" – that is, she consciously models herself on the French cosmopolitan fiction James clearly disliked. Greville Fane is popular because her characters "make love to each other from Doncaster to Bucharest" (220); yet, the narrator adds, "she was clever and vulgar and snobbish, and never so intensely British as when she was particularly foreign" (221). Her tone may sound cosmopolitan, and she may mimic fiction that claims to be cosmopolitan, but James makes clear that this is insufficient to make her so.

Yet this false presentation of the cosmopolitan spirit as an emptiness of tone and a vulgarity of style also becomes undermined as the story progresses. The tone of the narrative itself, begun in a sarcastic, almost condescending mode, succumbs little by little to the charm of Greville Fane herself, shedding its ironic asides and forgoing its jabs at Fane's fiction. In her everyday conversation Greville Fane is revealed to be as direct as her novels are far-fetched, readily admitting her fee for a novel amidst vastly elevated rumors, and brushing off expressions of adulation in favor of the simple desire to be paid. She never pretends to a higher art than the popular and speaks not of lofty issues but of the "price of a *pension* and the convenience of an English chemist" (226).

Thus the false cosmopolitanism belies a truer one, whose tone is direct and honest, loyal and "fine," if not enlightened. It is, as in "Collaboration," a question of the harmony of sensibility with a lack of pretension or artifice, whether in the realm of the lofty or the mundane, and it is in direct contrast to Bourget's female characters' sordid or aggressive speech. As in "Collaboration," this kind of tone clashes with the demands of both the literary marketplace and the ties of family as they are conventionally understood – but honest attachment to local habits bolster its integrity. Further, cosmopolitanism in these stories reveals itself to be not a fantasy but a practical response to the vagaries of cultural loyalty and the parochialisms of the literary marketplace as well as a defense of the possibilities of feminized conciliatory speech.[96] As in the version present in the American popular press, it is a cosmopolitanism, if such is possible, of the everyday.

In "The Velvet Glove" of 1909 we see a similar construction of the cosmopolitan female writer, here presented in a distinctly negative light. The story of the novelist Amy Evans, who beguiles the American writer, John Berridge, at a Paris party,[97] and then accosts him in order to secure a preface for the American edition of her book, presents this woman as a contradiction in terms. She is alluringly beautiful and properly subtle in her role as a princess arriving late at a *soirée*, yet in her appropriation of English and her aggressive use of it, both verbally and in print, she becomes vapid, mercenary, aggressive, and false: "I 'just love' – don't they say – your American millions; and all the more because they really *take* me for Amy Evans, as I've just wanted to be taken" (748). But of course she *isn't* Amy Evans – that is her pen name – and it is the public version of herself as princess that has entranced Berridge. This falseness so permeates the language of the story that neither we nor Berridge ever know her true name, and Berridge seems incapable of understanding much of what she says to him. Berridge finds himself going home with "Evans" in a cab which she directs to take a circuitous route, convinced he has embarked on what we might call a "cosmopolitan liaison." Thus he ignores the content of her talk, listening only to the touch of her gloved hand on his own and the "sweetness" of the conversation (753). When she bluntly and without chagrin requests that he write a preface to the American edition of her book, Berridge is not only astounded but mortified. The incongruity of so crass a request with the "exquisite intimacy" (754) of the scene in the cab becomes the ultimate of dishonesties, a moral failing occasioned by the gap between her motives and her tone.

Thus we see James's disapprobation of a false cosmopolitanism that would countenance this disjunction. Had the princess not taken on the language and style of the novelist Amy Evans, it is clear, there would have been no scene in the cab (and probably no intimacy at all between the two characters). On the other hand, had she been purely Amy Evans, in Paris in search of broader experience, her tone would have been forthright and direct, nothing like the more "Parisian" posturing of this character and this would have made her cosmopolitanism more true for James. In fact, in the 1899 story "Europe," it is the most unassuming and honest of the three American sisters who becomes the true cosmopolitan, never to return home. Europe brings her out, in a manner that presages Chad Newsome's transformation in *The Ambassadors*. However, this change is described as a heightening of the directness and honesty of her tone not her conversion to the evasive talk or hidden meanings of the French cosmopolitans: "'She told them, ... in a tone they'll never forget, that she was, at all events, quite old enough to be [on her own] ... she says she's on her own feet'" (75). James here privileges the American feminine honesty of tone and integrity of assertion over the crass assertions, manipulations, and crafted silences of the European women as the basis for "true cosmopolitanism." He seems to imply that the American woman's tone, style, and manner of speech contain the very combination of rootedness and travel, of assertion and conciliation, that constitute the cosmopolitan.

Thus, to return to the American context of the late 1890s, we recognize the extent to which the gendered language of jingoism expresses the very heart of the cosmopolitan conflict for James. James wrote in 1896: "The explosion of jingoism there is the result of ... a vast new split or cleavage in American national feeling ... the whole thing sickens me."[98] As he writes to William James in April 1898 at the height of the Spanish–American War, the conflict presents itself distinctly in terms of the disharmony, clumsiness, and general noisiness of contemporary American speech: "I do answer you, alas, almost to ... the foul criminality of the screeching newspapers. They have long since become for me the danger that overtops all others. That became clear to one, even here, two years ago ... when one felt that with a week of simple, enforced silence everything could be saved."[99] Clearly, there was to be no week of enforced silence and indeed no end to the screeching of the newspapers. The possibility of avoiding imperialist speech grows less and less as the 1890s wear on. The Jingo dominates discussion of international events, and nearly forces the possibility of moderate speech out of the public arena. The sound of a cosmopolitan tone seems lost in the clamor of imperialism, the delight in international curiosities is dropped in the rush to carry a big stick. Masculine martial instinct seems liable to rule the day.

Yet, on the other side of the table from the Jingo still sits his sister, calmly imploring him to marry sympathy with his nationalism and to consider the wounded on all sides – and yearning, like the sisters in James's story, to go to Europe. Kwame Anthony Appiah has claimed that "cosmopolitanism and patriotism, unlike nationalism, are sentiments more than ideologies." Thus one need not espouse any particular political doctrine in order to become a cosmopolitan. But a "cosmopolitan patriotism" would require that people "accept the citizen's responsibility to nurture the culture and politics of their homes" whether "they spend their lives in the places that shaped them" or move, taking their cultural practices with them.[100] It is just such a sentiment that we see begun in these 1890s efforts to distinguish an American cosmopolitanism from accidental traveling, or from Kantian idealism or universal expansionism. It is just such a cosmopolitan patriotism, fraught with all the complication of that dual identity, that James will increasingly enunciate as a feminine virtue in his late writing.

FEMINIZING THE NATION: WOMAN AS CULTURAL ICON IN LATE JAMES

> We really approach [the American woman] nearest in studying her full-blown ubiquity as that of the most confidently "grown" and most freely encouraged plant in our democratic garden. The conditions of American life in general, and our great scheme of social equality in particular, have done many things for her, and left many others undone; but they have above all secured her this primary benefit that she is the woman in the world who is least "afraid."
>
> Henry James, *The Speech and Manners of American Women*, 16[101]

In June of 1905 James, in the United States on the journey that would later be chronicled in *The American Scene*, addressed the graduating class of Bryn Mawr College on "The Question of Our Speech." To those New Women, emerging from their training ground with more formal education than the Master himself possessed, James railed against their ignorance of how to speak. "All life . . . comes back to the question of our speech," he tells them;[102] "There is no such thing as a voice pure and simple: . . . the voice *plus* the way it is employed [makes] not only the history of the voice, but positively the history of the national character, almost the history of the people" (34). In the following year James published a series of articles in *Harper's Bazar* treating the "Speech and

Manners of American Women." In these articles he expands the theme of his Bryn Mawr address, chronicling the inadequacies of American speech and calling upon American women to become able to discriminate among the various forms and tones of speech (25). In both articles James insists upon the connection between speech and the status of civilization, and locates the possibility of a vibrant national culture in the differentiations within its language.

In this sense, both the *Harper's* articles and *The American Scene*, written at the same time, evoke an America always in the process of being created and perpetuated by the utterances of its people.[103] If American nationality exists somewhere in the intersection of its historical narrative and contemporary performative utterances of its identity, as Homi Bhabha has claimed, then women, as James increasingly constructs them in these post-1900 writings, are the site of this intersection. For James women represent the only voices of the modern incarnation of America that have the potential to reconcile the tension between the history of the voice and its ongoing performance on the world stage, and thus mediate between the preservation of community and the reworking of nationality within a cosmopolitan frame.

All the writings from James's American voyage draw on common ideas, images, and habits of language, and, as Kenneth Warren and others have made clear, they all indict the same national excesses that James also condemns in the *Harper's* articles.[104] However, the articles about or addressed to women carry a more direct and powerful invective and insist on the role of women in improving not only the *vox Americana* but also the very "history of the national character," in other words, the intersection of the performative with the pedagogical in the voices of women.[105]

But James's writings from his 1904–5 American journey bring this redefinition of American womanhood into the international arena, renewing and expanding his excursion into cosmopolitanism by arguing for its continued enunciation. Because she is "the most confidently 'grown' and most freely encouraged plant in our democratic garden" (16) she represents its potential, but in order to enact that potential she must rise to an ideal that the nation as a whole can follow. Her discourse must display the individualism tempered by community, strength mitigated by soothing codes of conduct, cultural assertiveness bound to openness to Europe, and, most importantly, the ability to discriminate, that will make the cosmopolitan American nation possible.[106]

James's notorious difficulty in imagining a twentieth-century America in which the predominance of Anglo-Saxon blood and culture could no longer be presumed has been read as a sign of his xenophobic nativism.[107] Indeed, his racial notions of Americanness as evidenced in *The American Scene* and "The Question of Our Speech" often resemble many of the arguments being advanced by eugenicists in the first decades of the twentieth century.[108] As Kenneth Warren claims, on the issue of race, "the anxieties evident in [James's] fiction and criticism seemed to mirror the anxieties in American society at large."[109] These anxieties emerge within debates about the role of women both as nurturers of the nation and as perpetuators of its culture[110] and link the notions of race, gender, and nation inseparably. Not only does James locate the possibility of creating a cosmopolitan nation within the discourse of its women, but the fact that he does so demonstrates the degree to which these discourses were absolutely intertwined in the debate over Americanness in the first decades of the century and the extent to which James is intensely engaged with these debates.

At the same time James's ideal feminine speech, as evidenced in both his fiction and essays from 1900 to 1905, insists on a cosmopolitanism of tone which often comes into conflict with the inflated rhetoric of nativism even as it seems to rely on many of its assumptions about womanhood. This paradoxical stance may be seen as part and parcel of James's famously circuitous late style. It may also be seen to comprise the politics of the seemingly indeterminate modernist textuality of *The Ambassadors* and *The Golden Bowl*. In their indication of textual escape, as well as their implication within the discourses of ideal womanhood and Anglo-Saxon racialism, James's late writings present the increasingly polarized terms of nation and cosmos that will haunt modernist discourses of identity.[111]

James's *The American Scene* has elicited an enormous amount of recent commentary, most of it concerned with the construction of American nationality within its pages. Sara Blair has described it as a kind of theatrical space in which "James performatively meditates on American character and culture-building and on the limits of his own attempts to represent them."[112] Alex Zwerdling describes it as "nostalgia for an unrecoverable past and fear of the [American] present."[113] Beverly Haviland on the other hand characterizes *The American Scene*, as well as such late writings as *The Ivory Tower* and *The Sense of the Past*, as anti-nostalgic attempts to show "how important it is for the future of society to relate the past and present so that they are, as it were, on speaking terms."[114] Only Haviland, in her far-reaching study, however, devotes significant attention to the issue of gender and then mainly in relation to her reading of *The Ivory Tower*.

The American Scene presents us again and again with the issues of feminine ideals, which surface most immediately in James's descriptions of the national terrain. Within the first chapter of *The American Scene* James calls Chocorua Mountain "feminine from head to foot, in expression, tone and touch, mistress throughout of the feminine attitude and effect." The mountains of New Hampshire make you feel "as if the ground has gratefully borne you ... [and] that something intrinsically lovable everywhere lurks."[115] It is a literally feminine, nurturing landscape. As Virginia Fowler puts it, "James describes the New England landscape as a 'feminine' being who has been neglected by the 'masculine' forces of commercialism."[116] But here there is a Jamesian twist – the femininity of this American terrain derives from and presents itself in its "expression" and "tone" as well as its "touch." The passage continues:

It is like some diffused, some slightly confounding, sweetness of voice, charm of tone and accent ... There was a voice in the air, from week to week, a spiritual voice: "Oh the *land's* all right!" ... It seemed to plead, the pathetic presence, to be liked, to be loved, to be stayed with, lived with, handled with some kindness, shown even some courtesy of admiration. What was that but the feminine attitude? – not the actual, current, impeachable, but the old ideal and classic. (372)

The felicity of this feminine voice in the woods convinces him of a corresponding national felicity, if only here limited to its physical manifestation.

As in the earlier texts, the connection between the language of Americans and the constitution of the nation always plays itself out here within the realm of the feminine.[117] Over and over again within the pages of both *The American Scene* and *The Speech and Manners of American Women* James bemoans the fact that the American male has abdicated his social role in favor of purely commercial pursuits and has therefore given over to women the care and nurturing of American manners and language. Not only does his commercial focus leave the social sphere strikingly incomplete, but it makes the American male singularly incapable of a social or cultural utterance, reducing him in James's eyes to little more than a barbarian: "Of what sounds other than the yell of the stock-exchange or the football field does [the American male] himself ... give the cheering example?" (26). The sound of this male may be particularly American because it is created out of specific American circumstances, but it does not help to re-imagine or re-produce the nation. The pedagogical aspect of nation-building is here made to be solely the province of the feminine.

This passage, however, also demonstrates the gap James perceives between the actual American woman and the ideally feminine, a gap which always emerges within the realm of language and which exactly mirrors the gap between the existing nation and the cosmopolitan America he believes is possible. This particular idealized American landscape not only speaks sweetly and with proper distinction, as actual American women so often do not, but it also pleads to be loved and admired, rather than served. It is an undemanding landscape, majestic in its tender ubiquity, patient and mild in its calls for one's attention. It is also a landscape that observes the proper distinctions, speaking the subtly different tones of trees, rocks, and streams to the wanderer within it. This is female speech on a level that no real American woman can ever match – a paradigm for the role of the pedagogical. For James it represents a certain height of quality and degree of differentiation achieved by the physical nation but not yet embodied in its people.

Importantly, the faults of the women he encounters in his travels stem from the faults of America, not the other way around.

The world about the American woman has not asked of her anything of that sort – that she shall have definite conceptions of duty, activity, influence; of a possible grace, of a possible sweetness, a possible power to soothe, to please and above all to exemplify. It has simply, in its ignorance, its inexperience, its fatal good-nature, which has let so many precious opportunities, socially speaking, slip, taken her for granted as a free, inspired, supreme thing, nobly exempt, as I began by saying, from any sort of fear. (20)

If the American woman is not adept in the world of manners, then, it is because of the immaturity of America itself. It falls to her to develop some of the missing (feminine) social virtues, and in her performance of these virtues thereby to alter directly the course and tenor of the narrative of the American nation.

Thus, James's essays about and for women present this new assumption that women's speech is public in some crucial way. The idea that women are a fully functioning if not dominant force in the civic life of the country, and can *directly* alter the fate of the nation through the consistent power of their social discourse,[118] is crucial to the premise of the *Harper's* articles.

There could be no better sign of the social success, as I have called it, of our women, than the fact that it is of them we find ourselves speaking, and all irresistibly and inevitably, as soon as the question of American speech comes up. We take it, immediately, as most conspicuously lighted, over the social scene at large, by their example and attitude. (23)

James's June 1905 address at Bryn Mawr avoids the term "New Woman" but it shares the position of the editors of *Good Housekeeping*, who wrote that month: "The new woman is simply the one who, by experience, education and common sense, is qualified to make the largest and best use of her capabilities. She is more delightfully feminine than ever – the attractions of her womanhood more charming."[119]

For James, the prime ways that women must take the lead in the new century are as cultivators and mediators of social differences and distinctions. Like many eugenicists James rejects the status quo of democracy, writing throughout his life about the dangers of believing too wholeheartedly in complete political and social equality.[120] This obviously leaves him open to charges of elitism and hierarchical Anglo-Saxonism. However, much of James's antagonism to social democracy lies in his belief that it is the encounter with others who are recognized as different that makes for a rich social life and a mature culture. For James, in *The American Scene*, distinctions are crucial to the recognition of difference: "No kind of person ... is a very good kind, and still less a very pleasing kind, when its education has not been made to some extent by contact with other kinds, by a sense of the existence of other kinds, and, to a certain degree, by a certain relation with them" (705). Despite the fact that the dominance of the American commercial culture severely limits contact with other kinds of people, the importance of this kind of contact holds true not only in the international arena but also within the nation itself (727–8).

The problems James identifies within the speech and manners of American women, and by extension within the nation itself, then, both derive from and perpetuate this lack of respect for difference. American women who pay too little attention to their speech exhibit a "union of looseness and flatness ... a tone without form and void, without charm and direction" (29). They even mix all sorts of food, demonstrating what James refers to as "indiscriminate spooning" (67–8).[121] Such women are incapable of discriminating among either things or people. For James, who in his travels across America has been precisely concerned with discovering distinctions, with noticing the differences between the America he sees in New England and that of Savannah, and with adjusting to the differences he discovers between the America he once knew and the ethnically mixed new nation he encounters, this is the national failure.

This cultivation of differences and distinctions demonstrates the conflicts inherent in the discourse of woman in the Progressive Era, and the problematic inheritance of Anglo-Saxonism by modernist cosmopolitans. What has been called Anglo-Saxonist nationalism[122] or the Genteel Tradition[123] in the period from the Civil War to the turn of the century was a paradoxical mix of racial nativism and inclusiveness which ultimately rested on an assimilative notion of race. It must be clear that assimilation never implied social equality, nor did it extend so far as to include African-Americans. For some, the power of the American "race" was its ability to incorporate new arrivals without compromising its essentially English culture.[124] For others, it remained enough to speak of elevating the newly arrived masses in the settlement houses, thus instilling Anglo-Saxon virtues within the new, multi-ethnic democracy: "Instead of repudiating democracy, the older elite tried to come to terms with it by assuming the teachability and improvability of the uneducated common people."[125] The task of teaching and improving fell most often to women.

For James, as for many at the turn of the century, race was a broad notion, one that admitted not only the blood history of specific peoples but also the notion of amalgamation and assimilation. As Ernst Renan puts it, "Race ... is something that is made and unmade."[126] To many within the American context, "the notion that European immigrants might endanger the great inborn spirit of the nation strained credibility."[127] To assume that in the future there would indeed be an identifiable American race did not necessarily imply that one particular component of its ethnic mix would win out, but rather that the synthesis of many strains would breed a stronger people and dilute the influence of the weak. As James famously wrote, "We have exquisite qualities as a race, and it seems to me that we are ahead of the European races in the fact that ... we can deal freely with forms of civilization not our own, can pick and choose and assimilate and in short (aesthetically etc.) claim our property wherever we find it."[128] Even in 1905, *Cosmopolitan* still applauded this mix, claiming that 'the nicest of American women are incomparable in the world. They have the gracefulness and vivacity of the French, the refined beauty of the high-bred English, a Puritan sense of duty, and the warm kindliness of the descendants of the colonial settler."[129]

The American Scene, in its portrayal of James's intense reaction to the
new immigrants in New York, his stereotypically negative descriptions
of their appearance and their neighborhoods, and his apparent distress
at the disappearance of the New York he once knew, has often seemed
simply racist.[130] However, these descriptions must always be seen within
the context of James's continued belief in the power of the American
melting pot and within an ideology of the American race that stressed its
ability to incorporate new blood and thereby gain strength.

> [at] Ellis Island ... I was to catch ... the ceaseless process of the recruiting of
> our race, of the plenishing of our huge national *pot au feu*, of the introduction of
> fresh ... foreign matter into our heterogeneous system. But even without that a
> haunting wonder as to what might be becoming of us all, "typically," ethni-
> cally, and thereby physiognomically, linguistically, *personally*, was always in
> order. (408)

The operative words in this passage are "recruiting" and "plenishing,"
indicating James's sense that this is a positive strengthening movement
which will contribute to "our heterogeneous system" even when challenging our secure image of ourselves. Crucially, this kind of "race
improvement" is precisely women's role in the Progressive Era. According to Gwendolyn Mink, women reformers embraced their special role
in this national project, "shar[ing] Roosevelt's premise that immigrant
culture would yield to democratic habits, creating a distinctive American race."[131] For these reformers, replenishing the race would be ac-
complished by the female roles of education and social work, much as
for James the strengthening of American identity would rest on the
example women set within the realm of manners.

It is not surprising that James should wonder what is to become of
Americanness given the dramatic change in the people inhabiting his
beloved New York. What is more striking in this passage is the repetition
of the words "us" and "our," reinforcing James's connection to this
place *and* to these people. The race is not defined against these immigrants, nor is the nation described as under assault. *The American Scene* is
often falsely read as a marker of James's final turn away from his country
of origin; its fascination with describing the changes in the countryside
and populace seems to speak of James's sense of himself as an outmoded
outsider. But exactly the opposite is true. In *The American Scene* James
rediscovers the appeal of the American landscape and its people. Here
as elsewhere in these essays, James's personal involvement in the very
Americanness he is describing is striking. James, like the nation itself, is
being freshened by his encounter with these sons of unidentifiable

fathers. "Us all" is being re-cast in a way that further down the page he calls "thrilling." The American *"pot au feu"* itself never seems to be in danger; it is rather its habits of linguistic, ethnic, and especially personal self-conception that are, quite exhilaratingly for James, under siege.

Nonetheless, the Jews seem to represent for James a cultural life which even the American assimilative power, as embodied in its women, will not be able to overcome:

the unsurpassed strength of [the Jewish] race permits of the chopping into myriads of fine fragments without the loss of race quality. There are small strange animals, known to natural history, snakes or worms, I believe, who, when cut into pieces, wriggle away contentedly and live in the snippet as completely as in the whole. So the denizens of the New York Ghetto. (465)

The resiliency of the Jewish race threatens physically and ethnically but most of all it threatens linguistically.[132] As James puts it in "The Question of Our Speech":

All the while we sleep the vast contingent of aliens whom we make welcome, and whose main contention, as I say, is that from the moment of their arrival, they have just as much property in our speech as we have ... are sitting up (*they* don't sleep!) to work their will on their new inheritance and prove to us that they are without any finer feeling or more conservative instinct of consideration for it. (44–5)

Only the efforts of American women to preserve grammatical and tonal distinctions can prevent the new immigrants from diminishing both the tongue and the nation it signifies.

At the same time, *The American Scene* virtually overflows with reference to the diversity of the American land and people. This travelog often reads as if James were documenting the places as they flash by his train window, so acute is the sense of movement and change.[133] Throughout the book, the feminine landscape stands as both the cause and the overt sign of the population's diversity. These regional differences are always considered by way of differences of dialect and daily habit. Just as his best impressions of New York occur in the park where "the condensed geographical range, the number of kinds of scenery in a given place, competed with the number of languages heard, and the whole impression was of one's having but to turn in from the Plaza to make, in the most agreeable manner possible, the tour of the little globe" (502), so his best impression of America is as an almost global assortment of places, languages, and people. And as Virginia Fowler points out, it is Central Park, figured as the female hostess of an inn who has "never once failed of hospitality," that brings about this happy assortment.[134]

Despite James's loyalty to the Anglo-Saxon roots of American life, and his fear for its degradation, his cosmopolitanism reaches beyond the assimilative parameters of the Genteel Tradition. The threat of the immigrants is not that they will break apart a unified nation but rather, as the example of the Jews demonstrates, quite the opposite, that they will degrade the language into an ungrammatical, indiscriminate group of sounds, and thereby also erase the complexity of the culture. It is woman's role to advance the national culture by practicing the feminine virtues of conciliation, mediation, and community preservation. This is her participation in the pedagogy of the nation, re-iterating the values and self-conception of an ongoing version of national identity. But most importantly, it is woman's duty to establish an American speech with a variety of forms and tones, thus re-creating the nation as a multivalent, multifaceted culture. She must perform a version of national speech that will revise the narrative of a unitary America while also preserving its history. If the new ideal woman herself has an ability to mediate among a range of people, situations, and uses of language within both public and private domains, so the nation must be supple enough to accommodate, preserve, and formalize the various voices it contains.

This is not a resurgence of the old Anglo-Saxonism. In these late American essays, feminine nationality creates a realm of manners that rests on subtle distinctions, and a social world that recognizes the diversity of the American people and landscape. In the late novels, however, cosmopolitanism means interaction within the realm of manners but not within the biological sphere. Racial mixing becomes the limit, even in encounters with Europe, as it always was in encounters with black America, and women's special role emerges once again, this time as the propagators of an emerging American race. James's national conception emerges as a sort of cosmopolitanism resting on a white nativist base. The ideally feminized nation, in the late essays and fiction, becomes the icon of cultural syncretism bound to Anglo-Saxon gentility.

The story "Europe" from 1899 becomes a transitional text in the development of this new feminine role. As we have seen, it revolves around the desires of three sisters to go to Europe, and the ability of one of them to assert her voice and her independence in order to go and never return. Yet the story begins with a prolonged rumination on memory and the passage of time, which consigns the events to the American past: "It was another world, with other manners, a different tone, a different taste" (62). Within this context the sisters are described as being "much of the place" (62) and imbued with the distilled qualities of Puritan New England. Thus the mother's patrician desire to expose her daughters to Europe seems part of the old order, easily comprehensible to the narrator, a well-traveled young man who purports to "know everything" (66).

Yet the story does not allow us to remain secure in these assumptions. Structured around a series of visits the narrator pays to the sisters, which are separated by gaps of uncertain duration, the story describes a change within the sisters that is hidden both from the narrator and from us. He suspects that they avoid him because he has been to Europe: "It was as if they knew where I thought they ought to be" (69). Yet by the end of the story he (and we) are surprised that another sister has made it to the continent. It seems impossible within the context of her time and place, and the narrator assumes she cannot escape. My idea, he tells us, was that "I should never again see Becky. I had seen her for the last time, I believed, . . . that she had succumbed at last to the situation" (79). Thus the narrator's assumptions about these sisters' place within the New England domestic sphere belie the possibilities that they (and we) discover. On second reading we discover the narrator's perspective fraught with the same gaps that pepper its narrative structure, and full of unspoken challenges to his self-confident perspective. Even the manner in which the sisters depart becomes significant in this regard – they simply disappear from the text, leaving an absence to be explained to their ailing mother either in silence or in lies.

In the gaps of this narrative, then, we can see the new American Girl emerge. She comes into being in the dark corners of the New England sitting room, and in the fissures that open up in the narrator's construction of her time and place. Her behavior merits "not a word" (76), because there is no word that can explain her. Yet in a manner that clearly foretells *The Ambassadors*, she also comes "out" of that empty space (76), and of her silence, by encountering Europe. Jane in "Europe" is surely James's first version of Chad, becoming "different – different from anything she ever *had* been, or – for that matter – had a chance to be" (74), once left on her own in Florence. Like Chad's, her possibility is seen as both national and cosmopolitan at once.

In *The Ambassadors* and *The Golden Bowl* James transports this refigured Americanness back to Europe, creating both male and female characters who can open themselves to the otherness of Europe and at the same time maintain distinct personal identities and national affiliations. Even the restricted "center of consciousness" mode, which arguably reaches its height in *The Ambassadors*, becomes, in its insistence on the partial perception of events, a narrative elaboration on the necessarily incomplete status of national identity. Strether's Americanness constitutes itself as a continual process of re-creation which intensifies throughout *The Ambassadors*. As John Carlos Rowe puts it, "Instead of rendering French peasant life, for example, Strether expresses his own 'American' story."[135] The narrative of *The Ambassadors* becomes the accumulation of Strether's successive acts of signifying or imagining both his community and his nation. In this respect it is crucial that James forces his hero to revise rather then abandon his Americanness. Strether and Chad both return home changed Americans, changed particularly in their ability to be open to cultural difference, and to accept their perpetually incomplete and partial perspectives. In other words, they have become, in James's ideal sense, feminized.[136]

The Ambassadors, like James's other late fiction, seems to valorize this processual, partial, feminine kind of vision, particularly as it relates to national identity. Despite his continuing insistence on his Americanness, no one community seems capable of providing Strether with the complexity of perspective that he has established by the end of this narrative. Only Maria Gostry, the closest thing to an ideal American woman in this novel, can begin to broaden his understanding and fill in the gaps. However, Strether's evolving loyalties and shifting affiliations are not truly the kind of broad cosmopolitanism they are sometimes taken to be either. Strether's narrative creates a sense of identity, understanding, and connection based in an essential incompleteness and fragmentation, yet still firmly grounded in national belonging and loyalty. By tarnishing the image of the self-complete ambassador as invincible representative of his country, James rejects the perpetually determined and unified nation, and replaces it with its ideally feminized counterpart.

The question of nationality in this novel moves beyond the feminization of Strether in his encounter with Mme. de Vionnet and Paris. It raises the issue of the very sound of this feminization. If we turn to the Seventh Book, where, poised in the moment of waiting for Sarah Pocock, Strether realizes his independence, we see the issues of speaking, naming, and – their opposite – of silence, raised again and again. Waymarsh, in cabling to Woollett for guidance, has issued "the loudest possible call" for help in rescuing Strether.[137] As Strether remarks to Maria, "We shall have at last, in the consequences of his act, something definite we can talk about" (232). Of course this is precisely what they never have, what the novel as a whole avoids (to the consternation of its many unsympathetic readers). In this instance, the response Mrs. New-some sends her ambassador is supreme silence, a silence that brings her presence to Paris as no number of missives could possibly have: "What *was* remarkable was the way his friend's nature and manner put on for him, through this very drop of demonstration, a greater intensity ... the silence was a sacred hush, a finer medium ... he had never seen her so soundless and if he had never, on the other hand, felt her so highly, so almost austerely, herself" (238). Silence in this case becomes a danger-ous power, one which seems to represent the supreme capacity of the feminine art of persuasion. Strether struggles with the appropriate response to this silence, demonstrating the "uncertainty" about his position in Paris within the lack of concrete knowledge that comes with this indirect manner of assertion (247).

How to respond, what to call his position, how to name the change that has come over both himself and Chad – these are the questions that preoccupy Strether from this point to the end of the novel. As he arrives at the Cheval Blanc, in the Eleventh Book, Strether even characterizes his pleasure in Mme. de Vionnet as a question of tone: "One of the things that most lingered with him on this hillside was the delightful facility, with such a woman, of arriving at a new tone; he thought ... of all the tones she might make possible if one were to try her, and at any rate of the probability that one could trust her to fit them into occasions" (384). If it seems at first to be a simple matter of reading the text of the situation, the text, as both Strether and we know, refuses to give up its object simply. In this pivotal scene the question of tone, the object of a text, and international difference become linked, making it clear that to choose any one tone, or assert any account with certitude, is to miss the point.

The conditions had nowhere so asserted their difference from those of Woollett as they appeared to him to assert it in the little court of the Cheval Blanc ... They were few and simple, scant and humble, but they were *the thing*, as he would have called it ... "The" thing was the thing that implied the greatest number of other things of the sort he had had to tackle. (386)

"The greatest number of other things" include not only the range of possible experiences in Paris, but the range of possible ways of speaking of them represented by Mme. de Vionnet, who, when speaking English, had seemed to Strether to have a "language quite to herself" and a "monopoly of a special shade of speech" but, when suddenly heard speaking French, shifts "back into a mere voluble class or race" (392). It is she, then, who represents the cosmopolitan tone in this novel, one which is not only adopted by Strether but mirrored in the circuitous style of the text. If in the end we do not know whether we can call the attachment between Mme. de Vionnet and Chad "virtuous," it is because there has been so much said about it that makes a declarative statement of identity impossible.

The image of the nation presented in *The Golden Bowl* is more insistent on the specifically feminine ideal, if to a great extent because of the power of its female characters. By positioning Adam Verver within a family constellation primarily directed by its two women, James ensures that even the very real power of his money gets dispersed through feminine hands. Adam Verver is James's ultimate expression of the American commercial man. Yet he is rendered generally innocuous here because of his abdication of the social realm. His sole independent act, that of marrying Charlotte, may itself be seen as conditioned by the discovery of his own lack of identity when left on his own, a discovery manipulated by Maggie herself.

Thus, in *The Golden Bowl*, James portrays the appropriation of the masculine American commercial power by the feminized sphere of manners. Maggie acquires Amerigo in a feminine way. She is never brash or foolishly fearless, nor does she simply assert her superiority. Rather, she exhibits an extraordinary ability to perceive and understand the others around her without obviously objectifying them, and uses her perceptions to further her ability to manipulate the situation. When Maggie discovers the flaw in the golden bowl she also insists that Amerigo *see* this flaw, demonstrating the degree to which understanding and manipulation are combined in her: "She had said 'Don't you see?' on purpose, and was to feel the next moment that it had acted."[138] Perception, understanding, and control become rolled into one for Maggie, as the power of her gaze gets translated into direct power over Amerigo and Charlotte. James makes Maggie strong in an ideally feminine way,[139] insisting on the social power and success inherent in the interplay of discrimination and assertion.

The connection of this feminine power to the international situation of the novel is based partly on Maggie's new American blend of femininity, and on Charlotte's position as its other pole. When we first hear of Charlotte we learn that Amerigo found it difficult to determine "*her* race-quality. Nothing in her definitely placed her; she was a rare, a special product... It wasn't a question of her strange sense for tongues... The point was that in this young woman it was a beauty in itself, and almost a mystery" (40). As Amerigo tells us, "She doesn't like her country" (30). She goes back there to encounter a restricted role and thwarted desires. Still, in the end, like Chad and Strether in *The Ambassadors*, she realizes she can only establish the meaning of her identity in America.

But what of Amerigo? The Italian prince whose name can only imply the interconnection of Europe and America ends up separated from his desire by the distance of the ocean. He who at first appears as something exotic and unfathomable, as the ultimate adventure in difference, finishes the novel almost completely possessed by Maggie. If he takes after his namesake in any way it is in his adventure with an American family that ultimately absorbs him, imposing upon him an American version of the rules of propriety and property that come with marriage. He has thus, by the end, lost the power of his exoticism. His Italian heritage no longer plays a role in his social existence. He almost seems to be being punished for attempting to mix European and American mores, finishing with almost nothing of his own. According to William Veeder, "[Maggie] realizes that in reclaiming Amerigo for 'love' she has reduced them both to 'nothing.' Negation marks Amerigo forever, so Maggie too is negated" (244). While I do not agree that Maggie emerges so completely destitute, clearly there does not exist any possibility of Amerigo becoming once more a viable and appealing presence.

In Amerigo's possession and destruction by the Ververs and in Charlotte's banishment back to a homeland she professes not to love, James's nativism re-asserts itself. The international situation seems to have reached its limit in the connection between Amerigo and Charlotte which is both adulterous and adulterating. Maggie does not harm herself in marrying an Italian because it is she who possesses him by the power of her gaze, her money, and her social mores. There is never any real danger to her Americanness. Amerigo and Charlotte, however, who each contain within them the elements of a combined culture, pose a real threat to any national identity. While James may applaud American openness to Europe, he punishes Charlotte for acquiescing to Amerigo's desire to re-make her as half Italian:

Her account of the mystery didn't suffice: her recall of her birth in Florence and Florentine childhood; her parents, from the great country, but themselves already of a corrupt generation, demoralised, falsified, polyglot well before her... Such reminiscences, naturally, gave a ground, but they had not prevented him from insisting that some strictly civil ancestor – generations back, and from the Tuscan hills if she would – made himself felt, ineffaceably, in her blood and in her tone. She knew nothing of the ancestor, but she had taken his theory from him, gracefully enough, as one of the little presents that make friendship flourish. (41)

From the first, the attraction between these two hinges on their mutual admiration for the combined qualities of the other. That they switch back and forth from Italian to English voices the threat they pose to any discourse of nationality and underscores their inhabitance of a separate (mongrel) sphere. Still there are many characters in James's international fiction who do as much. The fault here seems rather to lie in Charlotte's provenance from a line already "corrupt . . . demoralised," and "falsified," her embrace of the idea of a mixed blood heritage, and, even more importantly, her subsequent rejection of America.

Thus here the question of a cosmopolitan language reaches its limit just as we might say the indeterminacy of James's style also nears a breaking point in *The Golden Bowl*. Corruption and misreading replace the pleasure in textual variety of *The Ambassadors*. All of a sudden it *does* matter whether Charlotte is innocent or guilty at least in terms of the action of the novel, and even more so, it matters whether the prince has presented a false story of his relations with her. In confronting him, Maggie reconstructs the history of the golden bowl, which itself presents a doubled scene of speech, resting as it does on the preliminary tale told by the shopkeeper about Charlotte and Amerigo. Amerigo is rendered speechless in this scene, not because of Maggie's command of the facts – but rather because she refuses to reduce the story to those facts: "It was still, for a minute as if he waited for something worse; wanted everything that was in her to come out, any definite fact, anything more precisely namable" (441). In her ability to control the flow of facts Maggie also becomes able to multiply her power still further, appearing to speak not only for herself but for her father, and using that opportunity to constrain the prince: "She would as yet, certainly, do nothing to make it easy. She felt with her sharpest thrill how he was straitened and tied, and with the miserable pity of it her present conscious purpose of keeping him so could none the less perfectly accord" (441). The power of female speech in this occasion seems far from the soothing conciliatory tones of ideal womanhood. The flexibility of speech becomes here a hazard and a weapon, and the proclamation of unitary identities seemingly the only solution.

James's use of the feminine ideal to re-make America rests on the assumption that the nation's cultural lessons must be learned from outside and that Americans must incorporate not only Europe's concern with manners but also its insistence on a certain pluralism. It is the dogma of a Mamie Pocock that undermines the possibility of an advanced American culture. It is the openness of Mme. de Vionnet's Paris that presents the best scene of instruction. Even if James applauds a kind of cultural mutuality, ultimately, like many in the Progressive Era who feared race decadence, he cannot sanction its extension to the biological realm. Miscegenation of the sort represented by Amerigo and Charlotte ultimately threatens Charlotte, who, from start to finish, is so open to Europe as to prefer a fantasy about her mixed heritage to the reality of her American identity. Charlotte is noticeably silenced and contained and is reduced to the level of ignorance which is "a torment" and this is how she is held (543).

Still Charlotte's negative containment, which in essence gives her nothing new to say, also affects the text as a whole. The long circuitous passages give way to short interrupted lines of dialogue; the construction of character and scene succumbs to their dispersal. The final chapters of the novel lack the accretion of detail and event that is the bedrock of James's late fiction. At the same time the narrative succumbs to the negative, presenting us with such passages as this exchange between Maggie and Mrs. Assingham in Chapter 40:

"I've told you before that I know absolutely nothing."
"Well – that's what *I* know," said the Princess.
Her friend again hesitated. Then nobody knows -?
. . .
"Nobody"
"Not – a little – Charlotte?" "A little?" the princess echoed. "To know anything would be, for her, to know enough." (543)

Gone is the potential for a positive construction of meaning in either the cosmopolitan scene or the speech to which it gives rise.

Thus, while in the late fiction James sidesteps the issue of race as such, it is as present there as in his essays of a few years later and as bound to the female incarnation of the nation. In the fiction Charlotte and Amerigo loom as dangerous characters because of their resistance to incorporation within the American sphere, a resistance that is symbolized by their use of Italian. In *The American Scene* the Jews threaten not only because of their resistance to assimilation but even more so because of their indiscriminate use of the American idiom. Both present the danger of a mongrelization that will not hide itself, blend into a pervasive American pluralism, or adopt the dominant Anglo-Saxon cultural and linguistic heritage. In this way James presents the early version of the nativist position that will inhabit much later modernism. As Walter

Benn Michaels tells us "miscegenation, the breaking down of difference becomes the privileged sex crime of nativist modernism."[140] From William Carlos Williams to William Faulkner, the notion of impurity or the disruption of difference carries with it a threat to the strength of American identity: "American modernism consisted in the set of ontological commitments that both derived from and made sense of the commitment to racial difference. The commitment to the ontology of racial identity was, in other words, internal to American modernism."[141] While James's position is much more paradoxical than this later version, the search for regional differences in *The American Scene*, the demand for discursive distinctions in *The Speech and Manners of American Women*, and, even more dramatically, the fear of miscegenation in *The Golden* Bowl, all mark the first step in that direction. It is in the hands, or more aptly, the mouths of American women that resistance to a distinctionless, mongrelized America lies.

On the other hand, the ideal feminine virtues that James urges on his nation resist reduction to a purely nativist position. The picture of womanhood presented by *The Speech and Manners of American Women* insists on the kind of female roles that also served many other purposes in the Progressive Era, and were often a vehicle to *combat* simple racism by counterpoising "assimilation to the politics of racial exclusion."[142] The American woman's discursive performance of the nation is one which forces a revision of the received notions of Americanness, improving it, in James's eyes, by forcing an expansion of its ability to respond and accommodate. For James, she fills the role that Homi Bhabha ascribes to the people in general: "[they] are neither the beginning or the end of the national narrative; they represent the cutting edge between the totalizing powers of the social and the forces that signify the more specific address to contentious, unequal interests and identities within the population."[143] Woman as the site of the intersection between the pedagogical and the performative, the historical narrative of the nation and its ongoing discursive expression, stands poised on that cutting edge.

At the same time, James uses the ideally feminized version of America to challenge the growing imperialism of this period. Placed in the international context, America-as-ideal-woman must temper its tendency to individuality, tone down its assertiveness, and become willing to learn the cultural lessons of other nations. At the same time, it must conceive of itself always in connection to others, never brashly asserting dominance or superiority. Just as in the domestic arena feminine discourse preserved distinctions without dislodging the ongoing unity of the national self-concept, in the international sphere the feminized nation cannot so assert its difference as to challenge the power of its co-existence with other nations or its interdependence on them.

It is precisely in re-creating the nation within a multivalent, difference-laden discourse, and in casting it as a feminized participant in an international community, that James's late writings resist the pull of simple nativism. And it is in placing women at the fore of the effort to create a mature and modern America that these writings challenge the restrictive codes of the domestic sphere. But the cultural icon of America that James creates is a woman who is both cosmopolitan and loyal native at once, both a powerful Progressive woman, and a well-spoken, community-minded, ethical presence. Within her figure and her voice the tension between a complexly differentiated twentieth-century America and the ongoing narrative prescriptions of an assimilative national identity will long persist. The paradox is inescapable, both in James's late writings and in the modernist discourses of gender, race, and nation that they illuminate.

CHAPTER 3

Marcel Proust

PROUST, BERNARD LAZARE, AND THE POLITICS OF PARIAHDOM

Les Roumains, les Egyptiens et les Turcs peuvent détester les Juifs. Mais dans un salon français les différences entre ces peuples ne sont pas si perceptibles, et un Israélite faisant son entrée comme il sortait du fond du désert ... contente parfaitement un goût d'orientalisme. Seulement il faut pour cela que le Juif n'appartienne pas au "monde".

(The Rumanians, the Egyptians, the Turks may hate the Jews. But in a French drawing-room the differences between those peoples are not so apparent, and a Jew making his entry as though he were emerging from the desert ... completely satisfies a certain taste for the oriental. Only it is essential that the Jews in question should not be actually "in" society.)

Marcel Proust, *A la recherche du temps perdu*, II: 194

N'ai-je donc pas le droit d'être Juif? Est-ce là le crime irrémissible? Et d'être tel, cela vaut-il l'éternelle haine de tous? ... Je suis Juif et j'ignore tout des Juifs. Je suis désormais un paria ... il faut que je sache qui je suis et pourquoi je suis haï, et ce que je puis être.

(Don't I have the right to be Jewish? Is that the irremissable crime? And if I am, do I deserve the eternal hatred of all? ... I am a Jew and I know nothing of Jews. I am henceforth a pariah ... I must know who I am and why I am hated and who I can be.)

Bernard Lazare, *Le Fumier de Job*, 25

Proust may have been closer in spirit to Bernard Lazare.

Julia Kristeva, *Time and Sense*, 145 [1]

"I was the first Dreyfusard" Proust proudly proclaims in a letter referring to his ardent early support for Dreyfus and his role in organizing the first Dreyfusard petition.[2] It was Proust who convinced Anatole France to take up the case, and he who helped turn Mme. Arman's literary salon into the province of the *cause célèbre*. However, Bernard Lazare, anarchist, symbolist poet, journalist, and Proust's contemporary, was by most accounts "the man most responsible for the public launching of the Dreyfus Affair."[3] His bold pamphlet *Une Erreur judiciaire* appeared in 1896, two days before Proust's petition and more than a year before Zola's *J'accuse*. Bernard Lazare was the prophet of the cause,[4] able to see as though with heightened vision the gravity and wide-ranging import-ance that the case of the Jewish officer would soon take on.

Of course Proust and Lazare cannot both be the first Dreyfusard. Publication history forces us to give the nod to Lazare, as does his obsessive devotion to the cause. Yet, the coincidence of these two claims reflects more than simple vanity. Proust's desire to be known as an early Dreyfusard marks the importance of the Affair not only as *the* defining event in *fin-de-siècle* France's changing national concept, but also as a crucial social delimiter, the reference point for identity and belonging within the intellectual spheres in which Proust moved. It is precisely this premise that the Affair marks within *A la recherche du temps perdu*, where, long past the days described in *Le côté de Guermantes*, the legacy of Dreyfusism is the demise of the social borders of the aristocratic salon. Whether nationalist or Dreyfusard, as Proust makes clear, the salon became determined by ideology rather than title.[5] While for those in elite circles it signified social suicide, for many within Proust's circle Dreyfusard identity implied bravery, prescience, social acuity, and moral intelligence – an ability to see in a manner not normally em-ployed in ordinary social relations. It implied not only willingness to be connected to the Jewish community but also willingness to separate oneself from France (without, however, relinquishing the right to call for a new verdict in the name of French justice).[6] Importantly, for both Proust and Lazare, it required construction of a subtle new mode of belonging, one predicated on the insight that comes from standing at the margins, from forging new community identities out of conscious pariahdom.[7]

The term "pariah" rings strangely when applied to Proust. After all, Proust was in his youth a gifted and committed social climber, a *parvenu* who valued the contact with Mme. Straus's famous salon over the friendship with Daniel Halévy that brought him there. These are precisely the kinds of assimilative behaviors that Hannah Arendt de-scribes as dangerous to Jewish life and contrary to a constructive use of pariahdom. While, as has often been remarked, the novel seethes with parody and caricature of the Faubourg, and its worst social excesses stand firmly outlined (Swann snubbed, the Duc de Guermante's ball held right after his cousin's death, the Verdurins' hypocritical treatment of Charlus, etc.), still Proust returns us there again and again, making the elite drawing room the privileged scene of the novel.

Yet, despite the ultimate triumph of Mme. Verdurin, the *parvenu* does not fully prevail in *A la recherche*. By the end of the novel we are as uncertain and off balance in her circle as is Marcel when stepping on the uneven paving stones of the Guermantes' courtyard. Proust uses his narrator's slip to the borders and his ultimate withdrawal from *le monde* to contest simple belonging as the means of constructing social identity, even before we learn of Mme. Verdurin's final triumph. In this sense he "extend[s] ... [his] condition of marginality" rather than trying to erase it, opposing it to the stultifying, bourgeois principles of group uniformity and upward mobility that predominate in *Belle Epoque* France.[8] The emergence of the Jew and the homosexual, the rise of the perverse and the secret, and the unfolding of the view from the periphery, where the gift of prophecy becomes both more plausible and less desirable, all clearly work to undermine the young Marcel's enrapture with aristocratic social codes. Neither the aristocratic privileging of the differences of rank nor the bourgeois concern with sameness (which ultimately unites the Guermantes and Méséglise ways), can, in the end, compel either the narrator or us.

In thus negotiating between the aristocracy and the *parvenu* within *A la recherche* we must turn back to Bernard Lazare. For it is in the unlikely connection between Proust and Lazare, constituted within the embrace and re-figuration of pariahdom, and of Jewish pariahdom in particular, that the political implications of Proust's constructions of community become clear. Hannah Arendt uses Lazare's writings to elaborate a theoretical dichotomy between the positions of *parvenu* and pariah in which the Jewish *parvenu* hastens his people's downfall; the lonely life of the wandering Jew is made more pitiful and more culpable by his efforts to be lost in the new national crowd.[9] The alternative tradition, which Arendt locates not only in Bernard Lazare, but also in Heinrich Heine, Rahel Varnhagen, Scholem Aleichem, Franz Kafka, and even Charlie Chaplin, provides the antidote. The "conscious pariah" – one who accepts, displays, and extends the condition of marginality – is able to see that indeed all Jews are pariahs, and that any new community must come from an espousal of that status. Thus "in their own position as social outcasts such men reflect the political status of their entire people."[10]

Lazare's conscious pariahdom becomes a call to solidarity on new terms, solidarity outside the realm of power. As Charles Péguy puts it, "this was a man, . . . for whom the entire apparatus of power, the reason of state, temporal powers, authorities of all sorts – political, intellectual, and even mental – weighed not an ounce in the face of a revolt, of a movement of the conscience itself."[11] Unlike other Zionists Lazare never uses nationalism simply to reverse the roles of insider/outsider. In fact it is his very refusal to re-create bourgeois society in a new Jewish state that eventually forces him to separate from Herzl and the growing Zionist movement. Both Proust and Lazare find their identities not merely in belonging to a comfortable circle but rather in connecting to it from a position of removal, a distance that can be achieved by traveling to Rumania as in the case of Lazare or by remaining inaccessible except by letter, hidden within the reversed time of Proust's upended nights and days. In Lazare's writings, as in Proust's, the movement beyond assimilation brings with it an enlightenment about past affiliations as well as a new paradigm for building future selves. While Proust does not follow Lazare down the Zionist path, nor – clearly – does he flaunt all political authority, his novel reflects a movement of the conscience like Lazare's, one that seeks to find, in the vision from outside, a means around the *parvenu*/pariah dichotomy and an ethical perspective on the excesses of the social world.[12]

By connecting such divergent writings this chapter seeks to demonstrate not only how *A la recherche* engages with the questions of social identity posed by the problem of Jewishness at the *fin de siècle*, but also how Proust's seemingly idiosyncratic fascinations with both *parvenu* and pariah, with exclusive places and circular routes, with hidden perversion and open voyeurism, imply an effort to situate the celebrated Proustian self within a new realm of political relation. At the same time, by relying on Lazare's category of conscious pariahdom, this chapter attempts to demonstrate how that thinker, so often written about[13] and yet so problematic even for Zionists, speaks not only to questions of Jewish identity but also to the narrative intersection of identity and political community. In this way both writers expand Arendt's critique of the social realm in twentieth-century politics along the lines suggested by Seyla Benhabib.[14] At the same time, because it is always both public and private, and because it comes into being in the creation of what Arendt calls "life stories," the notion of the pariah community in these writings also moves beyond Arendt's emphasis on public life, placing politics within both Lazare's social action and Proust's narrative contemplation.[15]

Lazare's idiosyncratic politics emerge in the period of Zionist awakening across Western Europe. From the time of the Dreyfus Affair Zionist writers sought not only to rehabilitate the status of the Jew within European civil society but also to restructure basic principles of affiliation whereby Jewishness might be seen as a new category of national identification. At the same time, by defining their separate allegiance Zionists continued to proclaim the outsider status of Europe's Jews. Rather than seeking to belong to communities which, after years of citizenship, were again excluding them, they abandoned the notion that assimilation was either possible or desirable. Following Teodor Herzl, they strove to create a completely separate sphere for themselves, re-emphasizing rather than combating their perpetual otherness within European society. In other words, Zionist Jews in Europe at the turn of the century chose to confront their increasingly embattled social status by avowing and building upon their pariahdom, even if ultimately the solution they proposed often reinscribed the same kind of nationalism that had been used to isolate them.

Lazare's anarcho-Zionism is unusual and difficult because it insists on interlinking the dissolution of all social hierarchies with the empowerment of Europe's Jews, and it is for this reason that he becomes so compelling to Arendt and others. Lazare, like Proust (who was only six years his junior),[16] responds with horror to the increasing power of the bourgeoisie in *fin-de-siècle* France but his anarchism drives him to promote the very kinds of social disintegration that Proust will bemoan. Lazare is able to see that assimilation into the bourgeoisie will ultimately disempower the Jews whose special identity is predicated on existing outside of and often in opposition to the machinery of the capitalist social sphere. Lazare urges Europe's Jews to resist upward mobility and to recognize that their status as pariahs links them to the disenfranchised everywhere, and that, as Arendt puts it, "one had to resign oneself to the fact that to be a Jew meant to belong either to an overprivileged upper class or to an underprivileged mass."[17] Over and over again his writings emphasize this point: only as a community of pariahs who do not seek to erase that status, either through assimilation or through the creation of their own bourgeois state, will the Jews become emancipated.

The debate about Jewish identity within France in this period reflects widespread and profound uneasiness with existing categories of national belonging. According to Eugen Weber, it is only in the ten to fifteen years before 1900 that France develops the unified, industrialized economy that allows its modern national identity to emerge.[18] More so than in England, French nationality at the end of the nineteenth century was based on a variety of ways of life and of allegiances. Inhabitants of many areas spoke French as a second language, if they spoke it at all.[19] Their manner of eating, working and constructing their houses belonged more to the region than to any larger entity.[20] And the *Patrie* to which citizens claimed allegiance could be the local *pays* where they were born as often as the nation at large.[21] Responding to Renan's contention that a nation must be founded on the desire to live together, Weber claims that "in 1882 consent might be assumed from indifference, but there could be little desire to live together with people who might as well have come from another world. The heritage of memories was not held in common but differed according to region and to social stock."[22] Belonging to the nation when one did not speak its official language, or when one felt as one entered Paris as if one were coming into a foreign city, required an ability to transcend concrete differences and imagine a broad, encompassing unity.

Having been granted the same rights as other Frenchmen at the time of the Revolution, Jews in France throughout the nineteenth century thought of themselves as French.[23] They permeated society, often leaving the confines of the overtly Jewish community. Even within the world of the *Consistoire*, which governed both religious and secular affairs, Jews identified themselves as distinctly French. Théodore Reinach wrote in 1885, "after 1791, there are not, properly speaking, *Juifs* [Jews] of France, but rather French citizens who practiced the *Israélite* [Jewish] religion."[24] Using terminology that anticipates Arendt's distinctions between "the Jewish notables" and "the Jews in general,"[25] they call themselves "*Israélites*" rather than "*Juifs*,"[26] hoping that the term will signal their distance from the Jewish stereotype, and mark them as distinctly French. In the years immediately after the Franco-Prussian War at least 5,000 Jews from Alsace and Lorraine fled to Paris, proclaiming the importance of their French identity, and seeing themselves as exemplary citizens. Despite the fact that they were "among the poorest and socially most backward of Western European Jewry,"[27] these Alsatian Jews were considered *Israélites*, not "Jews in general." They were potential members of what was referred to as a sort of "aristocracy of the blood."[28]

But the dichotomy between this elite group of *Israélites* and the "Jews in general" becomes clearly drawn when the Eastern European Jews begin to arrive in Paris in the 1880s and 1890s. The Jews of Alsace and Lorraine had been far from ideal *Israélites* upon their initial arrival in

Paris.[29] The refugees who began arriving from Eastern Europe in the 1880s, however, neither received so warm a welcome nor were so successful at assimilating themselves into French society. Over and over again, French Jewish writings from this period proclaim the vast differences between the Parisian community and these "backward cousins." While organizations like the Alliance Israélite Universelle pronounced their obligation to aid their less fortunate co-religionists,[30] they often did so with an air of condescension that insisted on the complete superiority of the hybrid French–Jewish culture.[31] In addition, assimilated Jews, many themselves immigrants from Alsace and Lorraine, began to fear that these backward refugees would besmirch their reputations and challenge their hard-won status. As anti-Semitic feeling began to rise throughout France, Parisian *Israélites* increasingly came to blame it on these Eastern European *Juifs*.[32]

The turmoil surrounding the Dreyfus Affair marks not only the height of anti-Semitic thinking but also the entrance of many widespread social and demographic changes into the sphere of public opinion. It consolidates concern about the place of religion in French society and brings out smoldering questions, left from Boulanger and the Panama Scandal, about the dangerous power of hidden forces in society. It re-ignites concern about France's decline as a world economic and military power, and voices the possibility that not only the degeneration of the French themselves but also their infiltration and control by foreign elements are to blame. If the Jewish community was closing itself in around its elite French identity, so was the wider French world. But ironically enough, the new conception of French nationality that began to emerge did not recognize the Frenchness that these Jews so prided themselves on. At the turn of the century, both among Jews and among the general French populace, affiliation with the nation became predicated on who one was not, rather than on who one was. Because even the hint of Jewish ancestry in those long assimilated branded them as other than purely French, the categories of the Jew and of the pariah once again came to be linked.

In France it is in this climate that the notion of Jewish community again begins to take hold. Although initially many French Jews reject Herzl's idea for a Jewish state (1897),[33] many soon begin to believe that the only escape from anti-Semitism is to constitute themselves as a nation apart. Most of the Jews who rally around Dreyfus are far from being Zionist, but their willingness to declare themselves as Dreyfusards displays a willingness to affiliate with a community that, despite the eventual exoneration of Dreyfus himself, is increasingly isolated and ostracized.[34] In the years from the eruption of the Dreyfus Affair to the First World War, many Jews, like Bernard Lazare, Swann in *A la recherche*, and the half-Jewish Proust, move beyond assimilation to embrace not only their solidarity with other Jews, but also the outsider status that their solidarity confers on them.[35]

However, not all Zionists at the turn of the century willingly embrace this outsider status, and even fewer accept the notion that it requires solidarity with all those who live on the fringes of society. Herzl clearly defines a nation in the terms of oppression, saying that "a nation is . . . in my mind a historical group of men of a recognizable cohesion held together by a common enemy."[36] The Jewish nation he envisions is consolidated by the multiplication of its anti-Semitic enemies:

The sentiment of solidarity with which we have been reproached so frequently and so acrimoniously was in the process of disintegration at the period when we were attacked by anti-semitism. And anti-semitism served to strengthen it anew. We returned home, as it were. For Zionism is a home-coming to the Jewish fold even before it becomes a home-coming to the Jewish land.[37]

This version of Jewish nationalism, which Herzl describes again and again in his addresses to the Zionist Congresses, may be seen as simply another version of the same kind of nationalism emerging in France at large as well as elsewhere in Europe at this time. Like the wider French variety, Herzl's nationalism is also increasingly linked to a bourgeois society, with capitalist enterprise a cornerstone of its edifice. While *A Jewish State* makes repeated references to the status of workers within the new Zionist society, Herzl's writings become less and less insistent on this point and more and more preoccupied with the creation of "The Jewish Company," the corporation established to finance the new Jewish state. At the Zionist Congresses, dominated by Herzl, the concerns of bourgeois Jews from Western Europe come increasingly to predominate over the needs of Jewish workers and immigrants from the East.[38] In reaction to the exclusion of Jews from mainstream society Herzl seeks to create a separate nation where Jews themselves make up the bourgeoisie and can therefore for the first time experience true belonging without denying their Jewish identities. By becoming a separate nation based on a single culture, Herzl hopes, Jews will be able to erase forever their feeling of being outsiders.

On the other hand, because it comes out of the anarchist movement, Bernard Lazare's Zionism recognizes this version of nationalism as immediately abhorrent. As a founding editor of the journal *Les Entretiens politiques et littéraires,* which published Lazare, as well as Proudhon, Bakunin, and Kropotkin, Lazare was involved in that strange amalgam of symbolism and anarchism that emerged in the years between 1890 and 1895, and that rejected the bourgeois world.[39] As Richard D. Sonn puts it, anarchist culture was structured analogically: "A work of art, the example of a saintly personal life, the terrorist's bomb, the martyr's altruistic self-sacrifice were analogs either of the revolution or of the anarchist ideal."[40] For Lazare, the symbolists' tendency to "extend their aesthetic aspirations beyond the production of works of poetry or prose, to seek correspondences with other realms of experience"[41] fueled his desire to create a new analogic kind of action through art.[42]

This anarcho-symbolism, however, was at first distinctly opposed to any sense of Jewish solidarity. Born to a long-established French Jewish family from Nîmes, Lazare arrived in Paris a non-believer seeking to escape the milieu of his parents. His French identity was clear, his Jewishness more ambiguous, especially since, for Jews among the left, affiliation with the religion of their ancestors often still meant connection to capitalism. In addition, the reaction to the Jewish involvement in the Panama Affair within the anarchist camp was to embrace the stereotype of all Jews as corrupt capitalists and to focus revolutionary activity against them. The Jew was once again a "class enemy," to those among the radical left, and Bernard Lazare shared in this opinion.[43]

Lazare's rarely read articles in *Les Entretiens* demonstrate his concern about his paradoxical identity as both Jew and anarchist as well as his effort to come to terms with the rising tide of anti-Semitism, and thus complicate the picture which Arendt has drawn of him. Ironically, considering what will come to be his position in the later part of the 1890s, in these early essays Lazare presents one of the most eloquent articulations of the assimilationist mentality, providing the key terms with which to elevate the "civilized" Jews of France. In two important texts in *Les Entretiens* Lazare codifies the distinction between French *Israélite* and foreign *Juif,* but, using anti-capitalist logic, he divests the *Israélite* from any responsibility for his money-grubbing foreign cousins.[44] The *Juif* "is dominated by the sole preoccupation of making a quick fortune which he gets more easily by fraud, lying and trickery. He despises virtue, poverty and unselfishness."[45] The *Israélite,* on the other hand, contains none of these vices:

Besides this despicable judaism, made worse by greed, and the disdain of noble actions and generous impulses, there are very different beings, there are *Israélites* . . . For years they have lived peacefully, attached to the land where they were born... (I'm speaking and only want to speak of French *Israélites*. The others are foreign and of no consequence to me.) They are poor or not very rich, limited in their desires, and have in front of them only the narrow horizon of relative well-being that belongs to the crowd.[46]

Clearly here the distinction between *Juif* and *Israélite* is based on participation in capitalist endeavor rather than assimilation into the surrounding populace, and this capitalist activity cuts across class lines. For Lazare, the great Jewish financiers of the period, though often well assimilated and proud Frenchmen, would certainly fall into the category of *Juif*, just as would any lowly unscrupulous pedlar.[47] Conversely the definition of the *Israélite* revolves more around the lack of *desire* for riches than any other quality. In this way, Lazare seems able to reconcile his own background with his anarchism, and at the same time to continue to revile the Jew as capitalist.

In similar terms Lazare derides Jewish solidarity in an article that callously rejects the Alliance Israélite Universelle's call for French Jews to support those from other lands: "What do Russian usurers, Gallician pawnbrokers, Polish horse merchants, second hand dealers from Prague, and money changers from France matter to me, a French *Israélite*? By virtue of what pretended fraternity should I preoccupy myself with the measures taken by the czar against subjects who seem to him to accomplish detestable work?"[48] Although much of this article works to demonstrate the demise of Jewish solidarity through the intermixing of races and the degeneration of the Jewish religion, it returns over and over again to the simple thesis that non-French Jews are mostly immoral and tainted by money-grubbing. In fact Lazare here, as in his 1894 book *L'Antisémitisme: son histoire et ses causes* (*Antisemitism: Its History and Its Causes*), even accuses Jewish religious texts of crass materialism. If the Talmud itself promotes trickery and the relentless pursuit of this-worldly fortune, then any Jew who lives within a practicing religious community must be tainted.[49]

Lazare's argument in *L'Antisémitisme* hinges on the assumption, first developed in "Juifs et Israélites," that Jewish community grows out of the national identity which is perpetuated by the laws of the Talmud as well as by persecution from without, rather than out of any racial Jewish identity. It is here that Lazare first develops the concept of Jewish nationality that will spearhead his leadership of French Zionism and which will influence a generation of Zionists to come.[50] Anti-Semitic diatribes almost always accused the Jew of disloyalty to France because of his blood ties to cousins in other lands, and Jewish groups like the

Alliance Israélite often supported this sense of racial affiliation in their efforts to argue for an indissoluble bond among Jews around the world. But Lazare insists that the Jews, as a nation not a race, are a varied group. They are thus not open to the kind of attack leveled by anti-Semites who accuse them of being an inferior race, nor are they born into any blood brotherhood that would prevent them from becoming as French as any one of their neighbors. By the time of *Antisemitism* Lazare no longer asserts the same kind of distinction between the two sorts of Jews as he did in "Juifs et Israélites." Instead he builds on his earlier claim that anyone, regardless of heritage, can become a *Juif* simply by espousing certain puerile values[51] and he insists that Jewish identity remains a chosen affiliation among a diverse lot. "The Jews are not a race they are a nation, they are diverse," he claims.[52] As a nation and not a race, Jews generate their own solidarity out of the consciousness that they need it to survive.

This non-racial understanding of Jewish life runs counter to the predominant view in French society at the end of the nineteenth and the beginning of the twentieth centuries and, despite its emphasis on assimilation, is far more supple than that prevailing in the Consistoire and the Alliance at the time. Clearly, the anti-Semitism that fueled the furor over the Dreyfus Affair demonstrates the power of racism among the bourgeoisie. As Michael Marrus points out, both the Jewish and non-Jewish communities, Dreyfusards and non-Dreyfusards, shared the tendency towards defining Jewishness as a race:

Although the notion of a Jewish race was subjected to a barrage of academic criticism at the end of the century, Jews for the most part stood by its basic premiss of some biological tie among the Jewish people... Jews often combatted anti-Semitic racism with racial information of their own... Scholarly refutation did little, even within the Jewish community, ... to eliminate all elements of racial thinking.[53]

Yet as Todorov makes clear, in this period racism undergoes a transformation. While traditional racism with its blood-based system of categorization still drew adherents, for many at the turn of the century race came to be a category predicated on shared culture rather than shared blood.[54] Concepts like Taine's milieu or Renan's linguistic group[55] diminish the importance of race *per se*, while creating a new system for categorizing humanity. In rejecting traditional racism, these writers create what Todorov refers to as "racialism," turning from biological determinism to a notion of the self as dominated by its hereditary culture. If Renan ultimately rejects the definition of Judaism as a race,[56] he insists on its existence as a socially significant, determining entity.[57] For the racialist, therefore, a religious, linguistic or cultural group, like the Jews, can function to guide behavior and attitudes much in the same manner as one might claim that race does.

On hearing the cry of "death to the Jews!" in the streets as the Dreyfus Affair begins to escalate in 1895–6 Lazare is forced to reassess the value of Jewish nationalism. He formulates the concept of the pariah not only to describe the identity automatically conferred on those who are hated and excluded but also to create it as a mode of being that can be avowed, elaborated upon, and used as the center for a new form of Jewish solidarity, just as Arendt will later do: "Don't I have the right to be Jewish? Is that the irremissable crime? And if I am, do I deserve the eternal hatred of all? ... I am a Jew and I know nothing of Jews. I am henceforth a pariah ... I must know who I am and why I am hated and who I can be."[58] In 1895, having been one of the very first to identify the campaign against Dreyfus as purely anti-Semitic, Lazare was silenced by Dreyfus's friends and family because of his anarchist affiliations. As soon as *Une Erreur judiciare* appeared, Lazare was also snubbed by his *confrères* on the left. The anarchist publications no longer wanted his articles, and the Dreyfusards themselves considered him too flamboyant to be of further use. Lazare, in identifying Jewishness as the source of the social condemnation of Dreyfus, thus condemns himself to ostracism, and in so doing discovers his solidarity not only with Dreyfus but also with other Jewish pariahs. It is in finding himself exiled from *all* camps that he discovers the power of outsider status. He therefore develops the notion of pariahdom not only as a response to anti-Semitism *per se* and to its anarchist version, but also as a critique of the behavior of those Jews like Dreyfus's family who so feared for their *Israélite* status that they could not stand up to injustice. The experience pushes him firmly beyond assimilation and towards further Jewish engagement, as he writes to Joseph Reinach: "I'm not saying anything about the injuries and the insults, nor about the accusations. Nothing about the attitude of the press towards me since that incomprehensible day. From one day to the next, I was a pariah ... You know that this did not discourage me, nor did it stop me in the work I'd undertaken."[59]

Out of this experience Lazare formulates a Zionism based on the principle that the Jewish community must not only remain a nation and strengthen its position as such, but must do so by consciously accepting its pariahdom and fighting all oppression from a position on the fringe. The result is a discourse that, paradoxically, is clearly nationalist, but also firmly committed to anarchist principles. The Jewish people must recognize how their plight makes it necessary for them to ignore internal divisions and to show common cause with all other social pariahs. They must abandon their bourgeois affiliations and build solidarity with society's outcasts, the working classes. Lazare repudiates the *Juif/Israélite* distinction and now bemoans the fact that in assimilation the Jews have come to be pitted against each other: "For Jews solidarity had been an acquired virtue... After emancipation ... the Jews were once again dispersed, fragmented, and even in the countries where they were not emancipated, the bourgeoisie separated itself from the people, having acquired privileges – the solidarity had disappeared."[60] Assimilation becomes the false road to *embourgeoisement* and away from community with the less fortunate. However, when assimilation ends in a roadblock, and the inevitable pariahdom of even the assimilated and "emancipated" Jews becomes clear, Jews will once again come to find solidarity with each other as with other pariahs: "Western Jews have lost the meaning ... [of the Bible] but they will find it again sooner than they think, when the country where they live becomes like the ancient city of Mizraim." According to Lazare's new formulation, if the Jews accept that pariahdom rather than continuing to escape or deny it, they will acquire new power, as will, by implication, any other pariah group that can transform its externally determined status into an openly avowed, conscious identity: "It is by their own power that they will liberate themselves, when they reconquer the dignity that others would have made them lose."[61]

For Lazare the fight for nationhood means not just the escape into a homeland that Herzl proposes at this time, but rather a constant battle against oppression of all kinds, and the constant reaffirmation of community that this battle provides. Henceforth the term "emancipation" in his writings means the Jew's coming into consciousness as a member of a community of outsiders, and all other forms of so-called Jewish liberation, like those of the Alliance Israélite Universelle, are only empty promises. It is for this reason that Lazare's Zionist writings have remained so persuasive in the twentieth century to those like Isaiah Berlin and Hannah Arendt.

Yet Arendt does him a disservice when she relegates his position to the simple opposition between pariah and *parvenu*. Even after his abandonment of the categories of *Juif* and *Israélite*, Lazare's writings consistently describe thoughtless pursuit of wealth as the grounds for unethical and self-serving behavior. It is not the fact of wanting to belong that injures the assimilated Jew but rather his refusal to see the injustice inherent in all distinctions within French society. Lazare's anti-statism implicates all who accept and wield cultural or state power; his condemnation applies not only to the notoriously anti-Semitic Rothschilds in the 1890s but also to the anti-clerical Combists of the early years of the twentieth century. Lazare's formulations thus do not create the sort of dichotomy that Arendt describes. He underscores again and again that justice is what binds Jew to Jew, and solidarity what unites the anarchist cadre with the outlawed monk and the ostracized pedlar. Pariahdom becomes the opportunity to form an ethical relation, a cosmopolitan linking of other and other, outside the corruption of established power, and beyond the parochialism of the conventional political movement.

On the other hand, in Lazare's peculiar form of Zionism the notions of "community" and "Other" become indissolubly linked, and emerge especially in the figure of the prophet.[62] In thus rejecting any rigid delineation of the two poles of social relation Lazare presents another possible mode of being in the world which in some ways resembles Arendt's "web of relationships." Yet for Arendt the problem of modern political life is the usurpation of the concerns of the public sphere by the private and social realms. Action for Arendt is distinct from what she calls "behavior" because it occurs in public and because it arises out of the effort of the individual to distinguish himself from others within a contest of achievement:

The public realm itself, the *polis* was permeated by a fiercely agonal spirit, where everybody had constantly to distinguish himself from all others to show through unique deeds or achievements that he was the best of all. The public realm, in other words, was reserved for individuality; it was the only place where men could show who they really and inexchangeably were. It was for the sake of this chance ... that each was willing to share in the burden.[63]

But for Lazare the prophetic role of the pariah moves beyond the contest of opinion and the need to distinguish oneself as an individual in the public sphere, into an insistence that political action is at the heart of both seemingly private Jewish affiliation and the public position of separation. This is an active work – not of mediation, as might figure in Arendt's model – but of being both in the community and always irrevocably apart from any claims or boundaries that it might establish. In claiming both of these arenas as well as both of these positions at once, and in crafting political action as the intersections of these concerns rather than the result of their conflict, Lazare expands the politics of community beyond Arendt's agonal public sphere.[64]

This coincidence of separation and belonging also resembles what Emmanuel Levinas describes as the position of the visionary Jewish prophet, who evidences "a simultaneous engagement and disengagement. The most deeply committed (engagé) man, one who can never be silent, the prophet, is also the most separate being."[65] Separation from society is placed at the heart of Jewish life, but for Levinas, as for Lazare, this separation need not always demand the removal of Jews to another country, nor the assumption that their status demands national borders. Rather, Levinas emphasizes Jewish education and religious observance as the means to a separate identity:

> Enlightenment and meaning dawn only with the existents rising up and establishing themselves in this horrible neutrality of the *there is*. They are on the path which leads from existence to the existent and from the existent to the Other ... which is the situation of the conscience ... the *manner* of the subject. This manner is the power of rupture, the refusal of Hegelian totality ... From this comes the power to judge history instead of awaiting its impersonal verdict.

Levinas proposes that in this rupture, which comes from rejecting the impersonality of belonging to a totalizing culture, one also comes to know the other. One must not only tear oneself away from totality but one must substitute "the relation with the other (Autrui)."[66] In this formulation, as in Lazare's, the Jew faced with anti-Semitism ruptures with society as he comes into consciousness; the experience of becoming other and coming into relationship with a community of others follows immediately.

Not only does the Jew who becomes a conscious pariah automatically create a relationship with other Jews and indeed with all pariahs, but he also enters into a new form of relationship with society. Clearly, there can be no pariah without the community from which he is separated; the relationship between the two is irrevocable. As Georg Simmel puts it, "the stranger, like the poor and like sundry 'inner enemies' is an element of the group itself. His position as a full-fledged member involves both being outside it and confronting it."[67] The distance between the *parvenu* and the pariah is therefore not so great as it first appears, or as Arendt paints it. Both categories of outsiders constitute their identity from an intimate relationship with society and both depend on affiliation with an Other, whether it be the pariah community or the dominant social group, in order to thrive.

For Lazare this simultaneous connection and pariahdom becomes a crucial part of Jewish consciousness. While, in reaction to the Dreyfus Affair, Lazare takes a stand firmly in support of Herzl's proposals to build a Jewish state in Palestine, the physical removal to another land and the apparatus of statehood (complete with its national bank) are abhorrent to him. His comments at the First and Second Zionist Congresses make clear that he is primarily concerned with the concrete benefits that Zionism will provide to the downtrodden Jews of both Eastern and Western Europe.[68] Indeed, after his break with Herzl, as he travels through Rumania providing support in the Jewish ghettos, he turns farther and farther away from Zionism as statehood and closer to a conception of the Jewish community as a nation within or on the fringes of general society.

The final incarnation of Lazare's Zionist consciousness, the incarnation most familiar to those who know him only through Arendt, moves back to re-examine the conception of the Jews as a diverse nation built out of both religious and cultural bases for solidarity. But this nation has no claim to roots in a particular soil or any commonality of blood and has little particularity as an ethnos. For Lazare the Jews become exemplars of the exile, actively connecting themselves to others on the fringe and reminding society of what Lyotard might call their "non-present presence" by continuing to assert claims to identity, solidarity, and nationhood without entering into any recognizable forms of social hierarchy.

This final formulation, which emerges in the fragmented dialog of the incomplete *Le Fumier de Job*, reaches back towards the anarchist theory that first inspired Lazare's activism. In espousing Zionism, Lazare suppresses much of the rhetoric of minority status and insists that Jews move from a nation within a nation to become a nation among nations.[69] Becoming emancipated but remaining within Christian society does not necessarily mean assimilating.

In addition, solidarity for Lazare does not necessarily mean the possession of common soil. Pariah communities can also be cosmopolitan communities because state boundaries are corrupt. While Lazare does not rule out the possibility of establishing a Jewish homeland in Palestine, and continues to participate in efforts to relocate Rumanian Jews there, he insists that this is simply an expedient measure. At the end of *Le Fumier de Job*, on the other hand, anarchist cosmopolitanism holds sway. Under the heading "Solutions" he asks "Where is our country (patrie)?" and replies "Where we have suffered."[70] What emerges then is a Zionism firmly grounded in cosmopolitan forms of connection, which seeks to counter the "International Brotherhood" of the wealthy Jewish elites with a notion of "patrie" as subjective and scattered, largely without form, yet nonetheless ethically compelling.

Le Fumier de Job takes the form of a series of fragments and dialogs between assimilated and nationalist Jews, cosmopolites and Zionists.[71] Here we can see the mature version of a cosmopolitan community emerge in the narrative play of the text, and the problem of the *parvenu* and the pariah erupt in the fragmentation of voice and perspective. Lazare will perform the issue as one that inheres in the narrative question of "qui suis-je?" the question the narrator asks himself upon hearing the cry of "death to the Jews!" in the streets. It is one that may thus ultimately be seen to inhere in the very same narrative question asked over and over by Proust's narrator, faced not with the prospect of violent death, but with one of the key threats to identity in *A la recherche*: passive, social acquiescence.

Like *A la recherche*, *Le Fumier de Job* does not so much argue a forceful historical or political thesis as display a wandering *topos*, a rumination on Jewish status and community within the context of several scenes of oppression. Like Kafka's fragmented texts, *Le Fumier* also destabilizes meaning by moving it, undercutting it, and by subjecting it to changes in linguistic register and resonance. Thus we might say, following Deleuze and Guattari, that Lazare's late Zionism emerges out of the strategies of minor literature, the first characteristic of which is a deterritorialization of language.[72] Yet just as it destabilizes language, Lazare's *Le Fumier*, like Kafka's *The Castle*, destabilizes or deterritorializes this social framework, embracing a minor position as the only viable one for a community which draws insight from its embattled status.

Le Fumier's opening description of a Jew coming into consciousness during an anti-Semitic attack during Passover is neither autobiography nor fiction but a strange combination of the two, a combination which, when paired with *Le Fumier*'s hortatory tone makes this piece truly unsettling:

> It is Passover night. The Seder ceremony is celebrated at a friend's or parent's house. They are all there, attracted by different motives (the poor person, the old man, the proletarian, unknown to each other, have taken their places at the table, brought from the synagogue by the master of the house who observes the rites). The story begins, interrupted by the clamor in the street, the cry of death to the Jews! Varied reactions by the people ... One of them trembles all over, he had heard the same thing (that is: the hatred and disdain). The first one says: "It is always like this. Someone who is not Jewish has forgotten and does not know."[73]

While Lazare's language is perhaps not so uprooted as that of a Czech

Jew writing in German, his refusal to settle anywhere in this text, his constant shift from personage to personage, fragmentary perspective to perspective, and from narrative to dialog to aphorism, disrupts not only our expectations of Lazare himself but also our ability to construct meaning in the text in any familiar way.

Le Fumier de Job works along other paths of minor literature as well: it expresses "the connection of the individual to a political immediacy, and the collective assemblage of enunciation."[74] There can be no doubt that political immediacy is the heart of this text. Lazare continually attempts to link each of his "characters" to others, and his own story gets caught up in its role within a dialog. Indeed, "the individual concern becomes thus all the more necessary, indispensible, magnified, because a whole other story is vibrating within it."[75] Clearly, the kind of solidarity that Lazare continues to insist on throughout this last work and that he inscribes into multiple occasions and subject positions within the text makes it a sort of collective expression. It is this kind of text that produces "active solidarity in spite of skepticism" and Lazare is precisely a writer "in the margins or completely outside" using his text to "express another possible community."[76]

Yet, the crucial difference here seems to be the impetus for change that virtually shouts through every one of the varied voices in the text and that questions any major/minor distinctions and insists on its strange anarcho-nationalist position. This text, as multiple as it may be in forms and personages, and as ambiguous as it is about its support for a Jewish state, ultimately leaves us with a message that is not meant to be destabilized. Its conclusion reads: "To participate in the human effort while remaining oneself, keeping one's personality, developing noble qualities, the characteristics of the best / To abandon all that depression has done, to develop into, to rebecome free men and not slaves."[77] This is the position that Lazare pushes on all Jews and on all others who willingly and consciously confront their pariahdom: to be both "oneself" and part of humanity at large. But, given Lazare's complication of both self and community, we cannot read this statement as an easy union between two common-sense notions. Rather, it is through a complex negotiation between a fragmented self-perspective and a critical, political belonging that Bernard Lazare exhorts us to move beyond assimilation into the community of pariahs. Political action comes to mean the process of creating a pariah identity out of the shards of narrative and of insinuating that identity into every aspect of a re-imagined Jewish solidarity.

THE COMMUNITY, THE PROPHET, AND THE PARIAH: RELATION
IN *A LA RECHERCHE DU TEMPS PERDU*

> For all his Parisian sophistication, there remains in [Proust] much
> of the capacity for apocalyptic moral indignation of the classical
> Jewish prophet.
>
> Edmund Wilson, *Axel's Castle*, 144[78]

Published after Lazare's death but born in the maelstrom of the Dreyfus
Affair,[79] Proust's *A la recherche du temps perdu* makes the move beyond
assimilation a central concern of the text not by means of Lazare's
political exhortations, but rather by inscribing the tension between
pariah and *parvenu*, between belonging and otherness, into all the circles
of identity that comprise the novel. If, as has often been claimed, the
novel is one of apprenticeship in interpretation, then the signs to be
interpreted, whether fully present, half seen, or seen from afar, form the
borderline between worlds that seem rarely to intersect.[80] Both *parvenus*
and pariahs are formed by the manipulation of social signs; both remain
subject to codes which require the unfolding of time and the unraveling
of seemingly "natural" identities to become clear. As Deleuze points
out, at each step Marcel knows only part of the picture, part of the
structure of identities that twist and turn through the pages of the novel.
In the light of these always only partially comprehensible codes, assimilation becomes an impossible task. Within *A la recherche du temps perdu* the
endless danger of pariahdom is as central to the formation of identity
over time as is the ominous specter of lost memories.

Thus in *A la recherche* the question of assimilation is not simply a class
or Jewish issue. It underlies not only both Marcel's efforts to enter the
Guermantes' circle and the eventual dislocation of that circle (as marked
by the rise of the Verdurins), but also Marcel's efforts to bring his past
subjectivities into relationship with his present "I," and the meditations
on the associative power of memory that result. Marcel creates a sort of
community of self – but one in which each subject position exists most
distinctly in memory. But like the Jews who most consistently and
forcefully question the value of assimilation for Bernard Lazare, Proust
not only challenges the viability of social affiliations and the identities
that they confer but also questions their value and recognizes their
paradoxical quality. Even for Marcel, affiliation with the other rather
than assimilation into a dominant group eventually represents both the
beginning of social ostracism and the means to self-fulfillment and

empowerment. By focusing on the hidden homosexual or *inverti* communities, as well as and in connection with the increasingly marginalized
Jews, *A la recherche* ultimately raises the possibility that identity is irrevocably multiple and that the potential for pariahdom lurks within all
members of society.[81]

But in this novel the view into this hidden world is not equally open to
all. It is precisely in the sighting of the pariah that he is created and that
assimilation is undone, but not always permanently or universally.
Swann's Jewish ancestry, the hidden race of the "men-women," Charlus's adventures in Jupien's brothel all reveal themselves in a moment of
privileged vision which at times also verges on prophecy.[82] The sight of
Swann's more pronounced Jewish nose, for example, reveals (to the
narrator in retrospect; to us, if we are attentive) his social future. The
glimpse of Charlus crossing the courtyard towards Jupien presages the
scenes of homosexual desire in the later chapters. Even the sight of
Albertine lost in the blurred image of the *jeunes filles en fleurs* presents in a
moment of gifted vision what will be her final disappearance in a
confusion of identity. Though the sense of prophecy that pervades *A la
recherche* stems in large part from its unique mix of prospective and
retrospective narrative gazes,[83] it is nonetheless responsible for our
ability to recognize, when the moment arrives, the truth in the (pariah)
identity that is finally revealed. As though taking a page from the
prophetic books of the Old Testament, or from the Racinian reworking
of the stories of *Athalie* and *Esther*,[84] Proust structures social identity
within a context of hidden truths, prophetic (or often voyeuristic) visions, and ultimate revelations.

However, it is only in avowing their status as either *invertis* or pariahs,
rather than simply being revealed as such, that the marginalized characters in *A la recherche* come to resemble turn-of-the-century Zionists,
moving beyond assimilation to the strength of membership in the
community of conscious pariahs. If Swann becomes a Dreyfusard it is
not only through atavistic return to the blood of his ancestors, as the
Guermantes presume, but rather through his control of his bodily
expression, his consciousness of his status. The same principle stands for
the other "cursed race" – homosexuals, who reveal themselves in
Jupien's brothel by taking on the roles of both gazer and gazed. Charlus
may reveal a glance inherited from "some grandmother" (I: 853) long
forgotten, but his presence amongst the young boys in the pseudo-
obscurity of the brothel is purposeful. Thus, the prophetic power of
Charlus's body is in a sense undone; the expression of identity and

acceptance of marginal status is made conscious, controllable, and willed. In this manner the overtly political work of those like Bernard Lazare and the belletristic tradition of those like Proust circle back towards each other. Unlikely as it may seem, both Proust's novel and the prophetic discourse of Lazare's Zionism converge on the same discovery: the false dichotomy of the *parvenu* and the pariah and the power of the view from the fringe.

The opening volumes of *A la recherche* develop Marcel's fascination with social worlds that do not include him. From his exploration of Swann's life at the time of his first love for Odette, an epoch dated before the narrator's birth,[85] to his fascination with *Le côté de Guermantes*, a realm that entices him most before he gains *entrée*, Marcel focuses his longing for social significance on communities that seem complete in themselves. In these volumes the collective identities of these social worlds wield definitive power and the individual dramas of their members remain less significant.

If the opening volumes of *A la recherche* are pre-occupied by the process of assimilation, Swann is its ultimate *parvenu*. He is the Jew who does not name himself as such; his Frenchness is so complete that Marcel's family, who define him not by his social successes but by his family origins, nonetheless never mention his Jewish roots. Nor do class differences limit him. Equally at home in the narrator's house in Combray, the inner sanctum of the Duchesse de Guermantes, and the bourgeois salon of Mme. Verdurin, Swann simply belongs. In these opening volumes he comes to represent not only a model for Marcel but also the paradigm of social mobility, a man so well assimilated that he no longer needs to attend to preserving his status and who can accomplish even that most difficult of social manoeuvres, associating with a lower class, without tarnishing his image.

Swann also represents the power of the social construction of identity. The individual becomes in a sense a receptacle for the ways that those around him look at him – rather than some manipulator of impressions. Assimilation for someone like Swann thus becomes less a matter of personal effort than the reflection of the common manner of seeing. As has often been remarked, Swann comes into this novel with barely a trace of Jewishness. The marks that ultimately come to shout his "foreign" ancestry from his face at first appear simply as elegant traits. In the Combray period, the narrator tells us, those impressed by his social success "see all the graces enthroned in his face and stopping at the line of his aquiline nose (son nez busqué) as at a natural frontier"

(I: 20). Marcel's parents fill Swann's face with the memories of their moments spent together. The narrator uses the description of Swann to explain to us that:

We pack the physical outline of the person we see with all the notions we have already formed about him, and in the total picture of him which we compose in our minds those notions have certainly the principal place. In the end they come to fill out so completely the curve of his cheeks, to follow so exactly the line of his nose, they blend so harmoniously in the sound of his voice as if it were no more than a transparent envelope, that each time we see the face or hear the voice it is these notions which we recognize and to which we listen. (I: 20)

If, in this period of his life, the line of Swann's hooked nose represents a natural frontier for his elegance, then it is only because others see him as completely incorporated by social grace. Even the foreignness of Swann's name goes unremarked in these opening volumes, despite Marcel's obsession with its sound and its spelling, and his growing suspicion of its innocence (I: 447). The narrator presents us with the Swann he knew and imagined, neighbor, father of Gilberte, and model of a desirable way of life. His Swann is the ultimate insider who travels with ease from Combray along both the Méséglise and the Guermantes ways, and whose alienation from society seems to derive not from himself but from his "unfortunate" marriage to Odette.

To introduce the Jew into a narrative without distinguishing physical marks and without a specific, determining past therefore implies a distinctly non-racial way of conceiving of Judaism and of identity in general. In the first volumes of *A la recherche* Proust consistently undermines any aspect of his characters that might demonstrate their determination by blood. This clearly runs contrary to Arendt's understanding of Jewish or homosexual heredity in Proust, yet I want to argue that physiology, behavior, and identity are not the same in this novel, and that identity, with which we are clearly most concerned, becomes a function not only of the individual's expression of what might have been called his "true" (physiological) nature, or even his conscious manipulation of that nature (in behavior), but also, importantly, of the ability of those around him to see that nature. This distinction between physical determinism and the manipulation of identity emerges not only in the fall of Swann but also in Bloch's assimilation. Bloch in the end is able to change how his nose appears, demonstrating his ability to affect how he is seen, and thereby his identity: "And thanks to the way in which he brushed his hair, to the suppression of his moustache, to the elegance of his whole figure, to his determination – his Jewish nose disappeared."[86]

His attempt to erase his otherness also erases its evidence on his body.[87]

Proust thus may be seen to participate in the same transformation of racial thinking that Todorov has well described and that we have seen stands behind Bernard Lazare's notion of Jewish nationalism. Proust engages in dialogue with nineteenth-century notions of race, persistently chipping away at the foundations of "natural" relationships and introducing unexpected connections among his characters based more on some characteristic or proclivity within their individual (physical and psychical) identities rather than some age-old blood tie. When Proust refers to the significance of Jewish blood (II: 388), he is clearly employing the term in a racialist rather than a strictly racist manner to refer to those who link themselves to other Jews by embracing a common heritage, behavior, or even relationship to scripture. As Marrus puts it,

By "race" they meant, to varying degrees, a sense of community with other Jews, a sense of some common historical fate . . . Almost invariably this sense of solidarity, this identification with other Jews linked the living and the dead; almost invariably it joined men who had no religious bond in common; and almost invariably it was associated with a historical tradition which transcended national boundaries and went beyond human memory. This was what Proust meant.[88]

Thus it is important that Swann's Jewishness becomes seen when he becomes a Dreyfusard and that Charlus's homosexuality reaches its *apogée* among the twenty-year-olds assembled for his pleasure at Jupien's. Proust connects his characters to communities of like-minded or like-acting selves, creating typologies that function within the novel much in the same way that cultural, religious, or linguistic groups do for Todorov's racialists. Throughout *A la recherche* social affiliations guide and limit the manifestations of physical identity rather than becoming subordinate to them.[89]

In contrast to the *jeunes filles* who continue to exist as a group even when forcibly separated, or the homosexuals, who can generally be seen with a discerning eye, the Jews in *A la recherche* only become a social entity when they draw together and engage in socially inappropriate behavior, an event which occurs rarely in the novel.[90] As a Dreyfusard Swann becomes denigrated to a type rather than what he had been, an unusual individual, who, as M. de Guermantes put it, "was a man of intelligence (avait de l'esprit)" (II: 703). Like Swann, Bloch appears without the indelible marks of a Jewish voice or appearance, and without being linked to the *Juifs*. For Bloch, the real *Juifs* are those at Balbec who use foreign words and go about in a group even more powerfully identifying than the group of *jeunes filles*. Indeed, only when Marcel *sees* Bloch with the group of Jews at Balbec does he become uncomfortably aware of his friend's background. The function of affiliation within *A la recherche* is, then, to adjust perspective or the manner of being viewed, which in turn determines identity. Mieke Bal describes the visual texture of the Proustian scene as a mottled screen, flattening differences and distances, even as it magnifies details. Like photographs the scenes in *A la recherche* often call attention to their perspective, destabilizing both the image and the viewer, and often multiply themselves through the insistently iterative quality of the narrative.[91] This scene of instability is repeated each time the object is seen again, creating the kind of vertigo that is so familiar to readers of *A la recherche*. Still the process is not limited, as Bal suggests, either to the visual plane or to the narrator's whirling subjectivity. Rather, we can see subject and object impinge on each other in the images of the Jews at Balbec, where both the images of Bloch and the way that Marcel sees him are two sides of the same picture.

This point is made clearer in a different domain when we consider the confusion which the first sight of Mlle. Vinteuil and her friend causes in Marcel (1: 160). The later scene of sadism, which he witnesses from outside the window, seems more complete and yet still not comprehensible. Rather than present itself as a whole picture it becomes instead "an impression" – one which is felt at the time but fully emerges only much later, when Albertine explains its significance. This "impression" writes itself on Marcel as it were, affects him in a way that he cannot perceive until the day when "the memory of this impression [would] play an important part in [his] life" (1: 173). There is then no complete picture of the object, the scene of desecration of the photograph of Vinteuil, even at the time that it is first narrated in *Du côté de chez Swann*. The truth of the scene is neither its personal meaning for Marcel nor its "objective" presentation of Mlle. Vinteuil's apparent lack of filial feeling, but some curious combination of those two, made possible only by the narrative foregrounding of the field of vision.[92]

Antoine Compagnon connects this very aspect of the scene to the theatrics of perversity, whether Jewish or homosexual, within *A la recherche*. As he points out, Mlle. Vinteuil is playing at sadism much as one might say Jews play at various perverse or non-perverse social roles: "Just as homosexuality is the homosexual's illusion, sadism is an illusion created when one observes cruelty; it corresponds to the point of view of a third party – who is, in fact, the voyeur."[93] Thus the scene of sadism has little connection to the essential nature of the person acting the role. It is the eye of the voyeur that discovers the connection to perversity, and it is a connection that implicates him, as guilty voyeur, as much as it does the object in view. In this sense social morality devolves onto the perspective of the viewer rather than on the essence of the player in the social theater. As Angela Moorjani claims, "the voyeur's sadistic interpretation of a scene is always only partial."[94] The position of the two "cursed races" – Jews and homosexuals – whose curse is that they must always play their roles several times over (Charlus the woman who plays Charlus the nobleman who plays Charlus the dominated, *ad infinitum*), is ultimately ambiguous. The scene and onlooker determine the perversity which depends upon the furtive process of secret unveiling.

The role of context in determining perspective also provides one of the primary principles of *A l'ombre des jeunes filles en fleurs*, connecting Elstir's paintings with the glimpses of the little band of girls and with our changing perspective on Bloch. For Elstir's genius seems to lie in his ability to heighten our understanding of perspective and of the way that changing the usual manner of seeing also heightens or changes both the viewer and the object in question: "Elstir had prepared the mind of the spectator by employing for the little town, only marine terms, and urban terms for the sea . . . On the beach in the foreground the painter had also contrived that the eye should discover no fixed boundary, no absolute line of demarcation between land and sea" (II: 895). Thus in switching the terms of "town" and "water" the detailed painting of Carquehuit harbor creates the viewer as the subject of art, because the painting is "about" her or his perspectives and preconceptions. The band of girls is seen as part of the Balbec landscape, appearing around corners or from beneath trees in a manner that Marcel hopes will be as predictable as the angle of the sun at those points at a certain time of day. The object of art then becomes the manipulation of our perspective of them in the landscape and, therefore, the manipulation of our understanding of their relationship both to Marcel and to us.

Yet as it concerns Bloch, the mode of seeing that unites viewer, context, and object within a change of perspective is more dramatic, because Marcel has already formed an impression of him at Combray, before adopting what we may call the Balbec way of seeing. At Combray, visiting Marcel without any of his family members, Bloch simply seems idiosyncratic, given to oddities of behavior that appear to belong to an eccentric individual. At Balbec, however, Bloch's identity, seen against the background of his relatives and their friends, begins to evoke the otherness of the Jews and therefore to change the simple manner in which Marcel has seen him:

Personally, I was not particularly anxious that Bloch should come to the hotel. He was at Balbec, not by himself, unfortunately, but with ... this Jewish colony ... Always together, with no admixture of any other element, when the cousins and uncles of Bloch or their co-religionists male or female repaired to the Casino ... they formed a solid troop, homogeneous within itself, and utterly dissimilar to the people who watched them go by and found them there again every year. (I: 794)

While Marcel busies himself about the task of trying to distinguish one girl in the little band from the other, he accomplishes the opposite for his friend by connecting Bloch firmly and irrevocably to this group of Jews. The type becomes more powerful than its components. All the Jews at Balbec who may be connected in any way with the Jewish colony become swept up into its collective identity which then determines what perspective we may adopt.

The theatrics of the Jewish scene at Balbec is one of collective choruses and grand movement: the dining room, the beach, and Bloch's house providing the scenes of a certain tragic downfall.[95] In fact, this is one of the implications of Proust's use of Racine's *Esther* and *Athalie* and of Halévy's opera *La Juive*.[96] The dining room at the hotel at Balbec is described both as a theater and as the temple from *Athalie*. The performances of identity that take place there are homosexual and Jewish, expressions of the constant connection between these two groups in the novel. The fact that most of the quotations from Racine's two last plays that appear in *A la recherche* are from the choruses, and, even more so, evoke collective forms of identity, makes the singling out of individuals within these types impossible.

And so I could not help reciting in my head ... lines of Racine ... from *Athalie* for in the doorway of the hall ... "a flourishing race" of young pages clustered ... like the young Israelites of Racine's choruses ... If one had asked of any of them, like the old Queen, "But all this race, what do they then within the confines of this place?" he might have said, "I watch the solemn pomp and bear my part." (II: 802)

Throughout the passage that follows the narrator constantly refers to the waiters in collective terms, as like "the young Levites," as " that 'young and faithful troop,'" and even more specifically as members of a chorus. The same principle holds true in the later description of Nissim Bernard and the young waiter whom he kept among the staff at the hotel. For there too the hotel seems peopled with "young Israelites" who rarely may be distinguished from their collective identity (II: 872). In fact, it is difficult to discover what differentiates the particular man who holds Bernard's interest, or if indeed we are meant to imagine a series of young Jews, collected over the years. The narrative is vague on this point, not simply because we hear only Marcel's version of Bernard's behavior, but also because the power of the chorus is an irremediably collective one.

Later Charlus, speaking about Bloch and his family in what Marcel refers to as "almost insane words," again makes the connection not only with Racine's Jewish plays but to the seemingly intrinsic theatricality of Jewish identity itself: "[Bloch] might perhaps hire a hall and give me some biblical entertainment, as the young ladies of Saint-Cyr performed scenes taken from the Psalms by Racine" (II: 298). The further suggestion, that Bloch and his family put on some more salacious and sadistic comic entertainment for Charlus, again returns us to the negative theatrics of Jewish social roles. Charlus wishes to see "a contest between your friend and his father, in which he would smite him as David smote Goliath" or " he might even ... give his hag ... of a mother a good thrashing" (II: 298). In Charlus's conception, the Jew who must play certain roles in society (as we know Bloch is wont to do) becomes the ready-for-anything actor, an improviser ready to play out the desires of the audience. His real relations with his parents, his actual sexual proclivities, or his personal response to violence play no part in Charlus's (Jewish) theatrical fantasy.

As Marcel's discomfort with Bloch's relatives also demonstrates, this mode of constructing identity displays the perils and vagaries of an assimilationist mentality, for both Jews and others throughout the novel. The type of the Jew becomes a paradigm for the status of the self, which appears singular and static when seen in isolation at one moment in time, but which hides a virtual infinity of performative versions, determining relationships, and social contexts. In order to release the potential of these many possible identities, one must manipulate and expand one's community, playing social roles that therefore multiply perspectives in ways that can be both dangerous and demeaning. Both Swann and Bloch use the power of association to remake themselves both personally and in the eyes of others, an activity portrayed as necessary for Jew and homosexual, and enticing for others like Marcel. Yet the "tendency towards blindness" (II: 641) which is the lot of the *parvenu* means that even the players in the social drama cannot perceive the whole scene, thus leaving themselves open to the gaze of a hidden viewer, who may construct a completely different meaning from the scene.

Bloch's anti-Semitic diatribe, delivered from the shadows of his beach cabana, provides a ready example of this paradoxical Jewish theater in *A la recherche*. If in both *Esther* and *Athalie* the Jews are hidden waiting for the moment in which their unveiling will also mean the coming of divine retribution, in this scene Bloch's unveiling only brings with it evidence of another level of subterfuge. Bloch inveighs against the Jews in a blatant attempt to identify himself as something else – "you can't go a yard without meeting them" (I: 793) – opening the assimilative spiral that takes him through the remainder of the novel. Yet Saint-Loup clearly recognizes him as a Jew, and blushes. The positions of the statement are thus altered, the "us" and "them" shift, and Bloch is unveiled as one of "them," an outsider.

But this is not the end of the story here. The situation in which we expect Marcel and Saint-Loup to discover "the truth" about the anti-Semite becomes instead a scene of self-revelation. Though Saint-Loup may blush at Bloch's efforts to distance himself from the Jews at Balbec, he nonetheless invites him to visit. The narrator on the other hand is overcome with the sense of regret that Bloch has not come to Balbec without that "Jewish colony that was more picturesque than pleasing" (I: 793). Thus, like the earlier voyeuristic scene outside Mlle. Vinteuil's window, the scene viewed in turn mirrors a view of the looker that irrevocably alters our understanding of him. Our attention leaves Bloch himself, now swept back up into the general group of Jews, and the importance of his not-so-hidden viewing, and his attempt to recreate himself becomes lost within a broader pageant of anti-Semitic stereotyping.

Bloch's family more clearly demonstrates the sway of typology and the difficulty that assimilation poses, especially when a class distinction also enters the picture. The members of the family are ridiculous not because they desire to improve their social standing or belong to the elite circles of French social life, but rather because they pretend to have assimilated when they so obviously have not. Here it is hardly a matter of perspective; or rather, in this scene manipulation of perspective becomes constrained by those Proustian circles of being which limit access to systems of meaning that lie beyond their borders. Bloch's father may discourage his family from using Yiddish words in Saint-Loup's presence, rightly understanding their significance to the aristocracy. Yet, when he tries to advance his own image by making allusions to exclusive social circles, he fails utterly because he believes that the notion of exclusivity has meaning in and of itself. He cannot understand that the word "club" (*cercle*) has no social significance as an unmodified noun. Saint-Loup on the other hand expects the defining adjective that never comes. Thus, when M. Bloch pretends to know Bergotte, whom he has never met, and then makes a pretence of having snubbed him at his club, Saint-Loup misses the point entirely:

> Saint-Loup blushed, for it occurred to him that this club could not be the Jockey, of which his father had been president. On the other hand it must be a fairly exclusive club, for M. Bloch had said that Bergotte would never have got into it if he had come up now. So it was not without the fear that he might be "underrating his adversary" that Saint-Loup asked whether the club in question were that of the Rue Royale, which was considered "degrading" by his own family, and to which he knew that certain Jews were admitted. "No," replied M. Bloch in a tone at once careless, proud and ashamed, "it is a small club." (I: 829)

Saint-Loup seems willing to consider M. Bloch as a successful *Israélite*, who might employ the terms of social belonging in the same manner as he. However, the membership in question here is precisely the opposite, the very one that *precludes Israélite* identity and inscribes M. Bloch into a circle outside of Saint-Loup's purview. Had he understood when M. Bloch spoke the word *"cercle"* that he meant *Juif*, Saint-Loup would have ceased, in a very real sense, to be able to see M. Bloch at all.

Of course, class differences play a part here. The group of Jews at Balbec are described as clearly middle-class, while the clubs Saint Loup mentions would only be open to wealthy Jews, like Sir Rufus Israels, or the Rothschilds. However, as Marcel's family continually points out, Swann, who gains entry into the Jockey Club, is the son of a stockbroker. He is far wealthier than the Blochs, but not truly of the upper classes. His social success demonstrates that here class is less significant than social behavior, manipulation of perspective, and appropriate deployment of terminology. Bloch is so far from Saint-Loup's world that he cannot even invent a story that will place him within the boundaries of the circle of the aristocracy, nor can he couch it in terms that will have the proper resonance.

As this passage demonstrates, the social world of these volumes turns around circles that only very rarely intersect, making movement between them again a question of complete assimilation.[97] We might call this kind of group identity "clannism" as it prevails in social circles like those of the *jeunes filles en fleurs*, the Jews at Balbec, the Guermantes salon, and especially the little clan at the Verdurins, which all create separate spheres, distinct identities, and exclusive social and linguistic codes. These clans only relate in order to define themselves in distinction from each other. They are, however, liable to be penetrated by those who are willing and able to assimilate completely, forsaking their old sphere in order to move into the next. But the novel would be only a series of fully fashioned images if these circles were not liable to inter-penetration and if the narrative were not constantly moving from one linguistic world to the next. The very whirl of Proust's sentences, whose circling subordinate clauses continually enclose and connect, ensures the interaction of the novel's many components and the eventual integration of the Méséglise and the Guermantes ways. Proust's frequent use of prolepse and analepse constantly connects events from different times and locations. The transformation of events and images through this process, an activity in many ways akin to assimilation, is precisely the problem the narrator explores and perpetuates throughout this novel.

But simple assimilation finally emerges as inadequate to meet the demands of a social hierarchy grappling with the Dreyfus Affair and its aftermath. Once Marcel is ensconced within the inner sanctum of the *haut monde* the fissures in its seemingly glorious unity begin to emerge. The fall of Swann and his eventual death also mark the disgrace of the entire community and although Marcel continues to inhabit this world he no longer entrusts to it the power to guide opinion or determine identity. Just as in this period, for Bernard Lazare, conscious pariahdom becomes a necessity and Zionism a hopeful possibility, for the narrator outsider status and the marginal community become constant and confusing preoccupations. Marcel's attention turns to those homosexuals and Jews, revealed through the prophetic figures and voices in the middle books of the novel, who themselves offer visions of another social reality. The prophet comes to look like a conscious pariah, one who shatters illusions of identity and unveils an inverted political truth as he himself lurks outside the window.[98]

Not only does Swann come to embody the cloaked differences hidden within the circle of his social community but he also moves from signifying the best within the Faubourg to marking its utter inability to accommodate his divergent identity. While the fall of Swann is partially attributable to his "unfortunate" marriage to Odette, it is his embodiment as a Jew that finally ostracizes him. Where once the features of his face seemed to testify only to his elegance and refinement, by the time of *Sodom et Gomorrhe* they are the indelible marks of Jewishness:

Whether because of the absence of those cheeks ... or because arteriosclerosis ... had ... deformed it ... Swann's punchinello nose, absorbed for long years into an agreeable face, seemed now enormous, tumid, crimson, the nose of an old Hebrew rather than of a dilettante Valois. Perhaps, too, in these last days, the physical type that characterizes his race was becoming more pronounced in him, at the same time as a sense of moral solidarity with the rest of the Jews, a solidarity which Swann seemed to have forgotten throughout his life, and which, one after another, his mortal illness, the Dreyfus case, and the anti-semitic propaganda had reawakened. (II: 715)

Swann's newly emergent Jewish features are paired here with the effects of illness. They not only proclaim his change in status but they also "deform" him, marking him as one about to die, physically as well as socially.[99] Where once he had what the narrator calls an "agreeable" face, it is now swollen and distorted; where once he looked French, now he can only be likened to an old Hebrew. As Sander Gilman points out, "the very analysis of the nature of the Jewish body has always been linked to establishing the difference (and dangerousness) of the Jew . . . In the nineteenth century it is more strongly linked to the idea that some 'races' are inherently weaker, 'degenerate,' more at risk for certain types of disease than others."[100] Because the other is seen as "the essence of Pathology,"[101] the physical degeneration of Swann's body becomes the mark of his religious and cultural otherness. In a sense, as Albert Sonnenfeld claims, the tumor "equating disease, Jewish self-conscious-ness . . . and moral fervor . . . contains the suggestion that Swann's renascent Jewishness is itself the disease."[102] It is in this capacity, as the sickening presence of the Jewish other, not simply because of the Dreyfusism he shares with many among the *habitués* of the Faubourg, that Swann becomes a pariah.

   This physical reassertion of Swann's Jewishness as degeneracy not only signals his ultimate distance from the Guermantes world but also triggers Marcel's revaluation of his former idol. It is in this very passage that Marcel tells us not only how much Swann had changed in appear-ance but "the much greater extent to which he had changed in relation to myself" (II: 716). Although Marcel himself has become a supporter of Dreyfus, and therefore receives Swann's confidences, at this stage in the narration he draws away from the glaring difference of the new Swann. Just as he had recoiled from meeting Bloch in the midst of the *juif* colony at Balbec, so, in the midst of his social success he cannot admire an obviously ostracized Swann. This is a position that can clearly be read as anti-Semitic. In fact Sonnenfeld claims that "Swann has lost his aura for the narrator because he has become a Jew" and calls this an expression of Proust's own fear that his Jewish ancestry will threaten his social success.[103]

Certainly what Marcel rejects in this Swann is neither his political position nor simply his lower social status. This episode marks the re-emergence of racist perspectives during the Dreyfus epoch. Just as in wider French society the furor over the Dreyfus Affair resurrects fading racial definitions of Judaism, so in *A la recherche* it prompts an abundance of remarks about the physical origins of behavior. However, these comments about race are *not* transparent expressions of Proust's own understanding of race, as so many critics describe them.[104] Not only is this simple equation of life with art problematic, the evidence from Proust's biography does not support the claim that he was anti-Semitic. Proust always preserves some distance from the overtly Jewish community and publicly responds to the Zola trial as a matter of abstract justice rather than as an example of anti-Semitism. Nonetheless he makes certain that his name is publicly connected to the Dreyfusard cause and that it becomes known that he has Jewish family. To Comte Robert de Montesquiou, a friend but a virulent anti-Semite, he writes at the height of the Affair, "If I am Catholic like my father and my brother, on the other hand my mother is Jewish ... I am happy that this occasion permits me to tell you what I might otherwise never have said."[105] When *La Libre parole* inadvertently omits his name from a list of the circulators of a particular petition he writes an outraged letter to the editor saying, "I know that my name will add nothing to the list but the fact of having appeared on the list will add to my name."[106] At another point one of the ultra-nationalist newspapers erroneously accuses him of having participated in an attack on Maurice Barrès, a fact that he chooses not to refute because he says that to object to being included would have been to say that he was not one of the Jews.[107]

Indeed, despite his conflicted connection to it, Jewishness was a remarkably empowering identification for Proust, one which comes to fruition in the salon, precisely the realm where Arendt claims its demise. His closest friends from his schooldays are of Jewish descent, and the colleagues with whom he creates a series of amateur literary reviews are from the same circles. However, Proust's emergence into both political and literary circles derives from his membership among the faithful of Mmes. Geneviève Straus and Léontine Arman de Caillavet, both prominent Jewish salon leaders.[108] Their salons become hotbeds of Dreyfusard activity. Not only do Joseph Reinach and Anatole France preside there, but these salons create arenas in which a whole generation of assimilated Jewish intellectuals can interact both with each other and with other French literati. Within the communities created by these two women, assimilated Jews, or those of part-Jewish descent like Proust, found the means to a political engagement that neither ruined their social standing nor forced them into isolation.[109]

These salons created the possibility of affiliation with a Jewish community for those who rejected the overtly religious Jewish world, and provided a means of political action from within the social realm. They thus represent what Benhabib describes, in writing of Rahel Varnhagen, as an alternative social realm. "The self-conscious pariah needs visibility," she claims, "to be seen 'as other' and as 'different,' even if only by a very small group." These salons provided that kind of social group. Like Rahel Varnhagen's they offered "a space of sociability in which the individual desire for difference and distinctness could assume an intersubjective reality and in which unusual individuals . . . could find a 'space' of visibility and expression."[110] Despite the fact that these salons were by no means all Jewish or, at first, all Dreyfusard,[111] they have been characterized by some as a "Jewish world" in which Jews often stayed instead of climbing further into the upper reaches of elite France.[112]

The bonds formed by Jewishness and the Dreyfus Affair in these social spaces were all consuming, long-term, and political. Proust's commitment to the Affair's politics, and to the solidarities formed in advocating action, persists throughout his life. Not only in the period of the Affair proper, when Proust sends personal pleas for Mme. Straus's assistance in circulating petitions, but also years later, the celebrated correspondence between these two lifelong friends is full of references to their common bond in Dreyfusism.[113] Even when no longer active in what we might call the public sphere, Proust's avowal of his Jewish background and his affiliation with these pariah communities continue to play into his political self-conception. In this sense we can see the social realm as both an instigator to political action and a mediator between politics as public contest and as private position.

Dreyfusism for Proust also clearly means affiliation with a marginal community. While, strictly speaking, these salons are not composed of pariahs, their early and ardent Dreyfusism, along with their open espousal of Jewishness, make them open to attack. As one critic puts it, "he welcomed social ostracism in some circles as a Dreyfusard, not only as a loyal Jew and a humane liberal, but as a victim of anti-Semitism."[114] The sort of political engagement that grips Proust in this period, and which is more transparently represented in *Jean Santeuil*, marks the same kind of attention to and affiliation with the pariah that emerges in *A la recherche*. As a Dreyfusard Proust not only abandons the *parvenu* mentality, he challenges it with an avowed and active support of the pariah.

We may see the incidents of anti-Semitism in the middle volumes of *A la recherche* as commentary upon the cultural ramifications of the Dreyfus Affair, and the importance of the social realm as a matrix of political identities, whether positive or negative. The prevalence of anti-Semitic remarks also serves as an indicator; they increase as old networks of affiliation disintegrate, pointing out the need for social terms of categorization and connection. In marked contrast to the early descriptions of both Swann and Bloch, almost every time that Bloch appears in *Le côté de Guermantes* we learn something about the Jewishness of his features and the effect they had on his status. His Jewishness has become something oriental that cannot be hidden by a European costume: "But Bloch, . . . remained . . . as strange and savory a spectacle, in spite of his European costume, as a Jew in a painting by Decamps" (II: 194). In much the same way the narrator tells us that Swann's Dreyfusism makes him "return to the paths which his forebears had trodden and from which he had been deflected by his aristocratic associations" (II: 604). The narrative gaze focuses on physical attributes, racial proclivities, and temperamental differences, as well as differing political perspectives that come to seem like the "natural" cause of the separate circles of Parisian social life. If, as we have seen, these circles describe different worlds of behavioral and linguistic signification, the Dreyfus Affair adds race as the first cause of these worlds of meaning and then pretends to find it always already implied.

Thus it is not simply because Swann has taken on a new Jewish ugliness that Marcel reappraises his idol. Rather it is that Swann has come to resemble an old Hebrew both in appearance and in his relation to society, forfeiting his insider status and forcing the first rupture that, as we have seen, Levinas describes as a function of coming into consciousness as a Jew. He also takes on that "simultaneous engagement and disengagement"[115] that Levinas also defines as the position of the prophet. But Marcel, having only just arrived in the Princesse de Guermante's salon, and ever-bent on classifying his acquaintances, interprets this prophetic stance as simply the aspect of a fallen *parvenu*. The Swann who commits himself to Dreyfusism succumbs to the Jewish identity that has been lurking behind his social success. "There are certain Jews (*Israélites*), men of great refinement and social delicacy, in whom nevertheless there remain in reserve and in the wings, ready to enter their lives at a given moment, as in a play, a boor and a prophet.

Swann had arrived at the age of the prophet" (II: 716). The Jew, the boor, and the prophet become irrevocably linked and opposed to the "fins" and "délicats" members of society. By positioning himself on the margins of the community, Swann becomes simultaneously an uncouth *Juif* and the voice of doom for a whole way of life.

Swann's position is prophetic throughout *A la recherche.*[116] Not only does his volume, *Un amour de Swann*, clearly prefigure much of the rest of the novel but Swann himself raises concern about many of the issues that will later confront Marcel.[117] However, it is by being erased that Swann functions most importantly as the predictor of social change and degeneration in *Le côté de Guermantes* and *Sodome et Gomorrhe*. To begin with, although often talked about, Swann is physically absent in the opening book of *Le côté de Guermantes*, where the general parameters of the Dreyfus Affair are discussed and the primarily anti-Dreyfusard positions of the Guermantes and their social acquaintances are outlined. This absence is significant here because he is replaced in the salon of Mme. de Villeparisis by Odette, up to then the very source of his increasing social ostracism. Odette, we learn, has broken into social circles previously closed to her by hitching her fortunes to the anti-Dreyfusard cause: "When he was not present she went farther and professed the most ardent nationalism . . . Mme Swann had won by this attitude the privilege of membership in several of the anti-semitic leagues of society women that were beginning to be formed and had succeeded in establishing relations with various members of the aristocracy" (II: 260). Odette becomes Swann's negative image, entering society only when he is not there, and only by expressing an opinion forcefully opposed to his own.

The most dramatic social upheaval of this central portion of the book, then, this shift in the character and composition of the Faubourg, occurs under the sign of Swann's absence. Swann's complete erasure after his death finally enables the social success of his wife and daughter. It is only after Odette's remarriage, when Gilberte stops using the name Swann, that she is received by the Duchesse de Guermantes, who makes a point of never mentioning the girl's real father in her presence. That Gilberte ends up becoming the wife of the anti-Semite Saint-Loup not only completes her dramatic social rise but makes clear that she accomplishes it at the expense of her father's memory.

In a further example of the paucity of the Dreyfus-era social world and of the increasing power of the bourgeoisie within it, Swann's position is ceded to Bloch who is so anxious to please that he constantly tries to express his Dreyfusism in a form that will disguise it. Bloch's attempts to hide his background are comical since those around him read his support for Dreyfus as an obvious mark of his Jewishness. In the same way, Bloch evokes laughs from the reader when, in trying to disguise his Jewishness he changes his name to Jacques de Roziers, a name that automatically evokes the rue des Rosiers, Paris's main Jewish street. These laughable "mistakes" so often attributed to Bloch are what make critics like Seth Wolitz see him as an inscription of simple anti-Semitism.[118] He appears to represent a Jewish atavism that is not only funny but uncouth, acquisitive, and threatening. But the *parvenu* behaviors of someone Lazare would have called the epitome of a *"Juif"* are what condemn Bloch here, not some essential quality of his Jewishness. In this sense he is laughable in the same way as is Mme. Verdurin – that is, as an example of the ironic shifts of social life and the demise of the propriety of society that accelerates in the first decades of the century. His lies, like Odette's betrayal of Swann or Saint-Loup's disavowals of his past politics, condemn the *monde* more than they condemn him specifically as a Jew.

Still the unveiling of the hidden Jew in *A la recherche*, like the unveiling of Esther or the presentation of Joas in Racine's plays, also serves to bring forth another truth, one hidden within this seemingly gloomy prophecy. As Goldmann claims, in his final plays Racine places his hidden God back into the world, allowing a certain justice to emerge from his unveiling.[119] In *Athalie* especially, the direct intervention of God in a depraved world seems to signal Racine's move beyond Jansenism, to another, less tragic, religious vision. The vision that emerges places the community back into relation with God, but within an other-worldly realm. The hero avoids tragedy by association with this community and this realm.[120] The chorus signals this transition, representing for Goldmann the clear return to communal frames of reference that were absent from Racine's earlier works.

As we have seen, it is precisely through their choruses that these plays enter *A la recherche*, in a manner that signals not only the collective aspect of Jewish identity, but also the vastly different terrain *A la recherche* stakes out. For, if the chorus/community represents the means of avoiding tragic isolation in Racine, what does it mean in *A la recherche*? It seems safe to say that God remains hidden, if not fully absent, within the novel.[121] Beckett long ago claimed that "Proust is completely detached from all moral considerations. There is no right and wrong in Proust nor his world."[122] Because of the absence of religious tenets or absolute moral claims, we cannot read the presence of the chorus as a sign of communal recognition of The Good. Rather, in a world of increasingly relative values, of ironic twists of identity and partially viewed, inverted truths, the choral voices of the Jews in the novel are ironic, signaling their very distance from any new communal perspective.

In fact, there is no new communal perspective that we can glean from *A la recherche*. In this sense, Swann's fall, and the emergence of the Jew in the novel, not only foretell the demise of the *Belle Epoque* but, in another ironic contradiction of the choral community, also speak of the coming of the age of the pariah. The novel shifts measurably after *Le côté de Guermantes* – where circles of belonging once predominated, degeneracy triumphs[123] and the figure on the fringe takes over.

Charlus becomes a different version of this same pariah figure – not because he is cast out – but because he revels in his separateness. He is what Kristeva refers to as a "solitary," one who exists as an exceptional being, beyond the possibility of mutuality and outside conventional social expectations.[124] He takes exception to the principles of national allegiance during the war, being, as the narrator puts it, without patriotism. Like the Jewish pariah, "he belonged, in consequence, no more to the body France, than to the body Germany" (III: 788). He is virtually expelled from the national community by Mme. Verdurin who calls him a Prussian (789). But there seems little need for his expulsion at this point in the novel, for he has of his own volition already become an outsider. "The bad reputation which Charlus was now known to enjoy made ill-informed people think that it was for this reason that his company was not sought by people whom in fact he himself made a point of refusing to see. So that what was really the result of his own spleen seemed to be due to the contempt of the people upon whom he vented it" (III: 788). This too we may term a kind of conscious pariahdom, and if Charlus is called a pre-war artifact (III: 787), his isolation as such also marks the coming of the age of the pariah.

The narrative's preoccupation with the homosexual as the ultimate example of the hidden pariah creates several links between homosexuals and Jews, but it also creates an alternative inverted community, one that rests on the ironic and the hidden for its common ground. A main principle that unites the denizens of Jupien's brothel is their insistence on secrecy and anonymity, even when that secrecy spawns wild speculation and conjecture about their real identities. Charlus prefers to invent jaded pasts for his lovers rather than know them for the unthreatening youths that they are. The very secrecy of their profession unites those youths, making of them a group indistinguishable like the *jeunes filles* yet even more so, because not even desire seems able to tell them apart. Even the narrator, standing in the shadows, does not bother to attribute lines of the conversation to individuals among them; though their talk is supremely banal, their isolated communion is profound.

But this community, the pariah community, rests upon the partial view of the voyeur who looks without being seen, yet not, it seems, without being implicated. To stand in the darkness and see without being seen is after all not only the position that Marcel takes up, on first climbing the stairs, but also that often occupied by Charlus in his habitual room in the brothel. The text is plain on this matter: Jupien places Marcel into Charlus's position and offers to open the ventilator – "a device which he has fixed up so that the Baron could see and hear without being seen" – precisely so that Marcel himself can see and hear without being seen (III: 852). If he had earlier cast himself in the role of the police, arriving in time to discover an "appalling crime . . . about to be committed" (III: 840), upon being ushered into its presence he does nothing to avert it, thus furthering his connection to the scene.

Voyeurism has been the vehicle for the truth throughout the novel, whose pivotal scenes are often overheard or glimpsed from the shadows. But only here do those separated from the dominant society by partial vision and ironic twists of meaning come together in this fashion. It is no surprise then that the narrative breaks off at this point, that a hiatus of several years ensues, and that we discover that during those years Marcel has isolated himself from society. Not only have we seen the ultimate level of vice displayed by a demeaned society, we have seen its threat to Marcel and his *parvenu* potential. The perspectives of voyeur and pariah seem to offer more than that of *salonard*. Certainly they provide more compelling stories, and it is from this realization that, it seems, Marcel beats a frightened retreat.

His stay in the sanitarium (itself a sort of inversion of Jupien's brothel) becomes an isolation that ultimately empowers Marcel, for it leads to the complete disillusionment with society that helps make him finally able to write. But what of the presence of Jupien and Charlus during that first trip to see the Guermantes in *Le temps retrouvé*? Like the second bookend on an empty shelf, these two dominate the first pages after this hiatus. Charlus, like Swann, has degenerated physically, and thus displays his otherness on his body. Where once an insistence on virility masked the walk of his ancestral grandmother, in this scene he is not only not-virile but practically unable to move. But whereas physical degeneracy had decreased Swann's social standing in the perspective of those around him, for Charlus it forces a recasting of his own elitism. He is described as bowing pathetically to Mme. de Saint-Euverte, whom he would never have deigned to meet before. Thus his illness not only "turned all social relations upside down" (III: 892), but also inverts the very principle of social degeneration. Charlus remains a member of the Faubourg, but one who (through physical inadequacy) no longer maintains its principles of snobbery.

From Marcel's perspective, the sight of this newly gentle Charlus appears as both warning and encouragement: Charlus has, in a sense, extended his inversion into the social domain, thus undermining the dichotomy between the principles he had adhered to in public and his hidden pariah behavior. His homosexual behavior has become more open and more voracious, yet we see him as beyond the desperation of the brothel scenes. The lessened Charlus has become less worldly; his aspect is of "detachment from the realities of life" (III: 892), yet he remains at the core of Marcel's social vision. He has moved further outside both life and propriety, but his detachment demonstrates to Marcel the self-reflexive power of the solitary and the other "truth" it can illuminate.

In this manner, the encounter with Charlus becomes crucial to the novel's final movement beyond the ethos of assimilationism, towards the detachment that appears to be its lesson. It is in the late pages of *Le temps retrouvé* that we see the final degeneration of the structures of belonging that guide the early parts of the novel, and the emergence of the pariah not only as prophet but as potential salvation, at least for a writer. We are tempted to turn back to Arendt and read again her tribute to the harsh pariah-hood of Bernard Lazare and applaud the narrator's journey towards, what pop-psychology might call "self-sufficiency."

Yet certainly neither Charlus nor even Swann individually seem to present a way that may be followed, or, indeed, that seems to offer Marcel a means out of the morass of contemporary social life, despite the narrator's realization that Swann has determined the course of his life. Indeed, the paucity of meaningful social categories available at the end of *A la recherche* might seem to point towards a need for stronger community, one which nationalism might perhaps provide. The kind of nationalist enterprise that emerges in the work of Maurice Barrès might even seem to speak to the kind of lack that the later volumes of *A la recherche* develop so eloquently. Marcel's explorations of places and names, of the implications of title and family background, and of the meaning and power of unknowable otherness within the community, all seem as though they ought to participate in the kind of project that Barrès pursues in *Les Déracinés*.[125]

Yet, *A la recherche* remains resolutely anti-nationalist. The demise of the meaning of social categories cannot be restored by ties to a home-land – the Guermantes after all are not saved by being rooted in a place. Even Charlus mocks this notion, in his constant reference to his German cousins. And as we have seen in the cases of both Swann the ardent patriot and Charlus the reluctant Frenchman, pariah status does not begin and end with the definition of Frenchness. Indeed, the dual status of the pariah community of Jews and homosexuals is a cosmopolitan condition. To remove these communities into their own separate sphere, the narrator tells us, would be folly: "I have thought it as well to utter here a provisional warning against the lamentable error of proposing (just as people have encouraged a Zionist movement) to create a Sodomist movement and to rebuild Sodom. For, no sooner had they arrived there than the Sodomites would leave the town so as not to have the appearance of belonging to it" (II: 656). The very concepts of Frenchness, and Germanness, meet their demise in these final pages, as post-war patriotic zeal is displayed as the false expression of any nation-ality:

Finally, to a certain extent, the germanophilia of M. de Charlus . . . had helped me to free myself for a moment, if not from my germanophobia, at least from my belief in the pure objectivity of this feeling . . . What in fact made it possible that this perversity was not entirely intrinsic to Germany was that . . . I had already seen in my country successive hates which had, for example, at one time condemned as traitors . . . those very Dreyfusards such as Reinach with whom to-day patriotic Frenchmen were collaborating against a race whose every member was of necessity a liar, a savage beast, a madman. (III: 951)

The fickleness of French patriotism comes to stand for the instability of its very terms.

Thus cosmopolitanism becomes a necessary corollary of the detached subjectivism of this final book in the novel. Marcel's realization that "it is only a clumsy and erroneous form of perception which places every-thing in the object, when really everything is in the mind" (III: 950) makes the objectification of any social boundary a ruse of the mind. The sphere of international relations comes to revolve around partial visions treated as though they were complete; the hatreds of international life emerge as though from the voyeur's insistence that what was seen through a small window through the shadows might constitute the whole picture as revealed in the light of day. It is not that the viewer has not seen *anything*. The narrator is quick to point out that the pure subjectivity of national prejudice does not mean that certain atrocities were not absolutely real (III: 952). It is the claim to a panoramic and objective view of the truth that undermines the nationalist cause.

The only possibility of community at the end of *A la recherche*, therefore, must be one which does not confuse subject with object. The subject who experiences a feeling of belonging may create from that moment a sense of community but never a static object to which he may return. As a matter of perspective, community is thus also intrinsically linked to voyeurism, but not in the false manner of the narrow national perspective. For, as we have noted, in the scenes of voyeurism the force of the scene lies in the impressions it engraves upon the viewer not in some truth it may disclose about those seen. The figure lurking outside the window becomes the vehicle for truth; his community is among those who, like him, are both removed from the scene, yet privy to its sensations.

Thus in fully abandoning assimilationism Marcel comes to take up this dual stance not only towards a social scene newly reconceived but also to the community of outgrown selves waiting for him on the paths of his past: "Was it not surely, in order to concern myself with them that I was going to live apart from these people, ... to concern myself with them in a more fundamental fashion than would have been possible in their presence, to seek to reveal them to themselves, to realise their potentialities?" (III: 1035). The strict opposition between self and other, isolation and community, pariah and *parvenu* seems to vanish in this final displaced reconnection with re-imagined others. Politics becomes an outgrowth of this contemplative process of re-imagination, one which acts as it looks down both private paths to the past and public paths to an uncertain future.

Finishing this novel more than twenty years after Lazare and Barrès began their work, and on the other side of the First World War, Proust seems prepared to accept the demise of the possibility of social plenitude where they were not. The search at the end of the novel is not for a means to recreate an epoch of solidarity but rather for a way to embrace conscious pariahdom without relinquishing the multiple and often inverted perspectives of a never completely divulged self. The narrative never attempts to present a new, all-inclusive version of identity or to connect the many strands of affiliation that trail behind each character.

A la recherche never seeks to posit another world where relationships remain untainted by a lurking otherness. The novel, on the other hand, not only creates worlds of belonging out of the *inverti* and the pariah, but presumes that these worlds contain only partial and subjective truths.

It is in this sense that Proust's contemplative pariah becomes an important political actor within a disintegrating society. If in removing himself from a world seeming bereft of meaningful identity the narrator becomes able to create an arena where he can connect with others "plus à fond," then he has recreated the possibility of community. What Levinas refers to as Proust's "battle with the ungraspable" is his effort to construct a world in its absence and to generate connection out of solitude: "In this battle the theme of solitude in Proust acquires a new meaning. It occurs in his return to communication, his despair is an inexhaustible source of hope . . . But Proust's most profound teaching . . . consists in situating the real in relation to that which will always remain other."[126] The pariah, in both his eternal otherness *and* his perpetual connection to the world, becomes the center of meaningful social relations in the new reality of post-war France.

Thus Proust rescues the social from the political ignominy to which Hannah Arendt consigns it. When she claims that the entrance of previously private concerns into the social realm, and the increasing predominance of the social over the political, are the downfall of modernity, Arendt neglects the possibility that new modes of affiliation might be born within that mix. On the other hand, the unlikely connection of Proust and Bernard Lazare demonstrates the possibilities of new pariah solidarities in the social spaces between public and private. For the conscious pariah generates an alternative scene of active community life, one where a personal politics may arise from contemplation, partial perspectives, and the view from the fringe.

CHAPTER 4

Virginia Woolf

"SPLINTER" AND "MOSAIC": TOWARDS THE POLITICS OF CONNECTION

For if there are ... seventy-six different times all ticking in the mind at once, how many different people are there not ... all having lodgment at one time or another in the human spirit? Some say two thousand and fifty-two.

Virginia Woolf, *Orlando*, 308

I admit fighting to the death for votes, wages, peace, and so on; what I can't abide is the man who wishes to convert other men's minds; that tampering with beliefs seems to me impertinent, insolent, corrupt beyond measure.

Virginia Woolf, Letter to Ethel Smyth, May 18, 1931, in *Letters*, IV: 373

But it is a mistake, this extreme precision, this orderly and military progress; a convenience, a lie.

Virginia Woolf, *The Waves*, 255

Art introduces between profound life and partisan action a confusion that sometimes shocks even the partisans.

George Bataille, "The Socerer's Apprentice," 226[1]

In October 1931, in the midst of national political and economic crisis, Oswald Mosley and Harold Nicolson called for political change in a new journal entitled simply: *Action:* "The nation demands action; the politicians seek a 'formula' ... we ask for policy they give us a manoeuvre."[2] Disaffected from mainstream politics by the inadequacies of the compromise among Labour, Liberal, and Conservative parties known as the National Government, Mosley and Nicolson present the nation in dire straits, not only inadequately ruled but lethargic to its very core: "We must create a movement which aims not merely at the capture of political power; a movement which grips and transforms every phase and aspect of national life to post-war purposes."[3] Not only is the National Government a travesty, the two proclaim, but it undermines the "real strength, vitality, and loyalty" of the British people, a people who need a movement in order to propel them back into the world's forefront. On the eve of the election, called in order to validate the national coalition government, *Action* and Mosley's hastily formed New Party sought to change the national course, to push for new legislation to combat the rising tide of unemployment and thereby to restore the international position of Great Britain. It was a program of directed reform, patriotic in its mission, yet resolutely international in its scope.

How very different sounds the political writing of Virginia Woolf, writing that in many ways grows out of similar disaffection with party politics and often a similar sense of contemporary peril. Perhaps the most celebrated phrase by Woolf casts her, somewhat more like Proust, as a cosmopolitan outsider, a practitioner of a studied indifference to the concerns of patriotism or the demands of any specific national crisis: "As a woman I have no country. As a woman I want no country. As a woman my country is the whole world."[4] Indifference she proclaims in *Three Guineas*, is the best route to cosmopolitanism, the best means of preventing war, the best way to resist the cultural systems that both deprive women of direct influence and contribute to the national habit of war mongering. Yet the mode of indifference here clearly does not imply inaction. Indeed the passage continues "from this indifference certain actions must follow." Woolf's indifference, as she presents it here in *Three Guineas*, is to the lure of national and "civilized" life, to the honors and benefits of participating in what she sees as a tainted society. Indifference does not, however, imply political lethargy.

To be sure, action seethes through the surface of *Three Guineas*, which is certainly the most vitriolic of Woolf's writings. Even as the narrator pauses to consider the question of whether or not to contribute her guineas – whether to join a political party or help establish a new movement – the sentences overflow with verbs of action, and with the facts, histories, and biographies that support them. If the setting of the book is the inaction of the narrator – not having responded to the entreaties for funds, not having answered the questions asked – and if the attack of the critics is that familiar cry of "lethargy" (43), the response is one of movement. As in *A Room of One's Own*, the narrator takes us to Cambridge, moves us outside, and asks us back in (63). We see the academic processions of hooded men march by, we hear the cyclical songs of children echoing the repeated demands of women (66), and we find ourselves from time to time perched on the edge of an abyss ready to plunge off the edge of a bridge between the restrictions of private life and the "possessiveness" and "pugnacity" of the public realm (74). We see the doors of the private house "forced open" yet without being able to "slam shut" again finally on the patriarchal realm within (138), and we stand with Antigone in the "craggy vault" (141) yet do not resign ourselves to being imprisoned.

So forceful indeed has been the rhetoric of *Three Guineas* that it and its sister essay *A Room of One's Own* have served as the cornerstones of the new understanding of Virginia Woolf's politics. In recent years, the social and political implications of Virginia Woolf's writings have emerged from the shadow of aestheticism. While critics were once guided by Leonard Woolf's comment that "Virginia was the least political animal that has lived since Aristotle invented the definition," and focused instead on Woolf's experiments in form and character, most recent work on Woolf makes clear how profoundly concerned with history and politics Woolf's writing really is.[5] In fact even the rarely quoted words following Leonard Woolf's famous statement undercut the summary power of his assessment:

she was not a bit like the Virginia Woolf who appears in many books . . . a frail invalidish lady . . . She was immensely interested in things, people, and events, and, as her books show, highly sensitive to the atmosphere which surrounded her, whether it was personal, social, or historical. She was therefore the last person who could ignore the political menaces under which we all lived . . . She took part in the pedestrian operations of the Labour Party and the Co-operative Movement. And by "pedestrian" I mean the grass roots of Labour politics.[6]

While she did not devote her life to party activity as did Leonard, it has by now become clear that Virginia Woolf committed herself to both investigating and influencing those "personal, social," and "historical" forces.

Yet within the context of the political turmoil of the 1920s and early thirties, the context within which Woolf's voice developed and matured, we may also hear engagement of a different sort. The process of writing *Three Guineas* begins when she first conceives its early version, "Professions for Women," in 1931, and owes its genesis to Woolf's experiences in the period immediately following the publication of *A Room of One's*

Own. Long before *Three Guineas* is published, action emerges as a primary concern of Woolf's fiction, not only in terms of her radical experiments with plot, fictional form, sentence style, and the expansion of the subject of narration, but also in terms of the limits and possibilities of real-world social and political action.[7]

Indeed these very limits and possibilities present themselves with the almost uncanny appearance of a positive review of Woolf's *The Waves* in that first issue of the New Party's *Action*. Harold Nicolson, *Action*'s editor, calls our attention to "the flux and reflux" in the novel, to the way that "this symbol [of the waves] cuts across her vision, intruding into her images its battering restlessness, its unplumbed mobility, its incessant renewals of shape and energy."[8] One might almost guess that Woolf was a direct supporter of the New Party agenda, a writer seeking to channel national energy towards the Mosley vision of "dynamic progress," or to harness that "battering restlessness" towards the New Party goal of "iron decision, resolution and reality ... which cuts like a sword through the knot of the past to the winning of the modern state."[9] If, given the lens of *Three Guineas* and the gift of hindsight, we discard this possibility immediately, in the context of 1929–31 – a period in which Oswald Mosley went from Labour cabinet member to disaffected outsider, when not only Harold Nicolson but several other prominent Labour intellectuals joined him in the New Party – this response is not so clear.

In fact this chapter will argue that Woolf's writings engage themselves directly with the political crisis in Great Britain in the period from 1929 to 1931, and with the entwined discourses of community and action so often in question in this period. In *Orlando* and *The Waves* in particular we can see the way in which narrative action becomes praxis, the expansion of the subject substitutes for the consolidation of personal political power, and the construction of alternative models of community pushes a cosmopolitan ideal. These novels may thus be seen to intersect with, and, indeed, to disrupt the contemporary call to political action and its discourse of "dynamic progress" – but not by substituting a marginalized indifference, no matter how perspicacious. Rather, by constructing new narrative models of cosmopolitan community, from the community of selves that come to make up the character Orlando to the community of voices that control the narrative of *The Waves*, Woolf creates an alternative discourse of feminist action and power, one which seeks to intervene directly in the political life of Britain.

In her 1930 "Introductory Letter" to a collection of life stories written by working women, Woolf expresses her dilemma when faced with working-class movements. Recalling a convention of the Women's Co-operative Guild (WCG) she writes:

These women were demanding divorce, education, the vote – all good things . . . And yet, though it was all so reasonable . . . a weight of discomfort was settling . . . in [our] minds. All these questions . . . leave me in my blood and bones untouched. If every reform they demand was granted this very instant it would not touch one bone of my comfortable capitalist head. Hence my interest is merely altruistic . . . I am a benevolent spectator. I am irretrievably cut off from the actors.[10]

Though Woolf may believe in the convention's political agenda she cannot join it. Her political solidarity cannot overcome the separation imposed by her own social sphere and the personal life she leads within it. The presumption of a false kinship with those of another class would be anathema to Woolf, who is nothing if not honest when forced to confront the question.[11] Rather than cordon off the personal aspect of the lack of connection she feels, Woolf allows it to affect her, positioning her behind the barrier of the proscenium, on the other side from the political actors of the world. This is repeatedly how Woolf responds to the question of political solidarity. She feels sympathy with the cause but cannot place herself personally among the actors.[12]

Yet the problem of solidarity is not simply written off as a disinterested snobbery or a peevish unwillingness to act. The "Introductory Letter" makes it clear that Woolf seeks some sort of empathy with the working women she has met at the meetings of the Women's Co-operative Guild, but is inhibited by her very bodily experiences, and she perceives that inhibition as a lack on her part. "Suppose one said . . . let's pretend," she proposes, taking on the voice of the women at the Guild conference:

Up I jump in the person of Mrs. Giles of Durham, in the person of Mrs. Phillips . . . But after all the imagination is largely the child of the flesh. One could not be Mrs. Giles of Durham because one's body had never stood at the wash-tub; one's hands had never wrung and scrubbed and chopped up whatever the meat may be that makes a miner's supper.[13]

The observer is inhibited, "shut up" as Woolf puts it "in the confines of the middle classes,"[14] and by the limitations which that bodily experience imposes on subjectivity. The presumption is that the middle-class observer ought somehow to know these experiences, to understand in her "blood and bones" what it is like to work.

Woolf's use of bodily metaphors here to refer to the dichotomy of flesh and imagination raises the question of her understanding of those terms and her reliance on what appears to be a determinist notion of subjectivity. The performance of an alternate identity cannot erase its alterity; if the body lives one way the mind is compelled to follow, she seems to assume. The body is thus the determinative term, and fleshly experience the matrix not only of the imagination, but also of empathy and community. This assumption also seems to accord with the maternalist ideology that has often been attributed to Woolf, and associated with the WCG, where pacifism was often seen as the natural domain of women and internationalism the natural mode of those who were more connected to family than to state. Yet, throughout Woolf's writings from "Mr. Bennett and Mrs. Brown" on, the power of the imagination is precisely the ability to undermine this bodily determinism, to imagine those lives glimpsed only in the corner of a train compartment or through the window of the bus. Woolf's tendency to accord the lower-class characters in her novels less opportunity to develop as separate consciousnesses may derive from the assumption that their lives are unknowable (to Woolf) because their bodily conditions are unfamiliar. Yet in *To the Lighthouse* Mrs. McNab *does* have her say; the barrier is not to be completely unbridgeable.

In fact, if we re-examine this performance of identities in the "Introductory Letter" we can see the fleshly experiences described as the barriers to common cause as those rooted in daily working life, and not in any essential bodily function. Woolf here seems conscious of the ability of capitalist patriarchal society both to alter bodies in such a way as to make them appear essentially different, and then to place priority on that bodily difference within social discourse. Woolf's imagination can circumvent that process, yet it cannot deconstruct the privilege accorded to the socially constituted body. Doing the washing up becomes an activity inscribed upon the bodies of the working-class women that not only marks them as different but that also makes them subject to their flesh.

Then, the determination of the imagination by the body emerges as an immensely important social situation to be overcome. The problem here for Woolf is not just that she is incapable of understanding the working-class women she observes but that she too is so limited by *her* physical experiences. The recognition she comes to – that her body, like those of the working women, is inscribed by class experience – is a recognition of commonality. Thus the political import of this "Introduction" is not simply Woolf's recognition of how class-bound she is, but her effort to discover a means to feminist community that would reject the determinism of culturally imposed bodily experiences. The limitation of middle-class consciousness, what Woolf refers to as being "shut up" in the middle class, is therefore not simply that of a particular bodily experience but, even more importantly, that of believing that experience to be an essentially determinative term of the dichotomy of identity. How to think "women" and "women's politics" without returning to the separate bodies of "woman at the washtub" or "woman in the parlor" is the problem here. The matter of the bodies is the very problem of the dichotomy of matter and imagination.[15]

But this dichotomy is also here a problem linked to a specific politics and in particular to the kind of cooperative/socialist agenda put forward by the Guild. For Woolf senses a force among the Guild members that might pierce that barrier between the bodies of the working women and those of Woolf's position, one which has the potential to join them in a community that will enrich *both* sides and ultimately dismantle their differences: "This force of theirs, this smoldering heat..., is about to break through and melt us together so that life will be richer and books more complex and society will pool its possessions instead of segregating them."[16] Unfortunately, Woolf remarks, this will happen too late for her to see. Action of this sort, which draws out the complexity of bodily experience and the possibility of overcoming its seeming tyranny, is, however, an action that compels her.

Even in the left-leaning political spheres in which Woolf travels, assumptions about identity often remain unexamined while the politics seeks to hide the problem of its agency. Yet in an almost grammatical fashion Woolf insists that we not separate the action from the agent, that we not presume a simple community even when the shared action seems clear. In 1920, after discussing the Fabian agenda with Beatrice and Sidney Webb, Virginia Woolf had written in her diary "But what is 'right' & who are 'we'."[17] This is precisely the question that would preoccupy her politics for the rest of the decade. In 1920 she was already bothered by the willingness of the voices of the opposition to create the same kind of univocal, exclusionary groupings as she believed inhabited the British ruling bodies.

It is for this reason that we must read Woolf's political agenda in the twenties within the context of her explorations of subjectivity throughout her career. Most socially oriented critics focus on Woolf's later writings and on *Between the Acts* in particular.[18] However, the kind of reconstruction of intertwined notions of self and society, community and nation that goes on in *Between the Acts*, and indeed in other writings of the thirties, certainly appears far earlier in Woolf's work and represents a constant preoccupation from the twenties on. As her "Introductory Letter" attests, Woolf sees political engagement as emanating from a specific, historically determined subject position, one that exists in a complex relation to its bodily experience. And when she experiments with this position in her fiction or challenges it in her essays, she is also perforce shifting her political stance.[19]

Woolf's radical attempt to reconstruct community in her fiction grows out of this knot of subjectivity and politics.[20] In *Orlando* and *The Waves*, community identity is not predicated on the traditional terms of kinship and proximity, nor on allegiance to a specific group or political party, nor even on participating in the broader groupings of region or nation. Rather, Woolf develops an expanded notion of personal identity, one that constitutes subjectivity as coming into being always in fluctuating relation to a small group of affiliated yet singular others. Out of this mode of what Jean-Luc Nancy would call "compearance"[21] arises a radically modern version of community, one which governs relations within, between, and among subjectivities while seeking to circumvent the tyranny of bodies. This sense of relation she calls in her diary in 1924 a "mosaic," implying by her use of that term not only a version of the psychologically decentered self as we commonly read it in modernist fiction, but also a model of a fractured yet coherent political life.

The context of her remark makes this social connection clearer – for Woolf writes about an invitation, which comes to her via the postman, for Leonard to speak at a Labour Party meeting: "The clock strikes 7, & I wonder if I hear Leonard . . . Here has the postman been, making me choke a little, born sentimentalist that I am, by hoping so honestly & sincerely that Mr. Woolf would address the ILP at Lewes on the League of Nations? This sort of thing counts."[22] It is this strange interconnection of people and events that surprises and pleases Woolf. The invitation not only demonstrates the pull of the Labour Party on Leonard but the appeal for Virginia of a form of inter-class connection represented by the postman's invitation. Having just returned from a visit with Vita Sackville-West and her father at his immense estate, Woolf appreciates the range of social horizon that this implies:

The swing from Knole & Lord Sackville's invitation . . . to postmen getting up the local meetings, which suddenly seem to me, matters of the highest importance. All this confirms me in thinking that we're splinters & mosaics; not, as they used to hold, immaculate, monolithic, consistent wholes.[23]

What is crucial in this response is the merging of personal, social, and political consequences in this event. In the last sentence, "we" might be read as a generalized reference to the individual self – all of us as individuals are really splintered beings – or as an evocation of the community at large, a mosaic which itself is constructed of individual splinters. Of course, it must be clear, neither of these readings would be sufficient here, and that's precisely the point. The combination of dissociated selves into a social mosaic that incorporates the realms of lords and of postmen, the concerns of the ILP and the League of Nations, as well as the relations of husbands and wives, while also continuing to splinter them, is the meaning of community for Woolf.

This may appear in some sense commonplace, and indeed on its surface it is. We all sense ourselves to belong to a vague conglomeration of those who have a claim on our lives and affections. Yet, what is significant in Woolf's writings from the mid to late twenties is the very distance she takes this image from the commonplace by following both the "splinter" and the "mosaic" to their logical conclusions. In other words, like the version of community elaborated by Nancy, Woolf's notion of affiliation stands in opposition to both atomistic individualism *and* to conventional modes of construing community in which the group exists as a "monolithic, consistent, whole." Like Nancy's notion of "compearance"[24] Woolf's version of community has clear implications for political organization as we know it.

In the political language of Woolf's day this kind of community would be more cooperative than collective, predicated on the continuing diversity of beings who nonetheless exist together. Indeed when Woolf writes directly about the concept, as in her 1930 essay "On Being Ill," she specifically chooses the word "co-operative" to refer to human commonalities.[25] But for Nancy each of these terms would be fraught with difficulty because each implies a second-order bond which is predicated on the constitution of a group. Community for Nancy is precisely the opposite, that which resists, that which undoes these kinds of groups because they falsely present community as an entity secondary to existence which is predicated on the free joining of separate subjects. It is just this other kind of community that Woolf's writings often create – where the day-to-day play of affiliation among a group of subjectivities supplants the "people" or "nation," and their continued though provisional being-in-common replaces the work of the political sphere. Just as Nancy insists that, while remaining inescapably political, the notion of being-in-common should never give way to the idea of a common being, Woolf's focus on the mosaic of inter-relationship can be read as an attempt to create a political community without resurrecting a suffocating unity.

In fact, Woolf almost seems to be confronting Nancy's political dilemma before the fact:

how can the community without essence (the community that is neither "people" nor "nation" neither "destiny" nor "generic humanity," etc.) be presented as such? That is, what might a politics be that does not stem from the will to realize such an essence? . . . How can we be receptive to the *meaning* of our multiple, dispersed, mortally fragmented existences, which nonetheless only make sense by existing in common?[26]

Both notions of community reject the collectivity as the repository of relationship, insisting on the possibility of fragmentation even within affiliation, and both attempt to resituate politics within that new mode of being-in-common. Importantly, both constitute the community as some form of action, whether an unworking that interrupts the false myth of group communion or a rewriting that articulates the call to community and its limits.

To begin, however, Woolf's recasting of community in the late twenties represents direct engagement with oppositional political groups between the wars. Alongside of and in conjunction with her feminist commitment, Woolf writes out of a sort of uncertain solidarity with the Fabians, the Labour Party, and through her connection with the Women's Co-operative Guild, with the Co-operative Movement. Even if such solidarity was not often easy or complete, and if Woolf had reservations about these political groups, the social rhetoric that emerges in her writings throughout the twenties and into the thirties converges with many of the terms of discussion about history and politics within those movements. At the same time, Woolf's reworkings of subjectivity by necessity challenge the rhetoric and the political agendas of these very movements, and in this way mark their separate project of action as the refusal of false community.[27]

Thus, rather than suffer nostalgia for the village community, or for the assumption of easy plenitude associated with it, Woolf's writings from the 1910s and 1920s welcome their twentieth-century urban environment. As early as her 1916 review of *London Revisited* Woolf expresses her appreciation for the richness of the city and its human history:

Personally we should be willing to read one volume about every street in the city, and should still ask for more. From the bones of extinct monsters and the coins of Roman emperors in the cellars to the name of the shopman over the door, the whole story is fascinating and the material endless . . . certainly this inexhaustible richness seems to belong to London more than to any other great city... But each Londoner has a London in his mind which is the real London ... and each feels for London as he feels for his family.[28]

As Susan Squier points out, the city remained of "lasting concern" to Woolf, "linking personal history to culture and yoking both to the literary imagination and her political analysis."[29] *Mrs. Dalloway* inscribes London within the lives of its characters and creates the world of Clarissa's party as well as Septimus's suicide within a distinctly modern, urban environment. As Gillian Beer puts it, "the contacts between Septimus and Clarissa are oblique and communal ... they are deeply embedded in common history – the recent past of the war, the longer past of English social stratification, the continuing presence of changing London." While that environment clearly harbors violence and alienation, along with the kind of richness described above, it does not proscribe the very possibility of community. In fact, Septimus's experience of war is part of what constructs community in this novel.[30] The experience of fragmentation becomes a common experience, the revelation of human finitude implied in Septimus's suicide creates a moment of communal recognition of the characters' shared fate. As Nancy puts it, "community is revealed in the death of others... A community is the presentation to its members of their mortal truth."[31]

Nor, with all the appeal of the rural settings of *To the Lighthouse* and *Orlando*, do we sense that village life along a smaller-scale or a face-to-face basis is free of London's potential for isolation. In fact, the chimes of Big Ben unite the London world in a way that the waves of the Hebridean Islands often do not: they mark the hours of shared activities and encounters, often disrupting any internal reverie with those moments of abrupt communal awareness. The suffocating (if false) presumption of the Ramsay household – that all must be truly present at the dinner table, that through the mediating influence of Mrs. Ramsay the thoughts of each can become commensurate with those of others – is precisely what does *not* hold sway in the metropolis.

Woolf shared this embrace of the social life of the modern city with Beatrice and Sidney Webb, principal architects of Fabianism and close friends of the Woolfs. Despite Woolf's many jokes about the Webbs' propensity to talk too often, too much, and with too much "efficiency" of purpose, she respected their independent spirit and their willingness to break with the verities of socialism. The Webbs' anti-utopian bent meant that they neither idealized past forms of community nor demanded that modern life conform to some idyllic model of social relations inconceivable within the modern city. The Fabians, and Sidney Webb in particular, loved cities and derided provincial towns.[32] Fabian socialism "was an idea, in [Sidney Webb's] word, of dense urban communities uplifted through the collective action of municipal organisation."[33]

Just as they rejected the kind of socialism that idealized the traditional village, the Webbs also dismissed revolutionary models of social change that promised cataclysmic shifts in political life. At the end of the nineteenth century the Webbs insisted that Fabians repudiate "the common assumption that socialism was necessarily bound up with Insurrectionism on the one hand or Utopianism on the other."[34] In a manner that betrays their grounding in nineteenth-century social thought, they insisted that social development itself would gradually tend towards "co-ordination among the units of each organism"[35] and that peaceful pressure towards this end would accomplish more than war. While not ideologically committed to pacifism *per se*, the Webbs' Fabianism, at least in the twenties, thus opened itself to those like Woolf who were opposed to revolution because they were opposed to war and who saw resistance as a powerful, alternative form of political engagement. Even if Woolf later became increasingly alienated from the Labour Party itself,[36] in part because of its unwillingness to recognize the limitations of its own self-concept, in the twenties her thinking about community seems to grow directly out of the promise of Fabianism.

Woolf's constructions of community also share the Fabians' vision of a classless society which nonetheless preserves a special role for intellectuals. The claims in her "Introductory Letter" that to "pool [society's] possessions instead of segregating them"[37] was the ideal might almost have stepped off the pages of a Fabian tract. The Fabians worked towards the eventual dissolution of class boundaries through the transfer of land and industrial capital from individual *and* class ownership into the hands of the community. They emphasized again and again that theirs was not to be a socialism based in class antagonism or achieved through working-class dominance but one that could only take place through the empowering of the community as a whole through the leadership of the intelligentsia.[38] Woolf's focus on female writers and thinkers and on the Daughters of Educated Men in *A Room of One's Own* and *Three Guineas* in this sense presents a particularly Fabian way of approaching the cause. In addition, while Woolf's fiction of the twenties and thirties does not concern itself explicitly with the *institutional* apparatus of socialism, it uses the city to construct a space for communities which often directly challenge the rigidity of class distinctions. When she develops new forms of urban affiliation in *Mrs. Dalloway*, or when she uses London's streets to write of the lack of connection among social spheres, Woolf is engaging in a political project aligned with that of the Fabians. The explicitly socialist, political rhetoric may be missing, but the impetus to use modern forms of social life slowly to revolutionize modes of human interconnection is ever-present.

Yet the Fabians' ultimate inability to separate themselves from both nationalistic and imperialistic modes of addressing Britain's social ills seems to have forced both Leonard and Virginia Woolf to distance themselves from the movement.[39] Despite the fact that the Webbs induced Leonard to become the Secretary of the Advisory Committee on International Affairs at the end of the First World War, they did not share his commitment to the end of imperialism. At one point Beatrice Webb even went so far as to call him "an anti-imperialist fanatic."[40] Leonard makes clear that he quarreled with the Fabians in the late twenties and early thirties partly because of their inability to pursue the anti-imperialist policies in which he believed.[41] Between the wars the Fabians moved from principles of small-scale co-operation to those of national federation and, finally, to a soviet-like hierarchical model of the state. For the Woolfs, both vehement opponents of rampant nationalism and imperialism, and critics of the soviet experiment, this change in Fabianism was disastrous.

Even outside of the specific abuses of the Fabians, the general location of community within the discourse of nationality in the early decades of the twentieth century becomes deeply problematic for Woolf. Within Woolf's writings the nation and its apparatuses are figured as distinctly masculine, inseparable from the patriarchal social structure that has kept women isolated and ignorant. From the Society in the eponymous short story to the Society of Outsiders in *Three Guineas*, Woolf consistently portrays communities of women that oppose the criteria of broad national allegiance. In "The Society," for example, a group of women seek to "find out what the world is like" (125) *not* why Great Britain is called "great." They are surprised by Parliament's declaration of war because they pay no attention to the House of Commons. These women who cannot even conceive of war are the ancestors of the pacifists in *Three Guineas*. As early as this 1920 story, Woolf equates the national with the patriarchal, war-mongering with the very structure of state institutions, and irrelevance with the sphere of conventional politics. Well before the Second World War and the abandonment of the pacifist camp by so many on the left, Woolf found herself building a feminist politics that opposed war and patriarchy by bypassing both the national arena and the oppositional groupings that played within it.

Woolf often found the Co-operative Movement more palatable than the Fabians precisely because it rejected the nation as the primary locus of community affiliation. Many of the oppositional groups of the nineteenth and early twentieth centuries build on principles of co-operation.[42] However, while the Fabians and other Labour advocates focused on infiltrating state institutions and on developing hierarchical national structures, the Co-operative Movement, and in particular the Women's Co-operative Guild, remained tied to its small groups of members. Unlike most of the trade unions, the Co-operative Movement at the end of the nineteenth century refused to merge itself with the Labour Representation Committee and its successor, the Labour Party, preserving its separate status and agenda.[43] Within the WCG federation each branch was self-governing and set its own rules. The democratically elected Annual Congress, which both Leonard and Virginia Woolf attended several times,[44] served as the governing body of the Guild as a whole. This Congress often debated resolutions on national policy, producing, for example, the WCG's celebrated and consistent pacifism throughout the thirties,[45] but according to official publications these resolutions were binding only on the Central Committee and Councils.[46]

WCG branches, such as the one in Rodmell where Woolf was active, were encouraged but not compelled to endorse the national agenda.[47] This meant that the WCG remained a federation rather than a collectivity, one which, in its day-to-day operation, often paid as much attention to the small events in women's lives as to the broader agenda of governmental reform. In this way it was different from the main Co-operative Movement which tended towards centralized activity, and it may have been precisely this difference that enabled it to become "arguably the most radical voice within the movement," taking strong public positions on such issues as female suffrage, divorce law reform, maternity care, etc.[48] Woolf expressed great admiration for the democratic operation of the meetings in which working women were encouraged to find their voices and in which few concerns were considered petty or off-limits. Indeed, her "Introductory Letter" makes clear that she found the power of these women striking and their movement a political force superior to any national political party. In fact the social policies that she was later to incorporate into *Three Guineas*, such as wages for maternal work,[49] owe much to the kinds of policies that were debated within the Guild in the 1910s and early 1920s.

Perhaps because of its lack of emphasis on the national sphere of activity, the WCG and the broader Co-operative Movement in general were also consistently supportive of the kind of internationalism that both Leonard and Virginia Woolf endorsed.[50] The Co-operative Movement was bold in its insistence that its movement absolutely required internationalism, and editorial after editorial, article after article in the *Co-operative News* emphasizes this point. For example, in 1913, a fairly typical statement of the cause reads, "The great and final achievement of co-operation must be the substitution of the present individualistic system by a co-operative commonwealth. This must be something more than a local or national accomplishment; it must be international."[51] In fact the economics of co-operation required a certain level of internationalism. In order for co-operative wholesaling to function it had to have access to goods and materials from abroad. Yet the internationalism of the Co-operative Movement contained a kind of zeal for internationalism that far surpassed economic necessity, as witnessed by the lessons in Esperanto carried in the children's magazine.[52] If the Movement was sometimes surprisingly blind in its acceptance of the British Empire, and in its loyalty to the British crown, it remained one of the few political forces in Great Britain to push consistently for international co-operation and peace throughout both the First World War and the inter-war period. As a 1929 article put it:

Co-operators throughout the world have striven always to promote the ideal of peace. That is a political as well as a social and economic ideal and the extent to which the international co-operative movement has recognized the importance of political action is measured by the hearty support it has accorded the political machine called the League of Nations.[53]

Still, it is clear from examining the pages of the long running *Co-operative News* that, under pressure from the public during the war, the general movement faltered in its commitment to international peace.[54] However, it is in the Women's Corner, the two-page spread given over to the WCG, that we see the most consistent and vocal internationalism. By the twenties the trend is predominant; the most frequent references to internationalism appear in these few (and last) pages of the *News*. The 1929 preparations for the celebration of Co-operator's Day (July 6) are a case in point. While the main section of the paper carries articles about the importance of the international arena, the focus is on how the recently founded British Co-operative Party might advance an international co-operative agenda within Parliament.[55] The women's pages on the other hand bear few references to Parliamentary activity, carrying instead resolutions to encourage international perspectives. "Co-operator's Day is a request to THINK INTERNATIONALLY, and to stretch our understanding of the word 'patriotism' until we realise that true patriotism is only expressed rightly when it sets out to safeguard the whole world instead of one bit of it."[56] The WCG did not restrict its discourse to the conventional maternal arguments for co-operation or peace, nor did it give way to men on legal or economic matters. On this issue at least, the WCG was the vanguard and the conscience of the Co-operative Movement.

The WCG was a real political alternative in another way: it belonged to women and arose from their concerns and perspectives. The movement that began with what was described as the "Woman with the Market Basket" was considered a female province whereas the trade unions were perceived as predominantly masculine. Woolf was never more than partially supportive of trade unions, as her lukewarm reaction to the General Strike of 1926 attests,[57] and that fact has often seemed puzzling given her sympathy for the working women of the WCG. Many contemporaries shared the opinion that the trade unions were a masculine domain, and that the Co-operative Movement was something separate.[58] For Woolf, already disaffected from the masculine institutions of power, as "The Society" and other writings from the twenties easily attest, the distance between the patriarchal domain of the state and the patriarchal domain of the trade unions must have seemed small.

The Co-operative Movement appeared less patriarchal in part because it focused on the power of consumers rather than on the forces of production. For many in the twenties, the Woolfs included, a *consumer*-based socialism seemed a likely alternative to reorganizing England's mechanisms of production, and a promising means of uniting intellectuals with the working classes. Because women were perceived to control their families' consumption they became central to the Co-operative Movement and vitally important actors for social change. For Woolf this meant that both middle- and working-class women could share a sphere of experience, influence, and power, despite their disparate lives. As the Guild put it, "In Trade Unions it is seen how the common interest of wage-earning has united men. So, in the Guild, married women have the common interest of wage-spending."[59] While the image of the "Woman with the Market Basket" leaves intact traditional assumptions about women's economic role, in fact many members of the WCG were *both* wage earners and spenders, as the stories in *Life As We Have Known It* attest. The WCG was revolutionary in that it constructed a sphere of belonging for working-class women outside of and often in opposition to the family. It demonstrated that women had an autonomous existence, had needs and desires not met within the home, and, most importantly, could wield a potentially world-transforming power, all truths that cut across class boundaries. The WCG women also demonstrated how solidarity and small-scale action could improve the daily lives of working women. As Margaret Llewelyn Davies proclaims, "How little it is realised by economists and others that Co-operation is the beginning of a great revolution! The Movement shows in practice that there is nothing visionary or impossible in the aspirations of those who desire to see the community in control, instead of the Capitalists."[60]

And yet as much as this sort of small-scale, pragmatic work seems to have coincided with Woolf's own politics,[61] the appeal of the WCG was ultimately limited because of Woolf's sense of distance from these women. The kind of community she seems to miss here, and that emerges again and again in her fiction, insists upon both personal and political affiliation without recreating the kind of exclusionary "we" that troubles her among the Fabians. It is precisely because Woolf's understanding of community does not stop at issues of national reform, and because it rests on the fluctuating connections within small-scale groupings, the importance of "non-historical" events, and the revisionary demands posed by recognizing a female sphere of activity, that it is both connected to and distanced from the Fabians and the WCG. The rhetoric of the Co-operative Movement may in many instances fail Woolf, but it re-emerges within the constructions of community in such fiction as *Orlando* and *The Waves*, bound up with the metaphysics of her push to move beyond the unitary subject.

From the writing of *Orlando* to the end of her life, Woolf's "characters" may never be reduced beyond a group of affiliated subjects, no matter how well developed individual differences become. We cannot finally separate the individual figures from the Society of Outsiders in *Three Guineas* any more than we can fully separate the individual speakers in *The Waves*.[62] Nor, in the end, can we separate these communities of characters from either their personal or their public histories. As Rachel Blau DuPlessis reminds us, "the late novels substitute ... a communal protagonist and a collective language" through which "the novel can suggest the structures of social change in the structures of narrative."[63] In terms of both their past and their present, these characters become socially and historically significant within a domain of affiliation. Woolf creates them in a sphere in which being implies being-with-others, and yet without reference to specific external social structures or shared political agendas. Further, as Bette London makes clear, the narrative voices that Woolf develops in the twenties "deauthorize the speakers, transgress the boundaries of individual utterance, and call into question the figures that mark the voice as a whole,"[64] thus expanding the realm in which character and community coexist.

Still, the transgressive quality of this extension of voice as it emerges in *Orlando* becomes more socially significant when we consider it as acting to interrupt and rework the cultural discourses surrounding character, community, and biography, in relation to gender and nationality. For example, in the latter portion of the novel the communal discourse surrounding motherhood is disrupted by the interjection of explicit questions about identity and empire. The flowery language leading up to the birth of Orlando's son is underhanded in its praise of the joys of motherhood. The narrator leaves us with the possibility that desire may be something else entirely, even a rejection of motherhood: "Hail, happiness! ... and all fulfillment of natural desire, whether it is what the male novelist says it is; or prayer; or denial; hail! in whatever form it comes, and may there be more forms, and stranger."[65] "More forms" here become "anything, anything that interrupts and confounds the tapping of typewriters and filing of letters and forging of links and chains, binding the Empire together" (294); "More forms" of desire are also the means of warding off those nightmares that "splinter the whole and tear us asunder and wound us and split us apart in the night" (295).

The fragmented language of the twentieth-century chapters of *Orlando* further this process as the city and its speed replace the idyll of the Victorian countryside. The prose is spare as we read lists of short declarative sentences that pick up pace much as the age itself seems geared for speed. The pace of the prose unsettles Orlando herself but it also unsettles the pastoral ideal that seems to occupy so much of this novel. As she drives out of London, fleeing the fragmentation of twentieth-century urban life, Orlando sees the country as not only a salvation for the mind but its actual metaphor, the "green screens" on either side of her representing the means of holding herself together (307). The idyllic rural scene stands for the place of origin that promises succor to the community of selves that people Orlando. Yet the disintegration does not stop upon entrance into that farmyard. The many selves still vie for the title "Orlando" and the quiet unification that seemed promised remains unavailable. Rather, the illusion of wholeness presented by her entrance into the countryside collapses back into the clamoring multitude of selves. The idyllic rural farm scene does not hold simple plenitude after all; the transcendence, if we can call it that, which comes at the end, requires yet another transformation beyond the available rural world of either past or present, to the moment when the landscape "shook itself, heaped itself, let all this encumbrance of houses, castles, and woods, slide off its tent-shaped sides" (326) and became a place beyond the human.

In this somewhat negative sense *Orlando* becomes a fictional model for the kind of community that refuses the prospect of self-imminence or nostalgia for a bygone era of wholeness or communion.[66] When it is remarked that "it was not to seek 'life' that Orlando went among" the people in the Elizabethan era, the novel is already parodying the notion that life was more intensely lived and more openly shared among the lower classes of that age, and that both we readers and Lord Orlando ought to seek out that communion (31). At the same time the novel also seeks to create a sort of obverse, where the character Orlando becomes larger than life by parodying the mythology of the noble hero. An alternate communal past comes into existence by refusing the communal mythos.

The parody of the noble hero thus unites social discourse with character in a way that revises both. In 1924, when she writes the essay, "Character in Fiction," Woolf seems to exclude all but character from fiction. As her famous line puts it, "I believe that all novels, that is to say, deal with character, and that it is to express character – not to preach doctrines, sing songs, or celebrate the glories of the British Empire, that the form of the novel, so clumsy, so verbose, and undramatic, so rich, elastic, and alive, has been evolved."[67] However, on the facing page Woolf seems to contradict her own rule. In novels like *War and Peace* and *Vanity Fair* she admires the very details of history or philosophy that she had condemned in the Edwardians, because in these works extra-literary concerns enter through the novels' characters themselves.

If you think of these books, you do at once think of some character who has seemed to you so real . . . that it has the power to make you think not merely of it itself, but of all sorts of things through its eyes – of religion, of love, of war, of peace, of family life, of balls in county towns, of sunsets, moonrises, the immortality of the soul. (426)

For Woolf, these concerns become appropriate in a novel when they are made intrinsic to the characters themselves rather than simply included as representations of its intellectual context, its material conditions, or its impact on the outside world. Yet enter they do, making clear that *Orlando*, as the most extreme form of character novel possible, is constructed not only against novels that "preach doctrines, sing songs, or celebrate the glories of the British Empire" but against the conventional understanding of character, and as a means of bringing broad social concerns into their appropriate fictional domain.

In this sense *Orlando* seems to substitute a supple and expanded notion of character for communal history, while at the same time resisting the consolidation of identity that underlies the mythic hero. Orlando's extraordinary series of connected identities makes it nearly impossible to read the novel without in some way conceiving of Orlando as a *multiple* figure with very different socio-historical roles. Orlando's essential quality seems to be that he/she knows, and is, all of her identities at once and cannot therefore be restricted to the progress of a hero/heroine – even one seen as supremely supple. We must resist the temptation to point out the "core" of identity that stays the same in Orlando – for there can be no core in so contingent a figure, no singularity when the character changes form (sex), dress (gender), language (poetic diction), state (marriage), and if not very often, age.

Indeed this notion is strenuously resisted in the novel especially by Woolf's use of the fantastic, in which, as Todorov puts it, "the limit between matter and mind is not unknown... The multiplication of personality, taken literally, is an immediate consequence of the possible transition between matter and mind."[68] This resistance becomes most apparent in the passage from the eighteenth century, in which social masquerade easily shields multiple identities, to the nineteenth, where the isolating terms of a romantic sensibility underscore the Victorian prescription of monogamous marriage, and inscribe its mental effects upon her material person. For if, as she discovers in the nineteenth century, "each man and each woman has another allotted to it for life" (245), then Orlando must not only choose to be wholly one sex or the other, but also only one self at a time. It is this aspect of the age that is so restrictive, and not merely because of the limitations imposed on women by Victorian married life. The possible modes of life that had required another relation between matter and mind, that had required that each operate at its limit – making the expansion of body(ies) a result of the expansion of minds, and the diversity of mind the consequence of the diverse sensual experiences of the body – become a thing of the past.

Fantasy recedes; Orlando is restricted because both mind and body are restricted to being singular.

At the end of the novel the narrator directly raises the possibility of Orlando conceived of as a community of subjects.[69] Confronted with the complexities of the twentieth century, Orlando calls upon a part of herself to take over and master the situation. The narrator describes this part of Orlando as if it were a wholly different person contained within the main character, thereby playing with the difference between the multiplicity of the internal self and the apparent unity of one we call Orlando: "For if there are . . . seventy-six different times all ticking in the mind at once, how many different people are there not . . . all having lodgment at one time or another in the human spirit? Some say two thousand and fifty-two" (308). We read a list of the possible characters that Orlando can call upon to help in her encounter with the twentieth century as though they might all exist at the same time, with no one of them precluding another, nor summarizing the lot: "These selves of which we are built up, one on top of another, as plates are piled on a waiter's hand, have attachments elsewhere, sympathies, little constitutions and rights of their own, call them what you will" (308–9). They come to exist together, forming a community that is never singular and a character called Orlando that is defined by always being both multiple and resolutely contradictory.

Indeed, in the prolonged period of instability after Orlando's sexual transformation, what becomes most salient and troubling to Orlando is how to make clear that she is not singular, that instead her name is the sign of affiliation for a great number of subject positions and their contextual situations. Orlando wonders: "How to tell him that she, who now trembled on his arm, had been a Duke and an Ambassador? How to explain to him that she, who had been lapped like a lily in folds of paduasoy, had hacked heads off, and lain with loose women among treasure sacks in the holds of pirate ships on summer nights?" (162). Desire becomes the principle of affiliation not in terms of a strict one-to-one, lover/beloved arrangement, but in a more open-ended social relationship in which the principle of desire itself serves as the connection between the subjectivities that make up Orlando. In remembering and longing for Sasha, Orlando clearly retains the emotions connected with that long ago Elizabethan lord, presenting a sense in which the desire has passed into a place between and among these figures, not available to the male Orlando because of Sasha's absence, only available to the female Orlando when conjured up as an embodied memory of an absent figure. But this is not figured in the terms of some primordial Lacanian lack, where the subject is split over that which is eternally absent. On the other hand, this motivational desire here is quite corporeal and present; like Orlando's legs, her/his sensuality is the primary link that unites the community that goes by that name.

This passage speaks to the power of Orlando's change of sex and to the pleasure of same-sex desire, where the passage into femaleness enables a kind of bodily memory of female bodies previously known. Still, on a more metaphysical level, this is also a passage of profound intersubjectivity, where Orlando presents us with an unlikely challenge to the philosophical problem of human finitude.[70] "She felt, scampering up and down within her, like some derisive ghost who, in another instant will pick up her skirts and flaunt out of sight, Sasha the lost, Sasha the memory, whose reality she had proved just now so surprisingly – " (163). More than just a memory, Sasha seems to exist within Orlando, if only for a moment, challenging our assumption that she is irrevocably lost, and presumed dead. The singularity of her being is thereby effaced because known and recreated, if not fully contained. She comes back into being through the possibility that the reality of existence is something beyond the presence of the body.

Sasha also reappears in more substantial form as we reach the end of the novel, another example of the way this novel responds to the challenge of human finitude. Sasha ages, thus forcing us to understand her presence as somehow "real": "She was shocked that she should have come to this; she had grown so fat; so lethargic" (303). For if we have long seen the novel as a projection of Vita Sackville-West's ancestral past onto a (single) character, the survival of that character, and of Sasha and Shel along with her, erases the pastness of the ancestor, and the possibility of seeing Orlando as a fantasy of origin.

If we see the premise of the entire novel in this light, we must then again raise the issue of community at the margins of finitude. This is the crucial question beneath the fantastical exuberance of Orlando's 300-year-long life. If we were to see her as one hero then we would have to read the community that she encompasses (at least all 2,052 selves) as in a sense the replacement for the communal life of England that never really was. If, on the other hand, as I would argue, the novel refuses the category of hero, just as it refuses so many other static categories of being, then what is rejected is not one particular version of the history of England but the very possibility of a foundational mythology, and the nostalgic version of communal plenitude that it engenders. The novel opens up a realm of liminal community which comes into being in the common experience of the possibilities and limits of being – in other words, in the experience of finitude, and in the inability of conventional versions of history and national belonging to account for or to accommodate this shared experience.

In this sense, then, *Orlando* is not simply a novel about the expansion of subjectivity or community in the abstract, for the history of England that we witness is specific. The community of subjectivities that make up Orlando also connect the character to realms in which both history and politics often intrude. Orlando as British nobleman trysts with the Russian Princess Sasha against the patriotic wishes of his countrymen. Her appeal as Other makes clear the limitations of Orlando's identity as a Briton. That Orlando later considers staying forever among the Gypsies extends this first critique of nationality. Although Orlando may not any longer "belong" to the pomp and circumstance of official England she found it "impossible to remain forever where there was neither ink nor writing paper" (150). She had, as the narrator puts it, "contracted in England some of the customs or diseases ... which cannot it seems, be expelled" (142). Her relationship to language seems to create a bond with her country people that all the good will of the Gypsies cannot break, one predicated on the use of description and metaphor to create a common past.

But how common is it? The reality of Orlando's return to England is one that demonstrates that the metaphors employed by Addison, Pope, *et al.*, are precisely *not* the metaphors used by the women below stairs or behind the locked doors of their rooms. The patriotic distinction thus proves again to be a false one – it may seem to Orlando abroad that all of England shares her rapture at the sight of a sunset, and that it must also provide a shared domain of experience because its language provides her with a term for beauty better than "good to eat" (142). The presumption in this section is that nationality must have meaning, at least within the domain of metaphor. Yet this proves not to be so, as the basis for national feeling drops away immediately, replaced by the common understanding of gendered social life that Orlando learns on-board ship. Orlando's re-creation as a woman among the Gypsies thereby pushes the question of common language and literary nationality into the realm of gender, making clear the extent to which patriarchy grows up alongside those other discourses of identity and participates in the perpetuation of nationality.

Part of the problem of a national parlance clearly lies in the class differences that emerge after Orlando's return. If we saw the lower classes quite literally at the margin in the Elizabethan era, tending their small fires at the edges of the frozen river while Orlando basked in the heat of national prominence, here we glimpse courtesans who, if not so low on the social ladder, nonetheless subsist there only through work. They do not own manors with 365 rooms as does Lord Orlando and therefore do not speak of houses as the source of metaphoric power, but rather as the reverse, as potentially debilitating objects to be hidden through deceptive practice. However, the deception does not work, and the practice creates first derision and then a tearing off of disguises and a break through to "the truth" (217). The bond that grows among these women, behind the doors that protect female society, is the bond of literal speech, behavior, and dress, an antidote not only to the glittering witticisms of Addison, Pope, and Dryden, but also to the assumption that the nation is united by a single elite metaphoric language.

Inscribed within this episode, however, also lies the issue of Orlando's relationship to female community, and it is here that we can begin to see the transposition of political rhetoric like that of the WCG into the novel. Orlando's tenure among the Gypsies may be seen to stand in for the historical experience of Englishwomen who were denied paper and ink, and who, like the Gypsy women, were looked at suspiciously when their meditations made them "less adept than before at milking and cheese-making" (145–6). In England, Woolf places Orlando within this community of women who join forces in much the same way that the WCG women co-operate, granting each member mutual support and encouragement to voice her own story. The strength of the union is the power to speak the stories of their lives without having to couch them in the language of the salon, and without having to deny their experiences as poor women or as courtesans. The stories after all revolve around the objects they possess; the tales of intrigue are rooted in material life. Outside the sphere of national importance and history-making then lies the sphere that beckons Orlando, yet which at the same time makes clear the gap in both language and experience that she must overstride.

This episode also re-enacts Woolf's difficulty with the metaphoric terrain of the WCG, for Orlando too finds herself limited in her ability to enter fully into this world, or to present herself in its language. She watches *outside* the windows of the salons, gazing at the shadows of Johnson and Boswell "roll[ing] out the most magnificent phrases" without either hearing them or being able to answer back (223). Community as a problem of the relationship of language to bodily experience thus re-emerges, heightened by the change of gender and the choices it forces upon the eighteenth-century Orlando. If her body does not create an automatic or natural community identity for Orlando, community becomes more an issue tied to the imaginative presentation of the self, in dialog with historical and gendered restrictions on language. Orlando-as-community comes to represent the potential past of women that cannot exist as a common experience to be remembered or drawn upon. It is this version of a potential common past that becomes "thinking back through [one's] mothers" (79) in *A Room of One's Own* and that, if it had been available to her, might have linked Woolf to the other writing women of the WCG.

In this sense we might term *Orlando* a "community biography," one which rejects the conventions of biography both to expand the possibilities of character and to recuperate community. Woolf belonged to the wave of revisionary biographers so important in the twenties, and to the company of those for whom writing a life occupied the middle ground not only between fact and fiction but also between the individual and the community writ large. Woolf began *Orlando* in the same month as she wrote "The New Biography," that essay in which she explores the method of Lytton Strachey and Harold Nicolson. Strachey, in the famous introduction to *Eminent Victorians*, writes of his own biography what might serve as well to describe much of Woolf's own project: "It is not by the direct method of a scrupulous narration that the explorer of the past can hope to depict [the Victorian Age] . . . [Rather] he will row out over that great ocean of material, and lower down into it, here and there, a little bucket, which will bring up to the light of day some characteristic specimen."[71] In *The Development of English Biography* Nicolson also insists that biography search for truth by expanding the facts into a more complete picture. The new biographer should use his imaginative and literary powers to mold and shape the story that emerges from the life: "[There] must result for the reader, an active and not merely passive adjustment of sympathy; there must result for him an acquisition not of facts only but of experience; there must remain for him a definite mental impression, an altered attitude of mind."[72]

If we see *Orlando* as an expansion of sympathy by the expansion of subjectivity beyond the determination of the body, we can also see it as an attempt to respond to the failure of sympathy Woolf experienced at the WCG Congress. The fantastical romp, begun as a joke, ultimately provides the hint of an answer to one of Woolf's most vexing problems by elaborating an alternative realm of community which makes a mockery of the possibility of being "shut up" in one's singular experiences. But the problem of the WCG is also a question of real-world action, a question not easily answered by Orlando's anti-heroism. Almost in reaction to the swashbuckling swordplay of the beginning of the novel, the novel ends in a misty state of watchfulness, rather than dramatic movement. While through Orlando's exploits we may perhaps recognize the potential for recasting our understanding of action in the world, the potential seems both unreal and unrealized. It is a force not fully to be recognized until Woolf recasts it in *The Waves*, moving the internal fantasy of *Orlando* towards "what is outside itself and beyond."[73]

OF OCEANS AND OPPOSITION: THE ACTION OF *THE WAVES*

"Symbiosis and oceanic feeling" Alice Kaplan claims "are produced in fascism's 'gathering' stages – produced in its rhythms, the intonations . . . What was liberating in aesthetic terms can look dangerous as soon as it is socially conceived."[74] It is no surprise that Kaplan should speak of fascism's gathering stages in aesthetic terms. For Kaplan, and others following Walter Benjamin, have persuasively elaborated on his claim that "fascism is the introduction of aesthetics into political life."[75] Indeed, the fascist desire to recreate society often emerges most powerfully in its utopian fantasies and in the mass spectacles organized to enact them. However, as Kaplan's analyses make clear, the fascist effort to make life into art was not confined to dramatic forms, nor did its nostalgia for pre-modern plenitude always imply a rejection of stylistic modernism.[76] In fact, we can point to any number of proto- or quasi-fascist novelists, from Céline to Wyndham Lewis, for whom the fascist aesthetic *was* a modernist one. As Russell Berman has claimed, "modernism articulated alternative models in which . . . life and art were to be merged . . . the social character of the various aesthetic endeavors was constantly underscored . . . [and thus] a fascist version arose."[77] We can draw no clear formal boundaries around the fascist aesthetic, especially in those gathering stages, just as we cannot easily judge, in its earliest days, the fascist potential of a political movement.

This difficulty becomes more salient when we consider that Kaplan describes the early fascist aesthetic as encapsulating "symbiosis and oceanic feeling," terms that are familiar to readers of *The Waves*. The ocean in darkness as the novel opens is an ocean without limits or boundaries, indistinguishable from the sky. As the sun rises on the children at Elvedon their monologues run together, with images spilling from one child to the next. The children are "edged with mist," in Bernard's celebrated phrase, they "melt into each other,"[78] and create the edenic Elvedon as a realm of symbiotic plenitude. The question of the politics of a certain communal aesthetic becomes then both less clear and more important. We must wonder, what makes the difference between a fascist and an anti-fascist text?

Yet, as the birds which first sang in chorus fly off, leaving only one singing "by the bedroom alone" (11), so the characters constantly come together and separate, quickly discovering the limits of connection even as they continue to desire it. *The Waves* begins and ends as a novel about the potential for plenitude in a group, about the forces, whether personal or political, that undermine it, and about the dangers, to both individuals and the group, of insisting upon it. Even more so than *Orlando* it evokes a notion of "compearance," of a being-in-common that is born in the absence of simple communion. Percival's imperial adventures, Louis's status-hungry strivings, even Rhoda's doomed quests for wholeness, all underscore the social forces which make the kind of unfettered community that Bernard craves impossible. The waves of the interludes may fall "in one long concussion" even as the sun sinks (207) but Bernard still wonders "Am I all of them? Am I one and distinct?" (288).

The Waves has long been recognized as Woolf's most poetic rumination on the problem of commonality.[79] What has not been adequately discussed is the extent to which, in *The Waves*, Woolf's aesthetic is bound up with the emergence of British fascism in the period of crisis from 1929 to 1931 – exactly the period of the writing of the novel. For this is fascism's gathering stage in Britain, the period in which the populist appeal of the proto-fascist movement is often indistinguishable from that of left-leaning political groups and in which fascism can be "especially appealing to the intellectual who dreams of gaining 'community' ... without losing 'self'."[80] In fact, in this period of rising unemployment, economic crisis, and dearth of leadership on both the right and the left, there were many British intellectuals whose quest for community brought them to the brink of fascism. Yet, even as *The Waves* expresses an oceanic feeling, desire for wholeness, and pressure for international community like that which pervades the proto-fascist rhetoric of Mosley's New Party (as well as much twentieth-century neo-conservative and fascist literature),[81] *The Waves* specifically confronts the limitations of this political and literary discourse.

As the sun rises further and further, the waves thunder on the beach, stamping and crashing,[82] but never dispelling the desire to be caught up in their flow (192). Klaus Theweleit has abundantly argued that oceanic images and particularly images of undammed, feminine waters which flow indiscriminately and transgress boundaries, ultimately *threaten* the fascist desire to "stand with both feet and every root firmly anchored in the soil."[83] The threat here seems to lie in a dynamic feminine aesthetic opposite to the masculine symbiosis Kaplan discusses in French fascism.[84] More specifically, *The Waves*, I argue, resists fascism first of all by enacting a more social version of that community based in compearance we saw in *Orlando*, a community which absolutely opposes most traditional models of family, proximity, and nation as well as the fascist call for the corporate state. Secondly *The Waves* resists fascism by rejecting the idea of the charismatic leader in the form of the character Percival. And thirdly it resists fascism by using gendered images of active natural power to contradict the ordered might of fascism. Within this context then *The Waves* may be seen as acting through its central imagery, creating a feminist narrative that swirls water against fascist boots. With the power of that narrative swirl, the novel presents us with an alternative model of both community and action, one which serves as a countercurrent within the crisis of 1929–31, both marking and resisting the gathering of political force.

It's not always easy to see the close proximity of Mosley's fascism and the left-leaning cosmopolitanism of Woolf's Bloomsbury cohorts. To begin with, fascism in Britain is often either written off as unsuccessful, or written up as a phenomenon that doesn't get underway until the mid-thirties.[85] In fact Mosley's version of fascism, which was to grow into the British Union of Fascists (BUF), came into being in 1931 with the New Party, a party that, at least at its outset, drew a startling number of adherents from the ranks of Labour, and held appeal for a wide range of dissatisfied citizens. If Zeev Sternhell is correct in claiming that "fascist ideology in all its essentials is best perceived in its origins,"[86] then it is to this party that we must turn to understand British fascism.

But the distinction between right and left within the oppositional movements of the late twenties, and even within the New Party itself, was very rarely clear.[87] Mosley was a member of the Labour Party's inner circle and a minister in its government until he resigned in 1930, and he began the New Party as a means to solving the unemployment crisis.[88] His ideas were therefore seen by many as an extension of Labour Party policies. In fact, "The Mosley Memorandum" that was rejected by the Labour cabinet in 1930, and which precipitated his resignation, was predominantly a Keynesian approach to solving unemployment through public works, regulation of the market, and the creation of new industries via expanded government credit.[89] Since the Labour Party had all but abdicated its agenda in the face of the international economic crisis of 1929, to many Mosley's New Party seemed to be a viable form of political action.[90]

The common bond among those attracted to Mosley seems to have been the desire for organized and decisive action that would wrest Britain's economic policy from the hands of the international banking community, action that would unite Great Britain even as it connected it to movements of the people in other states. For, as Mosley was to claim over and over again, fascism was "a worldwide creed. Each of the great political faiths in its turn has been a universal movement: Conservatism, Liberalism, and Socialism are common to nearly every country... In this respect fascism occupies precisely the same position."[91] Like socialism, Mosley's fascism was conceived as a people's revolutionary movement, but one which relied upon the corporate state as its vehicle. Thus its connection to a universal movement could not lie in the dissolution of national boundaries and international solidarity (as in communist internationalism). Rather, it would ultimately be in shoring up British trade barriers, granting almost unlimited power to the central authority, and drawing the people together as a "team" that Mosley's "Greater Britain" would become an example of the universal appeal of fascist principles.[92] "The human race is not prepared for internationalism," Nicolson writes, "for its fulfillment we require a similar attitude of sanity on the part of other nations. That sanity does not, at present, exist. Our sanity therefore must begin at home."[93]

In 1930, however, when Woolf was writing *The Waves* Mosley's politics were not yet openly fascist, and the claims of his followers were that they were continuing the work that the Labour Party had given up. The kind of action they were proposing was just the kind that many other Labourites had been urging on the conciliatory and slow-moving government. If we find Harold Nicolson giving up all else to edit *Action*, Vita Sackville-West writing a gardening column for the paper, and John Strachey and others intimately involved in its creation, then why, we might ask, didn't Virginia Woolf contribute as well?

The answer is not the simple answer that she was loyal to Labour, as we might perhaps argue for Leonard. As we have seen, in the twenties the Labour Party itself evoked mixed emotions from Woolf and the situation at the end of the decade was only more confused than it was earlier. Because of the variety of positions subsumed within the heading "Labour", those in power did not necessarily represent the Fabian perspective that had drawn her to the movement. Ramsay MacDonald was not a Fabian leader – in fact, the period of the twenties when he was twice leader of a Labour government was also the period of the Fabians' *least* influence in Labour politics. Woolf often felt quite distant from Labour especially as it continued to overwhelm and supersede the Co-operative Movement in this period.

Nor was Woolf's absence from the pages of *Action* a result of her unwillingness to conform to New Party political codes or to particular modes of writing. As the pages of *Action* attest, in its short run of one year Nicolson managed to assemble an exceptionally eclectic group of contributors. The editorial pages insist from the beginning that the paper was to be open to a variety of political perspectives and that all manner of contributions would be welcome. Thus along with Sackville-West's "Your Garden" columns there were weekly columns from Francis Birrell, and contributions from Osbert Sitwell, Christopher Isherwood, and Keynesian economist Rupert Trouton (who also published with the Hogarth Press). After the opening invective by Mosley, and Nicolson's corresponding editorial, there were reports on science, advice columns on housekeeping, and many reviews of general-interest books. One might have imagined Nicolson soliciting a review or two from Woolf – that he didn't, or at least that, if he did, she didn't deem it important enough to record in her diary, seems clear.

On the contrary, the only time Woolf appears in *Action* is as the subject of Nicolson's review of *The Waves* on the day of its publication in the premier issue of his journal. This review is worthy of mention for two reasons: not only does it attest to the openness of Nicolson's publication, but it also highlights the paradoxes inherent in New Party politics at the time, and in the proto-fascist sensibility in general. Just as Kaplan's French writers are swept away in the restless energy of fascist feeling,[94] so Nicolson admired Woolf's "battering restlessness," and the "incessant renewals of shape and energy" in her novel. Action in and of itself is a value for New Party members, from the metaphor of dynamic progress used from the first issue of *Action* to the later institution of a sports-oriented Youth Movement.

But clearly this is not flux and reflux of the kind inscribed on every page of Woolf's novel. There is no room for the sort of fluidity that the interludes in *The Waves* present or for a moment where "all . . . wavered and bent in uncertainty and ambiguity, as if a great moth sailing through the room had shadowed the immense solidity of chairs and tables with floating wings" (183). Rather, the kind of boundless energy that *Action* endorses is directed, unwavering, "co-ordinated, co-operative and controlled,"[95] action much more akin to the Hitler youth than to the young community at Elvedon. The watchword for the New Party is "VOLT": Vigor, Order, Loyalty, Triumph; its body is the corporate state.[96]

Nothing could be farther from Woolf's politics, and, particularly here, nothing could be farther from the version of it she expresses in *The Waves*. It is in this way that her novel may be seen as marking the limitations and the dangers of proto-fascism within her circle and in British political life in general, and especially its inability to admit any version of dynamic feminist force within its emphasis on action. When she writes in May of 1931 about political causes to Ethel Smyth she makes clear that what she "can't abide is the man who wishes to convert other men's minds."[97] If, as Jane Marcus has argued, *The Waves* critiques the imperial image of Britannia as ruler of the sea, then on the home shores it also presents the sea as pitted against the rigid and increasingly masculinized edifice of British nationalism.[98] *The Waves* presents an alternative feminist force of action that directs itself against the proto-fascist responses to national crisis, and to the system of party politics out of which that crisis arose. The action of *The Waves* – in the sense of a praxis that implies a moral and political goal – is thus the forceful substitution of the potential for a leaderless and anti-patriarchal being-in-common for the lure of fascist political communion.

The pages of *The Waves* not only critique empire through the fall of Percival but also contend with the domestic effects of international crisis. Woolf's account of her work on the novel states that she began it in earnest in September 1929, a month before the financial crash. In the period of the writing of the novel, that is from 1929 to 1931, British exports declined by one half, and unemployment went from just over a million in 1929 to $2\frac{1}{2}$ million in 1930. As a result, Labour fell from 288 seats in the 1929 election to 52 seats in the coalition government formed in the fall of 1931, just as the novel was published.[99] Although there are no legions of the unemployed in *The Waves*, material wealth often appears tenuous, especially in the bankruptcy of Louis's father "a banker at Brisbane," which forces "Louis the best scholar in the school" (92) to work in an office instead of attending university with Bernard and Neville. We also see occasional glimpses of London squalor, as for example, from Louis's window: "I see the broken windows in poor people's houses; the lean cats; some slattern squinting in a cracked looking-glass as she arranges her face on the street corner" (170).

The sense of collapse of the external social fabric may also be read in its general absence from the novel, as though it no longer exists as a realm of meaning, as though there is now no hope of social change through normal political channels.

We also see the sexual politics which for Woolf mark all aspects of British social life. Despite Woolf's intentions not to have any characters in the novel at all,[100] Rhoda emerges as a compelling portrait of the kind of woman who is maimed by patriarchal values, and, most especially, by the restriction of women to a certain sphere of manners. As the party scene makes clear, when Rhoda is deprived of a sphere of influence, importance, or comfort, she is deprived of strength and integrity of both body and spirit. Jinny finds ease in the social world by discovering the bodily communication among those at the party (101). Susan has discovered that "hard thing" (98) within herself away at school in Switzerland and brings it with her to her rural life. When she finds she "cannot float gently, mixing with other people" (98), Susan can turn to the natural world where she establishes not only connection, but also escape from the confines of her gender identity: "I am not a woman, but the light that falls on this gate, on this ground. I am the seasons, I think sometimes, January, May, November; the mud, the mist, the dawn" (98). But Rhoda has no alternative to being a woman, no other sphere where she can solidify her being, and so, while Susan and Jinny consolidate themselves in this episode, Rhoda disintegrates under the pressure of impending (and imposed) womanhood:

Here, twisting the tassels of this brocaded curtain in my hostess's window, I am broken into separate pieces; I am no longer one . . . I am to be broken. I am to be derided all my life. I am to be cast up and down among these men and women, with their twitching faces, with their lying tongues, like a cork on a rough sea. (106–7)

In these closely connected episodes Woolf's feminist critique makes clear that the political maiming of women is one which has corporeal consequences; without a means of enabling body and mind to flourish within the female sphere, both break up.

As Gillian Beer has pointed out,[101] each character in *The Waves* has a different relationship between body and world, and that relationship also governs the ephemeral give and take of the group's communal corpus. Still, the implications for the female outsider are more dire than for the male – than they are, for example, for Louis, who finds himself restricted by social codes of conduct but can nevertheless succeed within the masculine domain of business. This is partly because, while Rhoda is made marginal through the immutable fact of her sex, for Louis the expression of exclusion arises in his Australian accent, which he attempts to hide or transform over the course of the book. While language and body are strongly connected in this novel of natural, visceral, and often sexual images, the male figures Neville, Louis, and especially Bernard, reach towards a sort of idealized connection of the two realms. The possible uses of language hold out an ideal, potential wholeness of body and completenesss of interconnection that is not so available to the female characters. If Susan is at first content with the "natural happiness"[102] of motherhood, by the end of the book she wearies of it. On the other hand, as Beer points out, Bernard experiences a kind of physical well-being when his animal nature asserts itself in his final monologue, establishing a kind of "'gutteral, visceral' inner voice ... [as] the unreachable ideal language which Bernard always seeks."[103]

In the context of 1930–1, however, gendered images of the body also invoke the question of the body of the nation. The essence of British government as defined for many political writers at the time was perceived as a matter of establishing the cohesion of a group (party, House of Parliament, national government, etc.) which would preserve the unity and strength of the nation. Organic metaphors and reference to the body abound in these writings[104] making clear that the proto-fascist call for a corporate state was only one of many ways of conceiving of the nation as a wounded body in need of assistance.

The New Party writings highlight the inter-relationship between gendered images of the body, organic conceptions of statehood, war-mongering, and patriarchy that were also common within more mainstream movements. "What therefore, is the alternative between the flag-waving jingo and the pimpled pacifist?" Nicolson asks, "It is the belief that every man or woman is born into this world to fulfill a certain function. It is the belief in the Organic State."[105] Compared to those in both Italy and Germany, Mosley's New Party seemed better able to admit that women might serve a public function (as did, for example, Mosley's wife Cynthia, who was a Member of Parliament). Still, the rhetoric of physical "efficiency," "athleticism," and youth becomes increasingly masculinized.[106] The call to save the nation by shoring up the state, or consolidating party ranks, or changing leadership, all were calls to restore a wholeness and unity to the seemingly "natural" realm of masculine values, and to reinforce the system by which Louis triumphs while Rhoda disintegrates.

At the same time it is clear that the fascist fascination with the body, and particularly with gender distinctions as expressed by the body, is also bound up with desire to destroy particular bodies. Within the Italian context with which Mosley was aligned, for example, there is a tension between physical liberation and bodily discipline ever tied to the image of the body politic. If for the Italian futurists this aesthetic often implied a sense of *self*-destruction as well as the effort to overcome the demands of one's own body, for many German fascists the body to be destroyed belonged to another and was very often female. Klaus Theweleit's exhaustive compendium of male fantasies has made clear the extent to which the reduction of disobedient or potentially threatening female bodies to "bloody masses" was part and parcel of the fascist cult of the ideal body.[107] Even when not destroyed absolutely, the German woman within the Freikorps writings that Theweleit presents is deprived of her bodily sensuality, emerging as an amalgam of sister/ mother/nurse, dressed in uniform white, or else got up in the images of the united nation, Germania or Luisa of Prussia, safely de-sexualized and distanced by her symbolic role.[108]

From this perspective Rhoda's disintegration begins to take on more specific significance as an indicator of the potential corporeal destruction of the non-conforming female body within the proto-fascist situation. If Susan and Jinny can accommodate themselves to the available roles of mother and lover, at least enough to be able to preserve themselves intact, Rhoda becomes the equivalent of that bloody mass, dashed not by Freikorps blows or even the sword of Percival, raised in the imperial adventure, but by the false promise of a charismatic leader and the violence that emanates from his centralized authority. If the promise of plenitude held out by the proto-fascist, nationalist impulse is dual edged, verging on both liberation and destruction at once, then Rhoda's is the body that succumbs.

But the destructive aspect of the collectivist enterprise is not only limited to the female figures in the novel. While the cult of Percival is crucial to the development of the first half of *The Waves*, it is undermined as often as it is supported. If, as Melba Cuddy-Keane remarks, *Between the Acts* is a novel about the subversion of prevailing assumptions about leaders,[109] *The Waves* is its direct antecedent. Percival is not only laughable as a representative of empire, as Marcus has pointed out, but also very limited in his ability to act within the domestic arena. Woolf gives him no voice, so that we can only sense his presence in the effect he has on the others. But that effect is either illusory, or, as in the case of Rhoda, negative, created more by the function he fulfills than by the quality of his actions. This negative effect is especially clear after his death, as, for example, in Rhoda's comments: "now I will walk down Oxford Street envisaging a world rent by lightning; I will look at oaks cracked asunder and red where the flowering branch has fallen... Look now at what Percival has given me. Look at the street now that Percival is dead" (159).

This is not simply the result of the loss of Percival. In fact, he is missing before the fact, so that his charismatic appeal may be seen as a certain sort of communal misapprehension. Not only is he voiceless but he is always viewed from afar, leading the "smaller fry" or looking on with indifference: "His blue, and oddly inexpressive eyes, are fixed with pagan indifference upon the pillar opposite... He sees nothing; he hears nothing. He is remote from us all in a pagan universe" (36). He inspires devotion simply by laughing (38), love by "flick[ing] his hand to the back of his neck" (36), and poetry by "blunder[ing] off, crushing the grasses, with the small fry after him" (40). Even when face to face with him, Percival inspires Louis with resentment (39) and need (40). At the dinner scene where he is anticipated, the characters mutter a litany of negatives – "no it is not Percival" (118) or "he does not come" (119) – as the door swings open and shut. Their common experience is thus of the force of this negative, their common knowledge of his absence. Percival then is the sign of the negative, the opposite of the plenitude he seems to promise. His lack is felt before he ever leaves for India; the desire for him is for what is missing, in both self and other.

Indeed, Bernard begins the construction of this negative vision in the passage that opens the chapter. Having descended from the train, Bernard finds himself adrift, missing the sense of necessity that impels those around him (113). He seems not only without direction but also without self:

I have no ambition. I will let myself be carried on by the general impulse. The surface of my mind slips along like a pale-grey stream reflecting what passes. I cannot remember my past, my nose, or the colour of my eyes, or what my general opinion of myself is... People might walk through me. (113)

While we might find Bernard at times endearing in his misty aimlessness, in the context of 1930 his willingness to be led by the impulses of the crowd seems distinctly dangerous. The problem returns to the absence within the self that here is assuaged by the presence of others around Bernard. There is a "crack in the structure – one's identity" (115), he tells us: "To be myself... I need the illumination of other people's eyes, and therefore cannot be entirely sure what is my self" (116). Bernard desperately desires to be a self, and hence must be subject to completion by others. But the process is doomed from the start. Percival's presence at dinner cannot mirror back to Bernard his individual ideal self. On the contrary, it can only recast him as one of the many, birds massed singing together or "soldiers in the presence of their captain" (123).

In this sense *The Waves* comments upon the limitations of both charismatic leaders and their followers. It is also in this light that we must read the sections of the novel following the death of Percival. For, since he leaves the scene after the first third of the novel and dies by its mid-point, the group of characters that make up *The Waves* ultimately construct their community without him. Nor can either Louis or Bernard take over as the focus of desire or obedience, despite Louis's short-term appeal for Rhoda. As they come to adulthood the characters of *The Waves* form a group that has no static, organic identity and which no longer offers itself to a single leader. Theirs is a community that exists in fragmentation, that like Nancy's is constantly in the process of becoming, without ever resolving itself into a common being. As Bernard puts it, "We are divided; we are not here. Yet I cannot find any obstacle separating us. There is no division between me and them" (288).

From a political perspective, *The Waves* may be seen as a novel about the possibility of community not only without charismatic leaders but also without any structure like that of state, nation, or party. Woolf's social vision here moves beyond simply critiquing either the notion of empire or the problem of leadership. Rather, in the inter-connection of her community of characters she constructs an alternative model of social organization, which, I would argue, is directly targeted at those in search of political answers to England's crisis. It is a model that does not rely upon the renewal of nationalism or on the violent assertion of a party position and which paves the way for the possibility of cosmopolitanism.

Thus in *The Waves* Rhoda ends up not as a bloody mass but rather as fragments tossed into a current, pieces flung into the water that ebbs and flows throughout this narrative. If Percival's heroism is diminished both in the manner of his death and in the way it is announced in the novel "Percival has died; (he died in Egypt; he died in Greece; all deaths are one death)" (170), then Rhoda's is enhanced, but not because she is a martyr. Rather, the power of the river into which she flings flowers to the dead Percival (164), or of the waves into which she falls as if in a dream (206), is the power of a symbiotic connection that dissolves and disassembles, at the same time as it creates a network of connection that flows to all corners of this narrative. From the struggle of her isolation ("I have sunk alone on the turf and fingered some old bone and thought: When the wind stoops to brush this height, may there be nothing found but a pinch of dust" [206]) to the satisfaction of a fleeting communion ("Who then comes with me?" [206]), there is only a gap of a few sentences. The sense of the "we" is created the instant the dreamer leaves land and allows herself to fall into the sea; it does not matter what nation claims the cliffs:

> We launch out now over the precipice. Beneath us lie the lights of the herring fleet. The cliffs vanish. Rippling small, rippling grey, innumerable waves spread beneath us. I touch nothing. I see nothing. We may sink and settle on the waves. The sea will drum in my ears... Rolling me over the waves will shoulder me under. Everything falls in a tremendous shower, dissolving me. (206)

Just as the flowers flung as an offering to Percival travel with the waves to "the uttermost corners of the earth" (164), connecting Rhoda to her dead friend as well as to the woman and man she sees pacing the embankment, so Rhoda's body itself here reaches its utmost connection to other people and places as it dissolves under the waves.

Rhoda highlights the dispersal within the natural flux of human experience that pervades the entire community of characters. She provides an extension of the relationship between "splinter" and "mosaic" that lies at the heart of Woolf's political vision. For, just as her difficulties throughout are tied to the limitations of her feminine role, so are her strengths. The feminine, as presented by Rhoda, Susan, and Jinny together, begins to be seen as a power that works to manage that relationship, to create a different form of action out of its tension.

The female characters, even in their enormous differences, seem less insistent about the teleology of their lives than are their male counterparts in this novel, and are therefore more susceptible to natural, cyclical rhythms. In addition, the images connected to these female characters refer far more frequently to ebb and flow. Their metaphorical life within the novel touches far more often upon the presiding figure of the waves, which becomes in this novel the ultimate symbol for action and power. For example, Susan, who is perhaps the most conventional of the female characters and who claims to "have reached the summit of [her] desires" growing trees, fruit, and children on a rural farm, regrets ending up "fenced in, planted here like one of [her] own trees" (190). At night, however, remembering her childhood, she "can feel the waves of [her] life, tossed, broken, round [her]" and though rooted, still harbors the value of lives spent "eddying like straws round the piers of a bridge" (192). And Jinny, who finds her strength in the social whirl of London, experiences it not as the conquest of a realm or the launching of a career, but rather as the sense of almost limitless and directionless capacity: "I am arch, gay, languid, melancholy by turns. I am rooted but I flow. All gold, flowing that way, I say to that one 'come'... This is the most exciting moment I have ever known. I flutter, I ripple. I stream like a plant in the river flowing this way, flowing that way, but rooted" (102). To be rooted yet streaming in all directions is to be cosmopolitan in its most profound sense; it is to be the force of communal awareness without the limitations of either place or loyalty. Woolf here eloquently describes the same sense of "locational cosmopolitanism" or "rooted migrancy" that so many post-colonial critics struggle to express.[110]

So too in the interludes the figure of the waves promulgates an oceanic sensibility intrinsically linked to the rising of the sun and the cyclical progress of the lives of the characters, and thereby to the new cosmopolitanism of this novel. The waves that "thud like a great beast stamping" (150) are not simply symbols of imperialist violence as Jane Marcus would have it, but also part of the dissolving power of the natural world which sets to blazing an island "on which no foot could rest" (165) and lets nothing stand immobile, untouched. In fact, much of what is so striking in the interludes of *The Waves* is the very subtlety with which Woolf weaves together images of power and movement, sun and water, which all ultimately are connected to the feminist force of the novel. The sun, figured as a girl who rises from a watery bed to disperse her light, wears "water-globed jewels that sen[d] lances of opal-tinted light falling and flashing in the uncertain air like the flanks of a dolphin leaping, or the flash of a falling blade" (148). Her light strikes, "pierces," and "beats" even as it descends "in floods dissolv[ing] the separate foliage" of a tree into an indistinguishable mass (149). At times, the waves pound like drums (75, 109), the birds dart like warriors (74–5), and the sunlight shoots like darts (165), yet by end of day "sea and sky [are] indistinguishable," both feminine, fanning out over the shore and rolling back in a sigh (236). Warlike imagery is clearly not restricted to the waves: the mid-day sun shoots arrows into the water (165), even the clouds fling nets across the sea (183). Still, the sun in its descent dissolves and quiets all, working a power that continues even when it disappears.

There is no doubting the strength of this natural world, yet it is a power that cannot be categorized or compartmentalized – or rather, that is the very force of resistance to those categories. It changes with the cycle of the day and with corresponding events in the characters' lives. The waves move onward without direction, a force of aimless yet developing life, but a force nonetheless. In contrast to the direct line of Percival's life, the metaphors of the interludes mix modes, and dissolve boundaries between earth, sea, and sky, so that petals may be described as "shell-shaped," leaves might run, and "wave[s] of light" can pass through flowers "as if a fin cut the green glass of a lake" (182). As this last example makes clear, there is constant movement here from sea to sky and back again and it is this movement, sometimes thundering violently, sometimes rolling peacefully, that is the figurative thrust of *The Waves*.

This forceful current also moves through the structure of the senten-ces in the novel, which often slip from one word to the next, either clipping an intervening sound or smoothing it into an alliterative stream. As Garrett Stewart has pointed out, "a certain conjunction of words across the border or blank of their normal scriptive segmentation proliferates with unusual frequency in *The Waves*." In phrases like Susan's "the silver-grey flickering moth-wing quiver of words" (215), we can hear little distinction between the *g* at the end of "wing" and the *q* at the beginning of "quiver" which tend to run together as we pronounce them.[111] Even the *g* in "grey" and the *ck* in "flickering" participate in a stream of sounds whose distinctions have been elided. What Stewart calls "phonemic clotting or 'thickening,'" accomplishes the same goal.[112] When Woolf writes in an interlude "all the blades of the grass were run together in one fluent green blaze" (149) she creates linguistic echoes (blades/blaze; run/one) that help accomplish the meaning of the phrase, running sound fluently past the borders of the individual words, dissolving distinctions.

This is what I mean by the untrammeled, oceanic impulse of this novel – not a kind sweep of flowing waters which one might figure as stereotypically feminine – but an unceasing current of powerful change that moves through both the interludes and the episodes of *The Waves*. This current respects no boundaries, whether between natural realms or between individual characters. Nor does it respect life, often stranding fish (166) or washing the substance from the earth (236). Though the narrative moves with the image of the girl rising from her bed, it is not a stereotypically feminine force we see in the interludes but what I would call an alternative version of action, a feminist combination of "mus-cularity" (108) and flow. The interludes carry a power that neither can be directed nor has its own direction, and so despite its warrior drums

(75) it cannot be approximated to the dynamic progress of the fascist call to arms.[113]

The boundaries that are muddied by this active movement include the gendered roles and the forces of meaning-making that seem to threaten all the characters throughout this novel. If we know that Susan, Jinny, and Rhoda are far more than the phrases they become in Bernard's final soliloquy, we deny him the final word which he so craves. Yet, we cannot simply reverse the process, making Rhoda an anti-heroine, and Susan and Jinny images of natural maternalism or bodily freedom, respectively. The maiming action is the summing up itself, the need to make the outlines of life clear, and to anchor them firmly in English soil, which the receding waters of the waves are always eroding.

For Bernard, the dominant voice of the end of the novel, summing up seems to be the means to self-completion, to filling in the notorious crack in the structure of his identity. He seems intent on capturing his friends for his own use, rewriting them to construct his own life story, complete with beginning, middle, and end. Yet he too periodically succumbs to the force of an alternative logic. If the beginning of all sentient life, according to Bernard, is in the hands of a woman: "Mrs. Constable [who] raised the sponge above her head, squeezed it and out shot, right, left, all down the spine, arrows of sensation" (239); if the woman writing on the lawn at Elvedon is for him the "Stonehenge surrounded by a circle of great stones," ever-present, never to be dislodged from the center of his being; if life itself is "like a globe," like the feminine presence of the interludes; and if, in the end, understanding comes to him in the form of an old nurse who turns the pages of a book and says "'This is the truth'" (287), then Bernard himself must exist within a realm where meaning is gendered as feminine. Action for him, therefore, must derive from somewhere beyond the reaches of "that man, the hairy, the ape-like" within him that "mops and mows perpetually pointing with his half-idiot gestures of greed and covetousness at what he desires" (290).

Then, when we hear forceful metaphors employed within Bernard's final soliloquy, I would argue, it is not as a simple echo of Percival's ill-conceived heroism. Rather it is often the action of the waves seeping into Bernard's dying self, offering him the "sword ... with which to batter down the walls, this protection, this begetting of children and living behind curtains" (266). In other words it is the action that will sweep away the force and purpose of an isolated private life, replacing it with "rapture; [with] common feeling with death" (266). He recognizes the paucity of conventional images of power and order ("it is a mistake, this extreme precision, this orderly and military progress; a convenience, a lie" [255]) and instead returns again and again to the memories of his friends in an attempt to regain, control, and draw strength from their lives.

The waves must be a force opposed to the quest to assert a single life, which is first raised by Percival but then taken up at different moments by Neville, Louis, and Bernard. They must be a force that carries fragments of being, like the fragments of Rhoda's violets, off to far corners and hidden pools. Within the feminist realm of meaning created by the end of the novel, the "truth" spoken by Bernard's nurse must be the work of the waves to erase any single phrase written in the sand and meant to be followed. *The Waves* thus recasts action as a dissolving swirl or a thunderous crash which opposes summary truths, willful assertions of the narrative of identity, and violent attempts at heroism.

We can hear the challenge of Woolf's narrative even more clearly if we juxtapose it again to the pages of *Action* and its masculinist call for the corporate state. Mosley attributes the economic crisis to what he calls "the rule of the old woman" which extends beyond economics and politics into the social life of the country.[114] The nation, according to Mosley, is "hag-ridden," which means that there can be no forward movement, no efficiency, no discipline: "Liberty of life in this country is thwarted at every turn by the omnipresent grandmother. Strength, efficiency, modernism in Government are excluded, however menacing the economic situation. But the nagging whining voice of the universal grandmother is ever at our elbow to thwart and to impede every natural impulse of man."[115] The only solution is to hone the body and mind of the individual (man) into "disciplined moderation or athleticism of life" placed in service to the state.[116] By the end of 1931, and of *Action*'s short-lived run, the New Party's disciplined athleticism, promoted in the New Party youth groups and in Mosley's thuggish entourage, was only a step away from the hyper-masculinity of the black shirts.

Mosley's embrace of para-military youth organizations after his defeat at the polls seems to have forced many to recognize Mosley's fascist aspirations. John Strachey and several others among the founding members defected quickly in the fall of 1931. Nicolson ultimately followed suit, if only after accompanying Mosley on a trip to consult Mussolini. According to Nicolson's notebooks, Mussolini seems to have counseled Mosley not to try to import Italian militarism into Britain but rather to evolve his own homegrown fascism,[117] advice that would have stood Mosley in good stead had he heeded it. For it seems that the use of thugs at rallies and the para-military training urged on the young was to a great extent what disaffected his Labourite followers. At least to Nicolson, it didn't quite seem "suited to England,"[118] though he did his best to make it more so by suggesting to Mosley that the Youth Groups adopt grey flannels and white shirts as their uniforms.[119] The heightened emphasis on thuggish masculine power as directed towards accomplishing specific political action ultimately soured Nicolson on the entire concept of the corporate state, and he returned to the Labour Party, eventually becoming one of its most influential members.

Yet this all happens quite late in the game. In October Nicolson is still trying to mask the already severe disintegration of New Party consensus by shoring up its collective voice and empowering its proposals: "We believe that the intelligence of man is capable of creating a modern State as organic as the human body ... A State in which energy and efficiency are always rewarded, and in which the bungler and the sluggard must go to the wall."[120] Nicolson evokes a firing squad as a mode for dealing with those incapable of the right sort of "energy and efficiency" which are code words for masculinized, directed power harnessed to the goals of the state. As we remember, they are forces meant to combat the "universal grandmother," who keeps the nation from moving forward as an organic, unified whole: forces, in other words, meant to prevent the dispersal or free flow of social energy that Woolf associates with the feminist action of the waves.

Cynthia Mosley's ultimate rejection of the New Party seems to recognize this failing. As a self-described "ardent Socialist"[121] and member of the House of Commons, she traveled to Russia in 1930 to meet with Trotsky. Nonetheless, she supported Mosley's resignation from the Labour Party and was one of the staunchest campaigners in the elections of 1930.[122] She ran as a New Party candidate and garnered a larger margin than did her husband. However, after this election she seems simply to have ceased all political activity and rejected the New Party specifically. At one of her last public speeches, which was to a Women's Peace Conference, she said "There is only one way that people could stop war – by refusing to fight." Nicolson later responded: "Poor C[ynthia] ... She was not made for politics. She was made for society and the home."[123] When she makes specific objection to the New Party's tendency towards fascism, reportedly telling Nicolson and Oswald Mosley that she wants "to put a notice in the *Times* to the effect that she dissociates herself from [Oswald's] fascist tendencies," the two men assume it is a joke.[124]

A joke? Or sincere opposition to the increasingly ominous fascist rhetoric of the Mosley–Nicolson venture? That these men do not even engage with Cynthia Mosley's criticism, that they place it outside of sincere political or social commentary, despite her position as a twice-elected MP, demonstrates not only the misogynist dimensions of the New Party, but also its increasingly closed rhetorical world. While the first issues of *Action* were open to all political perspectives, the final ones are not. Nicolson begins by claiming the paper not to be fascist; by its demise it openly proclaims its allegiance. And this allegiance is to the masculinist principle of "VOLT": Vigor, Order, Loyalty, Triumph, on the way to the corporate state.

So if Nicolson admires the flux and flow of Woolf's "masterpiece," he cannot adopt its politics. For, in its insistence on community as fragmentation-in-coherence, on free flow and cyclical progress, and especially on the forceful border crossings of feminist oceanic movement, *The Waves* undermines action as directed progress. Woolf's work runs determinedly counter to the onward rush of fascism, presenting an oppositional cosmopolitan politics that resists the lure of the corporate state and that is prescient in its understanding of the danger of the fascist aesthetic. The gathering stages of fascism may produce rhythms, intonations, and oceanic feelings that hide its hard-booted political identity – but the waves of Woolf's novel, by moving according to another logic, uncover its masculinist, violent danger.

CHAPTER 5

Gertrude Stein

STEINIAN TOPOGRAPHIES: THE MAKING OF AMERICA

Suddenly you know that the geographical history of America has something to do with everything it may be like loving any man or woman or even a little or a big dog.

Gertrude Stein, *The Geographical History of America*, 84

East and west.
George Washington is best.
No one need leave out north and south.

Gertrude Stein, "George Washington," in *Four in America*

Stein's pages have become like the United States viewed from an airplane.

William Carlos Williams, *Imaginations*, 350[1]

Gertrude Stein's enormous early novel *The Making of Americans* grew out of the restlessness of loneliness, indecision, and displacement. When she began it in 1903, she had recently left Baltimore, medical school, and her unhappy love affair with May Bookstaver and, after a period in London, was living in New York City. By that summer she had moved to her famous apartment at 27, rue de Fleurus, and was writing what she called her "American" novel in the *atelier*, after her brother Leo had gone to bed.[2] The first four months of 1904 saw her back in New York where she wrote much of the early draft of the novel, which was not to be completed until 1908. By June she was back in Paris and would not return to the United States for close to thirty years.

According to a recent biographer, much of Stein's "nomadic life between 1900 and 1904 resulted from her need either to encounter or to avoid May Bookstaver."[3] The very concept of nomadism or wandering, which appears frequently in Stein's fiction, has often been linked to the theme of lesbianism and to sexual promiscuity in general. But as Lisa Ruddick points out, "one might easily reverse the emphasis and say that sex itself stands in the story as a metaphor for a certain type of mental activity . . . sexual wanderings become 'wanderings after wisdom,' after 'world knowledge,' after 'real experience.'"[4]

While their lesbian content is by now undeniable, Stein's writings also ask us to read these wanderings literally, as expressions of the import-ance of geography, (dis)placement, and movement within the modernist construction of subjectivity and community.[5] They inaugurate a com-plex series of connections between geography and identity, geography and nationality, and geography and nomadism that also ultimately raise the question of community and its relationship to cosmopolitanism. When Stein criticizes Oakland, California because it had "no there there," she is attacking its lack of community, yet, in a manner common within Stein's prose, she describes this fault in spatial terms, forging the connection between place and social life that will be elaborated throughout her work. When she claims that "America is my country; Paris is my hometown" she insists that national identity and community feeling are distinct though paired terms, and that community may ultimately develop in conjunction with, rather than in opposition to, the cosmopolitan condition. For Stein, "geographical history" may bring both individual and national identities into being, but movement in space changes their relation, forcing us to seek community in the network of lines on a map, or in the juxtapositions inherent in land-scape, or in the narrative extension of a shifting plural subject. From the linear, conventionally organic construction of identity that informs the opening pages of *The Making of Americans* to the map-based model of experience that will predominate in the late *Ida: A Novel*, Stein's radical narratives develop a topographical notion of identity, one that not only reconstructs the subject as nomadic and polyvocal, but ultimately chal-lenges the dichotomy between community and cosmopolitanism.

However, topography, or geography more generally, are disciplines undergoing enormous change in both Europe and the United States during the period of Stein's formation and maturation as a writer. The science of geography was moving from the categorization of conditions of landscape to the study of relations,[6] and especially new relations brought about through movement. The morphology of landscape was being connected to the morphology of human life, whether in terms of species movement, diffusion, or the development of language.[7] At the turn of the century this geographical interest in the relation between land and people often expressed itself in Darwinian racialist language; its understanding of human communities and their geographical needs often verged on a simplistic interpretation of *Lebensraum*, which could easily be appropriated for the geopolitics of nationalism. In the US in the early decades of the twentieth century the question of geography was increasingly polarized by the tension between this sort of organicism and more physically oriented map-based approaches, a tension which was only partially resolved by the demand for cartography during the Second World War.[8] It is in this tension and its connection to the politics of nationality in the period that geography serves to highlight the social implications of Stein's narratives. In other words, the pre-occupations shared between Stein's narratives and American cultural geography demonstrate not only the centrality of geographical representations of identity and their implication in the history and politics of nationality in the modernist period, but also the degree to which Stein's experimental narratives are inevitably entwined in that discourse.

Further, the pressure of movement which we may term "geographical" also infuses Stein's experimental narrative style, linking her notorious grammatical and syntactical shifts to their social implications. Grammatical play within Stein's narratives does not confine itself to hermetic concerns of the text – shifts appear in all kinds of discussions of relations, whether of self and other, individual and group, man and woman, woman and woman, old and new worlds, geography and mentality, or, importantly for us here, "nation" and "hometown" (which map loosely onto the French *patrie* and *pays*)[9]. The implication then is that in the mature work, from 1905–6 on, the Steinian subject exists on these several axes at once and creates community in the constant movement between and among them. Thus, claiming, as Stein does over and over again, that the geography of America determines the way its writers write, does not conflict with her insistence that the human mind or the writing "I" also moves beyond this identity. National belonging and mind wandering are not mutually exclusive, mind wandering constantly creates new cosmopolitan communities, and these new communities drive both narrative and social life.

Stein's later writings, and the *Stanzas in Meditation* and *Ida: A Novel* in particular, push this wandering "I" to its extreme, where the boundaries between subjects become unclear and the relationships among them often seem more metaphysical than political. Yet, in these expansions of a wandering subjectivity we may also begin to see a nomadic model of social affiliation, much like that recently adumbrated by Rosi

Braidotti,[10] which also evokes new feminist models of community. In the constant re-iteration of being within different contexts, which we can see literally in Stein's constant narrative repetition of the verb "to be," we can find the empowering shifts of a nomadic and polyglot existence.[11] In the insistence on writing as an activity shared between the "I" and the "you," we can find the evocation of an ethically inclined plural subject which may be said to form the basis of its own community. In this sense Stein's narratives, from *The Making of Americans* to *Ida: A Novel*, tie a feminist cosmopolitanism based in "dislocation, translation, and re-situation,"[12] to a new narrative version of community, one which gestures towards a geographical politics of the personal.

Having been dominated by tales of exploration and the description of new frontiers during most of the nineteenth century, geography in the US at the turn of the century began to turn away from simply mapping, cataloging species and terrain, or chronicling the conquest of nature by humans. Maps were becoming increasingly complete and standardized – so much so that by 1909 an International Congress could agree as to common methods and surveying procedures for producing an international map of the world.[13] Geography aspired to be more than "superficial instruction in the position of countries, places, mountains, and rivers,"[14] and came increasingly to be predicated on the observable relationships between people and land and on the multiple ways in which the two could be shown to interact. In 1903 the president of the newly founded Association of American Geographers wrote that "the essential in geography is a relation between the elements of terrestrial environment and the items of organic response."[15] As one British geographer put it in 1911, "The geography of today is in the act of escaping from the matrix of mere facts in which it has been too long imprisoned."[16]

The essential keywords in this new cultural geography were "relationship" and "change," especially as applied to human existence in landscape. While one of the nineteenth-century founders of modern geographical science, Friedrich von Humboldt, called his *magnum opus Cosmos*,[17] it focused primarily on the description and discussion of physical, not human, geography. While Carl Ritter's systematic study of humans within landscape, *Geography in Relationship to Nature and to Human History*, inaugurated the discipline of cultural geography, it was dominated by a religious conception of human systems as stable wholes with clear teleologies, organized by God.[18] But after 1859, which marks not only the deaths of Humboldt and Ritter but also the publication of Darwin's *Origin of the Species*, human geography becomes defined by study of the inter-relation of human communities with nature, and focuses on the incremental changes occasioned by that inter-relationship.

The influence of Darwinism on turn-of-the-century geography cannot be over-estimated. Source after source points to the galvanizing effect that Darwin's writings had upon the still-nascent science, in terms of both his addition to the storehouse of geographical fact available for study and his theoretical contribution to the principle of studying it. As one writer puts it, in 1911:

He showed that there is a delicately adjusted balance between organisms and their surroundings, taken in the widest sense ... in this respect human societies and settlements can be shown to behave like organisms. Therefore, we can hope to explain at least partially the manifold differences in man and his societies in different parts of the globe by the minor differences in their physical conditions ... the doctrine of evolution ... has ... for the first time raised [geography] to the level of a science.[19]

Most crucially here, we may note the relief with which geographers found a principle of scientific explanation in Darwinian thinking. This provided the essential causative element in an otherwise very nebulous theory of human/landscape relations. The appropriation of Darwinism within geography at the turn of the century, especially in Germany and in the US, thus hinged on the question of causation, and provided the means by which the environment might be described as a key determining influence on the behavior of human communities.[20]

This environmental determinism finds its most notorious and influential expression in the work of Friedrich Ratzel in the 1880s and 1890s.[21] Ratzel is most famous, especially in the US, as the coiner of the term *Lebensraum*, which was appropriated by Hitler to justify his geopolitical program of national expansion.[22] Indeed, the force of disapprobation is so strong that nearly all mention of Ratzel, and of his American student Ellen Churchill Semple, within the American geographical literature after the Second World War, appears with some caveat about their connection with Nazi thought. Yet, Ratzel may be said to be the key heir to Humboldt and Ritter, and a crucial link between the nineteenth-century science of geography and its twentieth-century incarnations.[23] His *Anthropogeographie* (1882 and 1891) and *Politische Geographie* (1897) inaugurated the sub-disciplines of anthropological and political geography and influenced a generation of geographical scholarship in the United States, well before their appropriation for statist aims.[24]

Ratzel's early work is straightforward in its application of Darwinian geography to the problem of human society. He begins his professional life as a zoologist and approaches geography with an already developed concern with the lives of organisms. Prompted by a prolonged excursion in the United States, his turn to geography focuses on the inter-connection of human migrations and landscape, and evaluates the combined results, in particular, of a transplanted German population in a new American environment. His enormous *Völkerkunde* (translated as *The History of Mankind*) is as much ethnography as geography, focusing on the many "races" of the world and their development in relation to their location.[25] So too, in *Anthropogeographie*, we can see the contrast between, for example, a people whose community has developed along a fertile river basin and their more isolated and less well-fed neighbors in the mountains. In this manner, human communities are seen to evolve in response to their environment, without significant distortions from their own agency, or statistical disruptions from variation in response.

Thus Ratzel's work is marked by a tendency to view human communities as complete organisms, subject to the same kind of pressures that Darwin would describe among other forms of biological life, in a way that clearly relies on over-simplified notions of race. Furthermore, he is never reticent about applying these rules to the political and cultural lives of nations:

The geographical factors in history appear now as conspicuous direct effects of environment, such as the forest warfare of the American Indian or the irrigation works of the Pueblo tribes, now as a group of indirect effects, operating through the economic, social, and political activities of a people. These remoter secondary results are often of supreme importance; they are the ones which give the final stamp to the national temperament and character.[26]

These claims are key in the development of organicism in both German and American cultural geography, and of the racism that often accompanies it.

However, it is also clear that Ratzel's work in the 1890s begins to turn away from a simple model of geographical determinism towards one in which several factors, both cultural and physical, come into play. He attacks the crude notion of the survival of the fittest in human life, and scolds Herbert Spencer for careless ethnography and vast generalizations.[27] In the two volumes of *Anthropogeographie*, published complete by 1899, "Ratzel expounded his great themes of human geography, those of human societies developing within a frame (Rahmen), exploiting a place (Stelle), needing space (Raum) and finding limits (Grenzen)."[28] In this sense, *Lebensraum*, as one concept among many in Ratzel's writings, works to circumvent pure environmental determinism, and to clarify the interrelationship between human communities and their geographical environments. Here the need for space for living is seen as a natural result of the growth of human communities in their geographical place, and as a factor in Ratzel's growing attention to the means by which humans not only respond to, but also interact with, their geographical environment.

Despite this expansion of the sociological dimension of geography, Ratzel still describes communities as wholes, often expressed in nationalist terms. The national community expresses the "spirit" of the people; the state becomes an organism needing room in space like any other. In Ratzel's work "The 'materially coherent' element of the state is the soil, with which the state, a group of men, has a 'spiritual connection' ... states can expand, contract, live, prosper, decay and die just as living organisms do."[29] It is this aspect of Ratzel's thought that opens the door to nationalist excesses, and which has been rightly decried as an invitation to a dangerous geopolitics.[30]

Ratzel's work gained him an "immense reputation" in Europe and the United States where the *Völkerkunde* and *Anthropogeographie* were both quickly translated and had a "formative effect on American geography."[31] Yet one might add that the kinds of thinking about the relationships among geography, land, and nation present in these works in the 1890s are to some extent already in circulation in the United States. Frederick Jackson Turner's celebrated 1893 essay "The Significance of the Frontier in American History" sounds something like Ratzel in its opening statements: "Behind institutions, behind constitutional forms and modifications, lie the vital forces that call these organs into life and shape them to meet changing conditions. The peculiarity of American institutions is, the fact that they have been compelled to adapt themselves to the changes ... involved in crossing a continent, in winning a wilderness."[32] Indeed, the idea that the frontier had provided one of *the* distinguishing features of American life, and that the nation might, in a certain sense, *need* a frontier, seems to verge on an American version of Ratzelian *Lebensraum*. Yet in another sense Turner concerns himself very little with the specific geography of the frontier, which of course does not have one single set of physical characteristics but rather shifts throughout history. Instead he focuses on the frontier mentality, which might differ from place to place, but which Turner describes as developing in the same stages throughout the country. The result, for Turner, is the creation of a people: "To the frontier the American intellect owes its striking characteristics. That coarseness and strength combined with acuteness and inquisitiveness; that practical, inventive turn of mind, ... that masterful grasp of things, ... that restless nervous energy, that dominant individualism."[33] As the final words of this statement make clear, the most important outcome for Turner is American democracy. In this sense Turner's is a different project from that undertaken by Ratzel, or indeed by any geographer of the time. It is a political history, not a geography, but one that might be said to derive from the recognition of the American need for a vast *Lebensraum*.

In the work of Ellen Churchill Semple, influential geographer and until 1984 the only woman ever to be president of the Association of American Geographers, we can find the direct transmission of Ratzelian principles into American cultural and geographical understanding at the turn of the century.[34] Her *American History and Its Geographic Conditions* (1903), and *Influences of Geographic Environment* (1911) which is a translation and adaptation of Ratzel's *Anthropogeographie*, were both widely read and influential, having been said to have "shaped the whole trend and content of geographic thought in America."[35] That they were published in the years that bracket the beginning of Stein's *The Making of Americans* and its publication is more than coincidental; it makes clear the specific contexts of geographical thought that would have surrounded Stein in the period of her formation as a writer.

Semple's work has been described as biological in its reliance on models of species movement and diversification as the basis of human history. Yet in Semple's preface to her translation of the *Anthropogeographie* we can see her distancing herself from Ratzel's most extreme determinism, from his racialism, and most importantly from his organic view of the state. She points out that the laws of geography "do not lend themselves to mathematical finality of statement. For this reason the writer speaks of geographic factors and influences, shuns the word geographic determinant, and speaks with extreme caution of geographic control."[36] In this way the forces of race also find distinctive treatment in her work. She separates herself from Ratzel's more extreme racial ideas[37] and rejects strict racial Darwinism:

If these peoples of different ethnic stocks but similar environments manifested similar or related social, economic or historical development, it was reasonable to infer that such similarities were due to environment and not race. Thus by extensive comparison, the race factor in these problems of two unknown quantities was eliminated for certain large classes of social and historical phenomena.[38]

In clear distinction from many of her predecessors, Semple never accords race a prime place in her study of the diversification of peoples over the surface of the world. The movement of peoples into new geographical areas with new demands comes to account for the variety of human life; adaptation is an ongoing issue of environment, not an embodied trait that characterizes a specific people.

In fact, as this passage makes clear, in many ways she seems to oppose the principles of geography and race, as though to claim that response to the terrain can only be sufficiently recognized if we consciously denigrate the effects of race. To imagine that ethnicity might predetermine a people's ability to persevere in a harsh climate, or to create a productive agricultural economy, would be to imagine that the human situation is always secondary to natural capacity – and that given almost any environment certain groups will develop along the path to "civilization" while others will not – a principle Semple rejects. Indeed it is almost the other way around – the main thrust of *Influences* is to insist that "man is a product of the earth's surfaces" and can only be studied as such.[39] The idea that one might identify some principal attribute of any human grouping outside of its specific environmental conditions is exactly the position she wishes to contest.

Semple's preface also points to another crucial area where she has modified Ratzel's *Anthropogeographie* in translating it: she removes all references to an organic state.[40] "This theory," she writes, "had to be eliminated from any restatement of Ratzel's system."[41] Even in her *American History and its Geographic Conditions* there is much less importance placed on the development of a unified national disposition than either Ratzel or Turner display. She concerns herself with the way the people of the Cumberland Gap developed in relation to the natural barrier of the Appalachian mountains, rather than with any general theory of "the frontier" or the national spirit. To Semple, geography is important because it marks the constant in "the long history of human development" and contrasts with "shifting, plastic, progressive, retrogressive man." It is a local not a state-based issue.[42] Semple demonstrates by example, and moves through her material regionally, concerned with issues of habit and culture more than with national spirit and rarely commenting on the role of the state or its political needs. Thus, though still prey to Ratzel's lingering racial organicism, Semple's geography avoids the pitfalls of both geographic nationalism and its use of *Lebensraum*.

It is just this kind of project that it seems Stein began when she took up *The Making of Americans*, even if she ends up on very different ground. Stein's early scientific writings and the early studies for *The Making of Americans* and for *Three Lives* proceed by similar methodology, eschewing the axiomatic and demonstrating by example. *The Making of Americans* begins as an attempt to describe the relationship of Americans to their long history of movement and migration across the country, and to demonstrate the various different kinds of Americans that have arisen in response. The novel begins with a genealogical conception of identity which seems to promise that the history of America will be the playing out of the relationship of racial and environmental factors much as it was for Semple. But the result of the migration and continued movement of characters, and of the experimental narrative itself, is to undermine specific human genealogies in favor of the more nebulous "kinds" or "ones" that populate the end of the novel.[43] The novel in this sense will ultimately reject the rule of biological genealogy and organicism, substituting instead a notion of affiliation rooted in place and experience, and inscribed within the play of "ones" who come to be Americans.

Stein hones in on only a few locations and attends to the variety of human response to which they give rise. Only after forcing us to witness her elaborate assemblage of types and kinds – a sort of intermediary step missing from Semple's work – do we advance to the realm of history proper. But the trajectory is much the same, as is the need for a materially based understanding of the making of the nation. In fact, I would argue, it is almost as if Stein is seeking to merge her concern with the typologies of human behavior with Semple's insistence on a geographically based understanding of the principles of human diffusion and differentiation. Semple claims that "a people or race which, in its process of numerical growth, spreads over a large territory subjects itself to a widening range of geographic conditions, and therefore of differentiation."[44] The result of that differentiation seems to be the assemblage of American personae presented in the early work of Gertrude Stein. To juxtapose Stein's geographical texts with the landmarks of cultural geography in the period is thus not to prove her intention to become a scientific geographer (though one might surmise that she'd have liked to have been read in their company), nor to demonstrate any direct influence of any specific geographical text on her writings (though one might expect her to be cognisant of the key debates within this influential, if evolving, twentieth-century science). Rather it is to understand her long-term project to describe Americans and their geographical history as part of this broad cultural concern with situating the changing American people in direct relation to their landscape.

Stein's much analyzed story "Melanctha" serves well as the place to begin reading *The Making of Americans* because it was written in the hiatus between drafts of the American book and demonstrates her continuing reliance on nineteenth-century organic notions of identity and race as well as her growing concern with geography and wandering. As Marianne DeKoven is quick to point out, this story contains "repeated passages of crude, profoundly offensive racial stereotyping."[45] These passages present us with a heroine who is not only determined by her race and her upbringing but who is drastically limited by them.

Thus from the very first "Melanctha" works to establish categories and kinds much like those that will propel *The Making of Americans*. We are meant to understand that Rose Johnson is a particular kind of black woman because she is "real black" but was "brought up quite like their own by white folks."[46] When the narrator informs us that on the other hand Melanctha "was a graceful, pale yellow, intelligent, attractive negress. She had not been raised like Rose by white folks but then she had been half made with real white blood" (86), it is to place her within a category that not only has the power to determine how Melanctha will think and act within the realm of the story's plot, but also attempts to tell us some bedrock truth about her identity.

Clearly this kind of stereotyping uses race, or, more broadly, ancestry, as a predictor of future action. Despite the fact that the intensity and frequency of racial descriptions diminishes after the opening pages of this story, "Melanctha" focuses on the ways that the bi-racial heroine is split between two conflicting ways of acting, much along the lines of the "tragic mulatta" stereotype. But the problem Stein introduces here is that Melanctha persists in acting, as one character puts it, "like that brute of a black nigger father" (112). She rejects Jeff Campbell in favor of a series of other, less "good" men and is always finding "new ways to get excited" (207). Melanctha acts more and more directly from her feelings, and in accord with her sexual desire and less and less in a way that, within this narrative, is attributable to her white blood. She wanders, both literally and figuratively, far from social expectations, and her wandering is presented as her distance from the center of white normative morality.

The narrative, however, is itself conflicted about Melanctha's "negroness." Not only does the center portion of the novel make far fewer references to race but the later sections increasingly undermine the notion that "whiteness" and decent behavior are better. Jeff Campbell has little of the appeal of Melanctha precisely because he does not allow himself to wander, which limits his range of experiences and makes him less interesting. Rose Johnson, the character who carelessly allows her new baby to die in the story's opening pages, is ironically given the last words on morality, as though to underscore her very lack of it. When it is Rose saying, "She don't never come to no good Melanctha Herbert . . . She didn't do right ever the way I told her," we question the value of "doing right" itself (235). The narrative reverses the movement of a typical nineteenth-century novel by pushing us to accept if not applaud Melanctha's deviance, her rejection of her suitor, and her movement *down* the social ladder.[47]

Marianne DeKoven reads Stein's emphasis on Melanctha's obvious preference for the lower-class world and for visceral experience as an indication of Stein's own effort to liberate herself both emotionally and sexually.[48] But the episodes with Rose Johnson also demonstrate a difference in the narrative that rests in its wandering structure and its circular prose. The story opens with the unnecessary death of Rose's baby, which is narrated more abruptly than the rest of *Three Lives*. This scene also reappears towards the end of the text, without indication of passage of time or development of perspective, and is the only section replayed verbatim: "Rose Johnson was careless and negligent and selfish, and when Melanctha had to leave for a few days, the baby died . . . Perhaps she just forgot it for a while" (85). In the midst of this we read (twice) "Melanctha Herbert . . . did everything that any woman could" (85, 224). This passage conditions the reader not only to prefer Melanctha but also to see her as a moral force in a world where just forgetting one's baby for a while seems to pass without remark. Importantly, this passage portrays a Melanctha who is not limited or tortured by her blood, but rather is able to act as strongly as "any woman." In a sense, this passage contains the pivot of the story, or its navel as it were, and the Steinian device of returning to it without linear development insists that our wanderings in this text revolve around this scene. "Melanctha" becomes then not just an exercise in the displacement of unspeakable sexual deviance onto the (for Stein) more admissible arena of racial difference, but also the construction of the wanderer as the prototype of the enlightened but doomed, moral and sexual subject. Melanctha in her tragedy is also then a heroine, a mulatta model for the combined perspectives created by wandering.

Thus, wandering in "Melanctha" beckons as a possible means of escaping the tyranny of blood and the sway of convention, on both the thematic and structural levels of the text. Carla Peterson has pointed out that the story itself arises out of Stein's wanderings in Baltimore, through neighborhoods where she would have overheard "coon" songs, rags, and the blues. The syncopation we hear in the story's verbal rhythms, and the sexualized slang we hear in its reported dialog, may thus be seen as Stein's deliberate straying into the genres of African-American popular culture: "As blues women, Melanctha and Jane Harden are headstrong, passionate, and deliberately flout social convention to insist on their geographic mobility and freedom."[49] Stein uses such common blues locations as the railroad and the common typologies of blues lyrics to highlight the connection between these characters. As Peterson points out, her use of blackface underscores the many levels in which wandering, and the play with identity that it encourages, permeate this text.

It is this complicated mixture of thinking about the relationship of ancestry and wandering in the development of behavior and feeling that informs the opening pages of *The Making of Americans*. The opening pages seem to promise that Americanness will be a family affair, its "progress" a microcosm for the development of the nation. Genealogy seems paramount as the litany of "mothers, fathers, grandmothers and grandfathers" (5) who appear to beget America proceeds. Yet even more than in "Melanctha" the wandering takes over, and pushes race and genealogy and even Steinian "bottom natures" to the periphery of a grammatically constituted community of Americans.

Stein's novel at first describes the Hersland and Dehning families as though this were to be a naturalistic multi-generational saga of immigrant striving and upward mobility. While there are none of the overtly racial terms that predominated in the opening paragraphs of "Melanctha," the first pages of *The Making of Americans* are filled with the specific marks of blood heritage. The characters are given family names, personal histories, and places of origin. Over and over again they are described with the phrase "One of these women" or "One of these men," as though to make immediately clear that each character grows out of a group with defined characteristics. The narrative insists that individuals within families resemble and belong to each other, and that family connections guide the actions of individuals over the course of several generations:

> There were very many of them and each one, of course, had his or her own individual way of feeling, thinking, and of doing, and with all of them the father and the mother were variously mixed up in them, and with some of them it was more the father ... And then in some of them it was the ... mother that was strongest in them.[50]

But these biological factors are quickly seen to intersect with geographical influences, as we learn the importance attributed to the east/west divide among these families and to their different places of settlement. Stein's narrative wants to situate individual characters within the context of biological and geographical milieux, using group resemblances, and family memberships in particular, to specify and define them. Settling in a particular place, as these immigrant families do in the first pages of this novel, seems only their first step in planting themselves in the new land, only the first step in a novel of natural assimilation.

In this sense Stein's novel expresses that same assimilative notion of the American race that also pervades Henry James's work, but here tied to a more definite geographical sensibility.[51] The possibility that the experience of immigration and settlement can become a family characteristic that is passed down through the generations, is implicit in this family saga. In the oft-quoted line from the opening page – "It has always seemed to me a rare privilege, this, of being an American, a real American, one whose tradition it has taken scarcely sixty years to create" (3) – the key word is "real," which at this point in the novel can only be understood as implying organically developing citizens who are American-born yet remember their foreign past. The making of these real Americans is presented to us as equal parts biological procreation and physical movement in a specific geography, migratory experience grafted onto the ever-growing family tree.

But the characters in *The Making of Americans* do not move as abstract objects on an undetermined plane, and it is in this sense that geography is always in play. In the first half of the novel the characters define and are defined by their relationship to place – to Bridgepoint, to Gossols, and to the space they must travel in between. David Hersland and his siblings are caught from the beginning between the city and the country and this conflict determines how they act: "The children had the same kind of half and half feeling that the people had around them, they had the living that was a country town living, they had the feeling that was a city feeling" (93).

In the inter-relationship between the people and the land here and throughout the novel, community may be said to develop in a traditional manner, tying the affiliations of the people to their location in a specific physical place. Because of its newness and its basis in immigration, this may not quite be the traditional community Tönnies longs for, but it deploys many of its forms and values, creating a newly naturalized connection among those living near each other which is based in the direct communication of face-to-face encounters. The Hersland children become part of the poorer kind of people who are around them, making clear that proximity begets belonging in this narrative, and that community develops out of the shared experience of place. This passage repeats over and over again in the course of several pages, and again at crucial junctures throughout the novel, building a slow accretion of belonging as the three children move from being "more and more of" the people around them to being simply "of them" (96) with no modifiers necessary. The mother of the family, however, persists in her "right well to do city being" (91), unable to bridge the class differences between herself and her neighbors, and thus creating the rift with her own children that forms one of the few axes of drama in this novel.

The appeal of Gossols for the Hersland children is not only that of discovering their connection to the families around them. They also respond directly to the landscape and to the "half-city, half-country" aspect of their home:

It was very joyous for all of them the days of the beginning of their living in the ten acre place... The sun was always shining for them, for years after to all three of the children Sunday meant sunshine and pleasant lying on the grass with a gentle wind blowing and the grass and the flowers smelling, it meant good eating and pleasant walking, it meant freedom and the joy of mere existing. (90)

If this passage is couched in the soon-to-be-superseded naturalistic style of the opening pages of the novel, it nonetheless expresses a sensibility that persists through to the end, where "experiencing being" becomes a crucial prerequisite for making meaning and, ultimately, for making community. If experiencing the freedom of the landscape is what makes the three Hersland children more a part of Gossols than of their mother, by the David Hersland section of the novel we learn that shared ways of experiencing are also what connect groups, or communities, to each other on a more general plane: "Certainly there are groups of men and women as to ways of experiencing things in being ones being living, certainly there are groups of them who in a way have the same ways of experiencing in them" (783). Like other immigrants who join the nation by being influenced by America's specific geography and who come to inhabit a community by sharing that geography with others, the Hersland children seem to become part of both community and nation by settling in the suburbs.

This description of experience then underlies the very notion of Americanness, and the development of its citizenry in this novel. Stein's characters move West in an almost paradigmatic fashion and in this movement create what Stein refers to as their "slow history" (63), very much in the way that Semple describes the slow growth of the geographical history of America. But Stein is also always interested in the ways that the generations repeat and resemble each other, even as they diverge in their specific actions and locations: "There is always then repeating, always everything is repeating, this is a history of every kind of repeating there is in living, this is then a history of every kind of living" (221). The repeating in the Hersland family is a sign of genealogical family resemblance, which will come to mark and also strengthen them as they feed into the general pool of American life. Stein seeks to develop as though by simple accretion a textbook of repeating behaviors of the phenotype "American."

It is in the context of Stein's seeming obsession with categories and kinds within this novel that much has been said of her reliance on Otto Weiniger and his 1908 book *Sex and Character*.[52] For Weiniger human nature could be broken down into typologies that in turn could be schematized, attached to males or females or discussed in racial terms. Stein's notebooks contain diagrams of personal characteristics much like the diagrams that the narrator yearns to be able to develop (595), and the use of terms like "independent dependent," "resisting," or "attacking" to describe the various characters seems to echo Weiniger's ways of codifying behavior.

Yet as both Priscilla Wald and Laura Doyle point out, Weiniger's influence on Stein here is limited. Stein is concerned with discovering what she calls the "bottom nature" of her characters, but in so doing she also discovers the curious mixtures of "bottom" and "other" natures within each:

Sometime then there will be a history of all women and all men, of all the men and all the women, of every one of them, of the mixtures in them of the bottom nature and other natures in them, of themselves inside them, there will then be a history of all of them of all their being and how it comes out from them from their beginning to their ending. (123)

It is as though in writing out her theoretical conception of bottom natures[53] Stein undercuts her own notion, subordinating it to a process of identity building that is based in progress and geographical movement, and the constant intermixing of subject and other.

In the extended digression about Mary Maxworthing and Mabel Linker, two dressmakers who live together in Gossols, we discover the beginning of a more flexible construction of identity that will mark the later Stein.[54] The friends, whom we also presume to be lovers, not only repeat their own bottom natures over and over, but also repeat aspects of each other, so that the boundaries between them seem increasingly unclear, as even the similarity of their names implies: "As I was saying pairing of friends and pairing in loving is always repeating of the coming together of the kinds of them, and this is not just general repeating but very detailed repeating" (221). While Weiniger would have described ways of distinguishing the characters, Stein is interested in what happens as they combine or impinge on each other.[55] The picture that emerges is bottom nature multiplied, repeated, combined, and ultimately unraveled, to the extent that Mary's nature implies Mabel's and vice versa.

The discussion of "singularity" also challenges assumptions about Americanness and procreation through allusion to homosexuality. Much as "wandering" in "Melanctha" may be understood as a code word for sexual promiscuity, and often specifically lesbian promiscuity, "singularity" can be seen as a veiled reference to homosexuality.[56] Within the discussion of middle-class values in the opening section of the novel, we learn "to a bourgeois mind that has within it a little of the fervor for diversity, there can be nothing more attractive than a strain of singularity that yet keeps well within the limits of conventional respectability." What follows is an entreaty on behalf of other "Brother Singulars" who "are misplaced in a generation ... [and] flee before the disapproval of our cousins, the courageous condescension of our friends who gallantly sometimes agree to walk the streets with us, from all them who never any way can understand why such ways and not the others are so dear to us" (21). The idea then in the portrait of Mary and Mabel is to reverse the utter singularity of the homosexual within this saga of middle-class Americana. The repeating, multiplying, and reproductive function of loving is not restricted to heterosexual families. The homosexual is seen as a mixed way of resembling and repeating, a kind of American indistinguishable from other kinds, and therefore no longer strictly "singular."

More than that, by becoming a paradigm for affiliation on a grand scale rather than a singularity contained within the conventions of middle-class life, homosexuality also contests the notion that nationality unfolds in a uniform direction, and thus is a direct result of the construction of traditional communities of proximity. "Singularity" then comes to exist under erasure and the repeated digressions into the lives of secondary characters, singular or otherwise, become central to a broadened novel, which wanders in many directions at once. Plurality becomes a value opposed not only to normative heterosexuality but to the linear national story to which it contributes. Stein's narrative comes to present the compendium as narrative alternative, thus challenging its own opening assumptions about the making of Americans.

At the same time, other marks of individual identity become less prominent over the course of the novel making it clear that family belonging, and thus the entire model of community which depends upon it, has been relegated to a backdrop. Rather than learn about the ageing of the immigrant families with which we began, we read at the end, under the chapter title "History of a Family's Progress":

Any one has come to be a dead one. Any one has not come to be such a one to be a dead one. Many who are living have not come yet to be a dead one. Any one has come not to be a dead one. Any one has come to be a dead one.

Any one has not come to be a dead one. Very many who have been living have not yet come to be dead ones. Very many are being living. (907)

Pronouns have taken over, shifting our attention from how specific characters exemplify Americanness to the ways that all Americans exist. Stein further underscores this movement away from the particular by replacing "she" or "he" with "someone," "that one," or "any one." Even the emphasis on "kinds" here disappears, as the final chapters of *The Making of Americans* attempt to create "a history of every kind of them and the many ways that one can think of every kind of men and women ... in the repeating that is more and more all of them" (180).

The voice that Stein adopts here is one that speaks from the position of plurality and community as it develops within the subject itself and thus as separate from the prevailing idea of nationality. The movement away from the genealogical in this novel also implies a movement away from the organic model of national identity, whereby the evolution of a people was seen as a result of a combination of racial and environmental determinants. The "one" we read about here, and which dominates virtually all of Stein's writing in the next period of her life, always bridges the gap between the particular and the general, merging a specific person with Stein's amorphous "any one" but never coalescing into the "spirit of the nation" or into a universal subject, untroubled by such characteristics as racial difference or "singularity." Furthermore, Stein's "one," as she repeats it over and over in a sentence, also works to designate several subjects with the same name. For example, a sentence reads, "Any one is one being one being living and any one is one having been in family living" (403). We may read this sentence as a simple statement about one particular "anyone," or we may interpret each new use of the word "one" as designating a completely separate person. Yet Stein's wider project pushes us to see a sort of amplification[57] at work here which augments the original subject as we move through the sentence, adding to it ostensibly other subjectivities. The "one" takes on several attributes, and several possible identities, within itself. It becomes a name for the plural subject in Stein's experimental writing, and a new basis for constructing community.

Thus, I would claim, the iterative experience of belonging that Bhabha describes as crucial to post-modern identity, and that Braidotti calls upon to support a post-modern feminism, here displays itself in this early modernist text, and thus challenges our assumptions about the distance between modernist and post-modernist social constructions. Indeed Braidotti recognizes her indebtness to Stein on this point, beginning her book *Nomadic Subjects* with an epigraph from her, and citing her several times in the text.[58] For Bhabha, Braidotti, and other current theorists, Stein's kind of "beginning again and again"[59] provides the possibility for shifting identities, perspectives, and loyalties with each new iteration. While this does not make Stein somehow post-colonial *avant la lettre* – she is after all always concerned with Americanness here, not with some much more nebulous worldwide migrancy derived from the pressures of globalization – it does help us to see this kind of iterative construction of identity as a core component of modernist experience in the early twentieth century.

But the final chapters of David Hersland underscore the particular qualities of the iterative experience of American life. Movement does not deny affiliation; wandering instead promotes a constantly renewed experience of the nation. Much as "wandering" and "singularity" had come to stand for key concepts, here "jumping" becomes a code word for the kinds of shifts in experience that make David Hersland important:

Some are jumping and some are then not jumping very much and some are not jumping well enough then so that they are interested in doing that thing, and some are jumping then and it is an extraordinary thing that they can do that thing so wonderfully... David Hersland was one of such of them. Certainly he was jumping and jumping very well and jumping quite often. (807)

David Hersland needs to experience life at different ages (817), in different places, and with different people (820). He is intent on under-standing what it means to be "going on being living" (892), but that is underscored as a constant process not only by the very fact that this phrase repeats in almost every paragraph for several pages before his death, but also that almost every sentence in those pages begins either "he was" or "he could." What he was or could be repeats and twists and revises itself; in one sentence "he was completely certain," in the next "he was almost completely certain" (810). On the same page he is first "sometimes wanting to be needing some other thing" and then "he was sometimes not wanting to be needing some other thing" (820). At the time of his death (rendered in classic Steinese by the phrase: "He had come to be a dead one" [903]), he has come to be "almost completely clearly feeling," precisely because of this twisted process of understand-ing. His life encompasses the searching, shifting notion of identity and identification that ultimately characterizes *The Making of Americans*.

Thus it is clear that, by its end, Stein's novel undermines the kind of geographical determinism of Semple's *Influences*, and of American geography of the period in general. The line by which Ratzel would connect geography to community and then to an organic national history is similarly distorted in Stein's work. Along with her rejection of linear narrative time, represented by the later principle of the "continu-ous present," comes a distortion of the physical line of influence pre-sumed by linear models of human history. As we have seen, Stein's final mode in *The Making of Americans*, most evident in the distinctive style of the David Hersland sections, always treats identity and identification as a group or series of particular repetitions in new contexts. Her constitu-tion of the American nation grows out of a perpetual process of enunci-ation, the slow accretion of those moments of intersection between being and belonging. It constantly creates itself as each generation iterates and reiterates its connections and resemblances to those who went before, and to those it encounters in new geographies – then it forgets them and moves on. The wandering of the text and the wander-ing of the characters force the novel's litany of personal and linguistic repetitions out of the closed circle of an endlessly recursive history and towards the slow discursive spiral that, for Stein, constitutes both per-sonal history and the American nation.

Further, as Stein later writes in *The Geographical History of America*, "the straight lines on the map of the United States of America make wandering a mission" (85). The kind of history that we've seen her develop in *The Making of Americans* depends for its basis not only on an iterative notion of identity but also, within a much more material realm, on the assumption that America and American nationality develop out of geographic pressure, but one different from Turner's version of *Lebensraum*. If the geographies of Gossols and Bridgepoint, and the distance between them, operate as the force which separates the Herslands and the Dehnings, they also provide the scene of cultural creation. The democratic impulses of the younger Herslands grow out of their becoming "more and more a part of the poorer ones around them" in Gossols, and out of the freedom to wander which the land represents. The possibility of moving to Gossols is then the possibility of this shift in perspectives, a shift that the novel constructs as paradigmatically American, and occasioned by landscape.

This is not the same, of course, as claiming that the nation is defined by its particular geographical borders, or even by the language contained within them. In this sense one might say Stein departs from what might be termed the strictly political realm, establishing her version of identity and belonging as that which takes place beyond the public sphere, or even the overlapping associations of Dewey's Great Community. As she put it during an argument with the University of Chicago's Robert Hutchins, "Government is the least interesting thing in human life ... creation and the expression of that creation are a damn sight more interesting."[60] She figures the interaction between geography and nation as between physical setting and the day-to-day lives of the inhabitants. By the end, the lives of the families she chronicles are conditioned by the geographical pressure to wander, which they do in an iterative, distinctly non-linear fashion, not by the directed goals of the nation-state, or by any concentric notion of belonging within a traditional community of proximity.

The prose of the very freely constructed final pages of *The Making of Americans* reaches towards the more finely honed experiments in the "continuous present" of the 1920s and 1930s, where physical metaphor becomes even more omnipresent, and always linked to the reconstruction of textual meaning. The many, many references to lakes and rivers, flat lands and borders, in *The Geographical History of America* make clear that Stein is still directly concerned with a specific geography, and with the understanding of its social effects. The fact that Stein chooses a title so close to that of Semple's 1903 work *American History and its Geographical Conditions* makes clear that she is in effect writing an alternative geographical treatise, meant to substitute her non-teleological, wandering history for the linear trajectories implied by Semple and her fellow geographers. In chapter 2 of *The Geographical History* (or the first of its many versions in this very circular text), Stein writes of the slow geographical changes in the land, where the water has either receded or advanced. She refers to the age of the terrain as determined by the fossils buried in it. All of these elements contribute to human nature and human mind: ultimately, to the place of "communism, individualism, propaganda" and war within that schema (68). What might seem like determinism here becomes limited because Stein's model not only minimizes the significance of these political systems, but also through her insistently recursive prose, minimizes any development towards them. The American landscape becomes only a variety of mapped spaces – the open sky of the prairies or the intersecting roads that wander endlessly in and around them. The only space that can be claimed for living in this geographical history of America is one with an "open-sky" mentality and a network of wandering paths as its location. Thus if Ratzel and to a lesser degree Semple were reaching towards an anthropological answer to political questions of human movement and differentiation, Stein will insist that we see the importance of geography – be it flat-land mentality or having no sky – as a broader question of the ever-shifting recursive location of being.

However, we must still return to the problem of the nation as the locus of community within geographical thought in the period, and to the potential problem of geopolitics and *Lebensraum* with which we began. For if the geographical history brings "communism, individualism, propaganda" back into play, what is to prevent us from understanding them as necessary conditions determined by environmental causes, no matter how metaphysically perceived? The potential for a return to organic notions of community and nation still lurks behind these geographical texts of the twenties and early thirties – it requires another dimension of narrative experimentation (that which emerges in Stein's later writings) to truly dislodge them.

WRITING THE "I" THAT IS "THEY": GERTRUDE STEIN'S COMMUNITY OF THE SUBJECT

To leave Stein on the question of geography here is to miss the better part of her experimental vision and the complex politics that may be said to be implied within it. The portraits in *Four in America* as well as several of her landscape plays and poems are themselves experiments in geography, but geography seen as encompassing subjectivity, social identity, and narrative structure within the process of map-making. The hypothetical situations of *Four in America* may read at first as comical nonsense. Yet by asking "If General Washington had been a writer that is a novelist what would he do," Stein is clearly positing a possible relationship between writing and politics. That this portrait begins with concern about scenery and by its seventh page begins again with the subtitle "Or a History of the United States of America" (166), further cements this narrative connection.

The issue of narrative here, however, clearly revolves around the question of subjectivity and its relationship to the American national story. The very idea of posing alternate identities for Grant, Wilbur Wright, Henry James, and George Washington revises the pedagogy of the nation by undermining the status of unitary identity within it. It poses no problem for Stein to recreate Grant, or to assign him an imaginary twin, Hiram Grant, who might just as easily have existed. Not only that, this substitution comes to be construed as an essential component of American religion, which, Stein claims, is directly related to the land. Grant, Stein writes, "was or was not an only child but he had to be one of some one." In other words, he had to have a family, even though, like most Americans, he wants to be an only child, valued in his individuality. This is a key aspect of religion here: "Think every minute if that might not be religion American religion that any one could be an only child or of some one or more than so."[61] Yet this is the moment when the twin appears on the scene as a leader in religion, negating the possibility that the only child is ever really an only child, unique and in full possession of his identity. Nor does he own his own name, although the construction of him within the national narrative might present him that way: "And now I know it makes no difference whether his name was Hiram Ulysses or Ulysses Simpson" (33). Hiram is not Ulysses; they look completely different. Yet when one says simply "Grant" it is impossible to distinguish – hence the constant play here on our need to know which Grant is which: "Have you forgotten what he never did. Have you forgotten what he never said. Have you forgotten. Which Grant . . . Think of the two not as Grant but as each one" (34). We may then hesitate when we write the history of the period – was President Grant really U. S. Grant? Can we distinguish a leader of war from a leader of religion? If not, what does that say about individual identity (only children) and the history of America?

The George Washington portrait makes clear the historical dimension of this rewriting of American identities and its relation to American geographical characteristics. From the familiar rumination on names and the possible connection between George Washington and the writer George Wickham, Stein turns back to national narrative by taking quite literally the idea that George Washington was the author of the story of America. But he is not the author of America because he won battles or was a strong president. Rather it is because he understood the implications of geography for national identity, and that, in an almost reverse version of *Lebensraum*, America had to define its own identity because it had so much extra space.

What is the United States of America.
It is not a country surrounded by a wall or not as well by an ocean. In short the United States of America is not surrounded.
He knew.
He knew that.
And what was the result of his knowing that.
The result of his knowing that was that he said this and in saying this he began a novel, the novel the great American novel. (169)

Americans had to delimit their nation because of a lack of natural boundaries and they did so through the stories of those like George Washington.

In some cases they even did so directly through naming, as Stein is quick to point out: "Is there anybody who does not know that the city of Washington is named after him" (204). The circularity of reasoning here – that Washington writes the national story which makes him the founding father but the nation only exists after it is named and it is named for him because he writes the national story – must always already be contained within each use of the proper names in this text. The name thus stands for the problem of America – how to delimit itself when its landscape refuses to do so – in other words, the problem occasioned by the lack of a determined organic national identity.

What is intriguing about the concern with landscape and nationality within the texts of the twenties is the transition from landscape as object of inquiry, with its implied notions of identity and nation, to map as principle of narration, with its concomitant unraveling of unified versions of the American national story. If the American landscape must be named to be delimited, then naming is mapping. Yet as we know from so many Stein texts, naming not only calls up the question of multiplicity ("which Grant") but makes of it a principle of narration. The connection between naming ("Americans," "Italians," etc.) in the early work of *Geography and Plays* and the prose of the text itself, which is a kind of instantiation of national sensibility, also demonstrates ways in which naming a nation here gives meaning to a diffuse set of verbal performances rather than to the static stereotypes we might expect. The line from mapping to narration lies submerged beneath this name-based prose from the 1910s and early 1920s only to emerge as a direct vehicle or mode of narration in the geographical texts of the late 1920s and 1930s.

In *The Geographical History of America* this is presented as an abstract philosophical problem. Yet we recognize Stein's insistence that the problem of knowledge and the problem of being, here "human mind" and "human nature," are immediate questions of relationship in the world. The celebrated quip, "I am I because my little dog knows me" continues "I am I why / So there / I am I where." (99). There is no separating out the problem of human nature (which is what the dog perceives) from its specific situation: "Of course the human mind. / Has that anything to do with I am I because my little dog knows me. / Has that anything to do with how a country looks" (103). Identity in the outward, traditional sense is insignificant.

The human mind, on the other hand, is able to know that the world is not necessarily as it appears, objects may be other than as they present themselves, and identity is thus not verifiable from perception (74–5). It is the human mind that can make sense of the history of geography while human nature responds to the way the land looks (as from an airplane – the most common geographical image in the text). By being able to perceive the places where the oceans were or being able to understand the implications of the big flat open spaces that, for Stein, typify America, the human mind distinguishes itself from human nature. The difference between how the land looks and "the way any land can lay" (79) – in other words how it comes to have meaning – is thus key to the abstract argument of *The Geographical History* and indeed, for Stein, to the very question of human knowledge.

Beyond that, this question of knowledge and the human mind is connected to the American landscape through the vehicle of writing: "Why the writing of today has to do with the way any land can lay when it is there particularly the flat land. That is what makes land connected with the human mind ... and so America is connected to the human mind, I can say so but what I do is write it so" (79). America, that flat, borderless, no-sky country forces the mind to consider more than what seems obvious. It requires a certain effort at distinction, at creating identity and making meaning, all aspects of what Stein is attempting in her own prose. It also requires that we are able to encompass the relationship of the part to the whole, for, as Stein puts it, "the geographical history of that country [is] . . . the way one piece of it is not separated from any other one" (85).

This wholeness does not imply a return to organic nationhood. The fact that America cannot be divided into pieces creates it as the space of wandering rather than linear development for Stein, and in that way the connection to writing is clear. Thus we see Stein presenting the origination of her mode of narration in the connection between the idea of "wandering attention" and the realities of landscape: "What has wandering got to do with the human mind or religion. But really wandering has something to do with the human mind" (93). America is important to Stein, here then, not because of its politics or its specific history, despite her interest in its founding figures, but because it forces the issue of the relation of human mind to human nature and the relation of landscape to wandering, out of which comes modernist writing and modern community.

The very next passage in *The Geographical History* brings politics back into question by raising the issue of the First World War. "Any time after a war any one is nervous" (93) and nervousness promotes wandering. It is for this reason that wandering in this text becomes linked to a specific political situation and historical period. War is also here figured as the result of human nature, that is, of "individualism and communism" (56) which are for Stein the same thing – emotional ways of being that have no relation to the human mind. Landscape also comes back into play again as we learn, somewhat cryptically, that "Europe is too small to wage war because war has to be waged on too large a scale to be contained in a small country" (69). The American landscape is presumably big enough for war, big enough for nervousness, and big enough for wandering, which as we have seen *does* have a relation to the human mind. Stein's relentlessly circular logic then brings us back to the possibility that politics and writing may indeed exist in relationship, but only through the mediation of both literal and textual wandering.

How does this nexus of politics, geography, and narration connect back to Stein's insistence on *naming* as both mapping and narration? The answer seems to lie in the constant intrusion of the question of multiple subjectivity into Stein's prose. From *Three Lives* and *The Making of Americans* on through *The Geographical History of America*, the narrator continually intrudes, insisting that we reckon with her. Her intrusions sometimes appear as snippets of overheard conversation or concerns about the weather, in addition to the more usual ruminations on the text itself. Critics often mark these as areas of cubist *bricolage* or moments of free play between personal and public discourse. Indeed Stein rarely seems to demarcate her discursive zones: just as snippets of a play appear in the "philosophical" *Geographical History* so snippets of conversation appear in the poems of *Stanzas in Meditation*. It is often tempting to mark a difficult passage with some real-life association that Stein allowed to seep into her literary voice. Certainly her sexual puns demand that we not separate absolutely the pleasure of the text from the pleasures of the author.

However, the question of Stein's real life also raises thorny political questions that refuse to be answered simply. There has been much speculation about Stein's politics, which she rarely expressed directly. Her friendship with Bernard Faÿ, her written appreciation of Pétain,[62] and her ability to remain in France unscathed during the Second World War have led to speculation that she was friendly to fascism. Yet she was published in the resistance magazine *Confluences* along with Jacob, Aragon, Sartre, Gide, and Malraux;[63] several sources point to her disdain for Hitler and her sympathy for the opposition;[64] and after the war she was awarded a citation for her service to the French Resistance.[65] Still, beyond liberation of her beloved France, Stein seems to have had little use for the politics of the left; throughout her life she generally embraced bourgeois political values, even if she rejected the patriarchal restrictions of marriage and heterosexuality. As John Whittier-Ferguson has claimed, Stein's conservative politics may tell us more about the way in which she accepted "a widespread set of attitudes . . . ideas that fit comfortably with the conservative politics she had long been embracing" than about any more idiosyncratic modernist critique.[66]

But to leave it at that is also too easy, for the moments of seepage between "real world" situation and textual performance almost invariably raise the question of identity in what we may call politically provocative ways. In particular, within a feminist framework we may see Stein's insistence on bringing her domestic life with Toklas into her literary texts as an attempt to privilege the domestic scene as a place of potential meaning-making and (literary) power. Further, she enlarges this scene by bringing it back into the more public space of a text meant for publication. Thus in an abstract sense she here accomplishes the kind of fracturing of the borders between public and private called for by feminist theorists such as Benhabib and Fraser. Yet if Benhabib searches for a new public universalism that might arise from this sort of dialogic perspective, Stein's writing continues to insist on the specificity of both its language and its situation. It thus takes up the key feminist question of the inter-relationship between public and private spheres, and forges subtle new means of addressing them.

Further, we can understand the private scene of Stein's garden, or her *atelier*, or her living room, as also providing a specific new space for the construction of community, which in the texts of the thirties and forties emerges within an intimate, female polyvocality. Indeed issues of inter-subjectivity and of twinning arise again and again when female relations enter the prose (as we've seen with Mabel and Mary), and when questions of social or political representation demand to be addressed. But this intimate scene of community also brings us back to the question of physical space, geography, and its politics. In particular, the very idea of *Lebensraum* as it develops in Germany in the twenties and early thirties, prior to its appropriation by Hitler, comes to describe this sort of welcoming, empowering domestic space. Claudia Koonz describes this more abstract version of *Lebensraum* as a social sphere in which women could define their function as "beyond the materialist and abrasive 'masculine' world of business, class struggle, and high politics."[67] It was for these German women a positive version of the separate female sphere that Hitler's regime would later transform and emphasize. As Koontz puts it, "*Lebensraum* provides a useful metaphor for analyzing the variety of competing views on how women ought to enter the modern world."[68] For Stein the *Lebensraum* of the living room she shares with Toklas serves as the sphere in which a new version of female community can come into being.

It seems valuable then to counterpoise briefly the very personal and seemingly non-referential poems in *Stanzas in Meditation* with what we might call the national prose of *Four in America* and *The Geographical History* – all thirties texts. In *Stanzas in Meditation* Stein quite explicitly includes herself and Alice B. Toklas in the poetic mix, playing with the transformation of "I" and "she" into "they." Part of Stanza xxxv, PART v, reads, for example, "What is a landscape / A landscape is what when they that is I / see and look."[69] As one critic puts it, what emerges in the *Stanzas* is the "they" as a kind of joined mind of Toklas and Stein.[70] Both Ulla Dydo and Douglas Messerli have also astutely described this volume as an alternative memoir meant to be opposed to the written-to-be-popular *Autobiography of Alice B. Toklas*.[71] If the *Autobiography* is read as

Steinian ventriloquism then the *Stanzas* are distinguished by their dual-voiced quality, which might best be described, *à la* Irigaray, as "two-lipped." Opened practically anywhere at random one finds lines that switch between singular and plural pronouns, especially where followed by verbs of thought or emotion ("Could I think will they think that they will" [PART II, Stanza xvi, 59]), and sections that play constantly with issues of numbers ("Not two will give / Not one will give one two / Which they can add to change" [PART II, Stanza xvii, 61]).

This plural discourse begins a connection between these meditative writings and the social discourse of the national narratives, a connection that is mediated by Stein's emphasis on wandering and landscape. Stein elevates intimacy and the plurality of subjectivity as an important literary and social category, which becomes a basic structure in her mature writing, even apart from implying any reference beyond her text. But plural subjects always wander within a geographical domain, creating in their wakes paths of affiliation and networks of community.

The first stanza cited above demonstrates this principle as contained within Stein's use of geography. The stanza is a rumination on likeness as it concerns intersubjectivity as well as objects in the world. The search for relations of likeness is occasioned by the paired events of "wondering" and "wandering" which ultimately lead to comparisons of geography:

> As very much alike
> As when I found it very much
> I did then not wonder but wander
> And now it is not a surprise as eyes
> Nor indeed not if I wonder
> Could it be exactly alike.
>
> (PART V, Stanza xxxv, 178)

The eyes see likeness easily as they become accustomed to new landscape, negating the assumption that terrains which are colored differently on the map differ inherently. The stanza circles around and around the issue of color (landscape) and otherness, asking us to see that if places are not exactly alike they are "as very much alike":

> As I am wandering around without does it matter
> Or whether they oblige that they see other
> They can if they manage or at best
> Either a color
>
> (PART V, Stanza xxxv, 179)

The "they that is I" wander, see the object, the landscape, and question its likeness to what they know, and in the process create themselves as paired viewers. The question of likeness in landscapes occasions a question of likeness in the subjectivity who is wandering in that landscape, which becomes the wider topic of the meditations at large.

Importantly, by the end of this stanza, we return to the international scene and the question of the nationality of landscape. The stanza turns to the question of Stein's fame in America in the moment before the huge success of the *Autobiography*. She ruminates on a "there" where map color is a different question, and where water raises the issue of whether the places are strictly apart or part of the same. It is for "them" – those who have denied her fame – that Stein "will try to tell very well / How I felt then and how I feel now" (PART V, Stanza xxxv, 180). This is a continuation of the process of asserting likeness taken now into the national arena, a process which Stein marks here with the verb "to gather," which is also the opening verb of the stanza. To gather together likenesses, to extend the wandering/wondering about landscape to that different place across the water, is also to continue to gather together subjectivities (I/they as Stein and Toklas; I/they as Stein and the Americans) into a plural perspective that is not obliged to "see other."

Thus in a way we see here Stein's meditation on the naming of self and other, self and self, self and object, which broaches the question of community in its most intimate and abstract sense. Much has been made of the relationship between Stein's writing and French feminist thought. As Lisa Ruddick has put it, "'French feminisms' . . . helped to ground much of the work on Stein in the eighties."[72] That work according to Ruddick was often utopian and focused on linguistic play in isolation from historical concerns.[73] Yet what Stein's writings of the thirties and forties make clear is how very historical indeed are the concerns with polyvocality and female subjectivity in her work. For if in the *Stanzas* the self becomes an intimate community of perspectives (the "I" that is "they"; the gaze that wanders from self to other), it is a community that exists not only within a broader geographical or national community (which for Stein are not the same thing), but also in counter-distinction to it.

In other words, I want to read the concern with intersubjectivity in the texts from the latter part of Stein's career not only as simple ventriloquism, experimental language play, or even the inscription of a complexly plural female subject position into writing, but as the creation of an ethical model of social community. What if the portraits in *Four in America* were an attempt to take the lessons learned in *The Making of Americans* and use them to recast the "subject" of the national narrative?

What if the *Stanzas in Meditation* push that project *both* into the intimate/ feminine domain *and* into the ethical sphere of the community? The nuanced attention to the problem of intersubjectivity in these texts may thus be read not as simple theft, or even the loving incorporation of Toklas into a plural Steinese, but as the coming to terms in writing with the Levinasian ethical problem of being-towards-the-other. In this sense they raise the question of both ethics and community textually. We see Stein here taking on a responsibility to account for Toklas that insists upon her constantly revising any possible presentation of her own self. In her refusal to specify the personages in these verses, Stein also extends this I/other relationship into a potentially universal realm. As Levinas puts it in *Otherwise than Being*, she creates "the substitution in responsibility, signification or the one-for-another ... the intention *toward another* ... [which] turns out to belie intentionality."[74] For Levinas being towards or for another is other than being – not simply a condition of a morally inclined self. In this context Rimbaud's phrase "Je est an autre" – "I is an other" – is crucial for Levinas.[75] But Stein's *Stanzas* operate in much the same way – where the I is another – constantly rewritten. For Stein in these writings, being for another always predates and revises any possibility of writing "I."

The meditations thus become an instantiation of the predicament of writing otherwise, which always raises the specter that in language this otherwise-ness cannot be said. When Levinas raises the question of the distinction between the saying and the said, that is between the approach to another in language and "the giving out of signs,"[76] he privileges the saying, making clear that in saying one is denuded of intention and more than laid bare. Thus, in the performative utterance, the "I" is always in question: "The subject is not *in itself*, at home with itself ... it becomes a sign, turns into an allegiance."[77] When Stein writes the "they that is I" or the "either/or with/and" of Stein and Toklas, she is creating this sign of allegiance that is not a theme, a thing communicated, but is the process and effect of what Levinas calls the saying or what we might call the performative.

However, the scene of this "saying" in the *Stanzas* is also specific and intimate, an expression of the intense, personal, and sexual interconnection of Stein and Toklas. In this sense it raises the possibility of an alternative, feminist version of the ethical perspective, one which derives from intimacy rather than from radical alterity, from eros and the caress rather than from the abrupt impersonal encounter with a foreign face. This is the kind of ethics that has been posited by Irigaray within the domain of sexual difference, and by Tina Chanter more generally, as an ethics of intimacy, one which critiques and revises Levinas. One of the main thrusts of Levinas's work, of course, is to rewrite the possibility of ethics as an opening up to alterity. Much of Levinas's writing insists upon the other as "infinitely foreign"[78] – the responsibility one feels in the face of the other must arise from beyond the call of the known. Yet, if we turn back to Levinas's earlier writing on eros and the caress we can see the intimacy at the heart of Levinas's theory and the possibility of accounting for the Stein/Toklas encounter as ethical.

In the sections of *Totality and Infinity* entitled "The Phenomenology of Eros" and "Fecundity" Levinas places filial relations at the heart of the ethical perspective. Paternity and its converse, filiality, are, for Levinas, the model for all love which liberates the "I" from itself by constituting it as also another – the child. As he puts it, "The I breaks free from itself in paternity without thereby ceasing to be an I, for the I *is* its son."[79] In this dialectical relationship of father–son Levinas finds, in a sense, the aim of eros, the creation of an "I" in the person of the son, who is both unique and not unique, individual and, because he owes his individuality to the father, not separate. Hence, the son, who, as the above passage attests, is for Levinas, *the* "I," exists as separate from others yet always in orientation towards them: "The I as I hence remains turned ethically to the face of the other."[80] The son emerges as the very origin and possibility of ethics.

For Levinas this model is crucial because the erotic relationship between an I and other (here always figured as both foreign and female) works against ethics and thus demands the complement of the child. The phenomenology of eros takes place in a space, figured as feminine, that is beyond the social, since for Levinas the "feminine is an other refractory to society, member of a dual society, an intimate society, a society without language."[81] Further, "the relationship established between lovers in voluptuosity, fundamentally refractory to universalization, is the very contrary of the social relation."[82] The erotic caress is beyond the face and thus beyond the stark recognition of alterity that the face-to-face encounter accomplishes in his work. For Levinas voluptuosity is "love for the love the Beloved bears me, [and] to love is also to love oneself in love, and thus to return to oneself."[83] Because the Other/Beloved is in the erotic embrace merely a mirror for the self, the only possible transcendence of this egotism emerges for Levinas in the child: "the I is in the child, an other."[84] Though the model is revised and extended in *Otherwise Than Being*, this reliance on the non-social position of the feminine, the anti-ethical nature of the erotic and its transcendence in the ethics of the paternal/filial continuum remains.

In *An Ethics of Sexual Difference* Irigaray revises Levinas by emphasizing the importance of the realm of sexual difference for ethics. She reinstates the possibility that the voluptuous embrace is not an erasure of alterity or a mirroring of one's love for oneself but rather an acute encounter with alterity. There is therefore a possibility of ethics within eros: "Who or what the other is, I never know. But this unknowable other is that which differs sexually from me. [There is] this feeling of wonder, surprise and astonishment in the face of the unknowable."[85] As Spivak makes clear Irigaray is here providing the "ingredients for an ethical base to rewrite gendering in the social sphere."[86] For Irigaray, the embrace or caress becomes the "(im)possible threshold of the ethical" which creates the "possibility of two spaces, un-universalizable with each other," yet always implicated and intertwined, each with each.[87]

As Tina Chanter makes clear, this rewriting of alterity within the domain of eros also cancels Levinas's insistence on procreation as its ethical outcome. If the realm of eros is not one of mirroring or sameness, it need not be transcended in order to become ethical. Reproduction is not essential for Irigaray as it was for Levinas; the erotic embrace is productive in its own manner.[88] Further, for Irigaray the embrace does not presume the active/passive, heterosexual split that lies behind Levinas's writings on eros. It can stand in for the original procreative embrace, as well as for the intimate intersubjectivity of what Spivak describes as "being-in-the-mother." Importantly, because it need not be focused on reproduction as its outcome, it can also include the homosexual embrace: "By insisting on the otherness of eros as such, . . . Irigaray both resists reducing the feminine to the maternal, and opens Levinas's model of eros to the possibility of homosexuality."[89] By reinstating the difference posed by the very position of the loved one within the embrace, Irigaray makes possible a multiplicity of ways of understanding that difference as ethical.

This is precisely the ethics of the Stein/Toklas embrace in the *Stanzas*, where the subject becomes ethical in its embrace of the other/beloved who nonetheless remains other. Rather than subordinate the beloved to the mysterious passivity she takes on for Levinas, Stein uses grammatical play to revise the ethically inclined self into the female "lover-beloved."

> They will never differing from will refuse
> And remain meant to please
> ....

> All meant in adding mine to mine.
> ....
> And to add bless and caress
> Not only ought but bought and taught
> In kindness.
> Therefore I see the way
>
> (PART V, Stanza xxxiv, 177)

The intimacy and difference of Stein's relationship with Toklas, as written into the shifting plural voices of the *Stanzas*, challenges Levinas's being-towards-the-other. It arises from within a specific intimate realm of difference, where encounter with the other need not necessarily aspire to the universal experience of the neutral face. And it pushes the ethical relation to become both an expression of the caress of the beloved, who may be at times the same and the other, and an initial movement towards living and writing otherwise.

Stein's *Stanzas* then leave us on the threshold of community, a community that begins not from an external social stance but from an intimate realm of encounter with the possibility/limit of embrace. For Irigaray the caress both describes and transgresses bodily boundaries; its gesture is not one of surprised recognition but of recuperation of a universal human experience that is intersubjective and social. But any universalized position is always being constituted and undermined within Irigaray's scenario by the reassertion of difference within the lover/beloved relationship. The community that begins in the connection between them must then rest on the constant question of one or two that is present throughout Irigaray's writings and that we have also seen throughout *Four in America* and the *Stanzas in Meditation*. The community must be predicated on engagement with this border – whether we define it with Irigaray as a body limit, or with Stein as what seems to be a language limit, the border between the voice of the "I" and the "you." The ethical question of Stein's ventriloquism appears with the familiar accusation of her "theft" of Toklas's voice in *The Autobiography of Alice B. Toklas* but ends by becoming a question of a new communal (I/you) voice. In this confusing of voices in *The Autobiography* and the *Stanzas* Stein writes the intimacy and difference of her relationship with Toklas into an ethics of intimate community.

Thus when we see Stein's ventriloquism also appear in *Four Saints in Three Acts*, for example, as it does in so many, many texts from the mid-twenties on, we can see it not merely as a parlor trick or a meditation on the possibilities of language but as an instantiation of a social relationship which carries implications not only for language use but also for forms of social/ethical connection. Stein uses grammatical play to write the lover–beloved, or the ethically inclined self, as a shifting plurality of subjects.

In *Four Saints*, however, a further connection becomes clear. While the distinctions between saints' voices and Stein's voices are being elaborated, questioned, and eroded, so are their geographical distinctions. Stein's comment in *Lectures in America* that in "Four Saints [she] made the Saints the landscape"[90] has often been taken to mean that the saints and their voices exist on the stage as elements of a landscape do. The specific landscapes of Avila and Barcelona, the primary locations of the main characters Saint Therese and Saint Ignatius, are, however, also being evoked here in order to establish them as the causes of, and markers for, the different identities of the saints, as well as, by the end, to raise the question of position: "There is a difference between Barcelona and Avila. What difference."[91] Any number of differences between the two cities might be claimed – language, cultural prominence, terrain, and, as the play remarks, longitude (591). Yet the position of Saint Therese as specified by landscape seems to be the play's primary concern. In other words, we read "Saint Therese half in and half out of doors" (587) along with a description of the climate of Avila which "can be rain and warm snow and . . . if to stay to cry" (586). So the question is raised, if Therese stays in isolated Avila does she suffer? Therese is always separated, whether because she is seated while the other saints are standing, because she claims that "nobody visits" (587), or because she is set "in place" somewhere apart: "Away away away away a day it took three days and that day. Saint Therese was very well parted and apart and apart apart from that . . . Saint Therese in place" (596). On the other hand, Ignatius exists in movement and connection: "Saint Ignatius and more. / Saint Ignatius with as well" (594).

However, within the course of the play the intercutting from saint to saint, with short echoing lines moving from one to the next, elide these basic distinctions. If the geographical landscape of the play differentiates the saints, the play *as* landscape connects them. "Can two saints be one?" the play asks in the first version of "scene two" (589), which seems to be almost the same question as the later "might it be mountains if it were not Barcelona" (603). Indeed, the last version of "scene one" begins "Might they be with they be with them might they be with them. Never to return to distinctions" (605), and the final pages insist in familiar Stein fashion on the play of identities and numbers ("Saint

Ignatius. Two and Two" [607] or "who makes who makes it do. / Saint Therese and Saint Therese too" [612]). The meaning of this play then, if it may be said to have one, hinges on the transition from position to position, and from saint to saint, as we move from understanding them as distinct to understanding them as juxtaposed as they would be in a painted landscape.

It is difficult to assign an ethical or even a social value to the work here. This is less the case, however, with the trio of interlaced texts that make up Stein's writings from 1938: *Ida: A Novel*; *Dr. Faustus Lights the Lights*; and the children's book, *The World is Round*. In that year of profound upheaval, which saw her displacement from 27, rue de Fleurus, and her growing awareness of the Nazi menace, her texts become concerned with placing the shifting subjectivities of her earlier work within a plane of both local and national importance. Stein's work of the thirties becomes not only more representational, but more overtly social. *Doctor Faustus* is surprising in its obvious inscription of Hitlerism – as well as in its use of the Faust theme – but perhaps most so because of the way that it places the plural subject in the center of that setting. The character "Marguerite Ida and Helena Annabel" enters amidst a controversy about her name and her identity. If Dr. Faustus insists that he knows that she is not, or at least, that she is not who she says she is (Marguerite Ida and Helena Annabel), he does nonetheless save her life. Marguerite Ida and Helena Annabel seems secure in the knowledge of her name ("I am I and my name is Marguerite Ida and Helena Annabel") but it is the question of place that bothers her ("I am here and am I here or am I there"), especially at the moment of her fateful viper-bite.[92] Further, it is the intermingling of these concerns that arises in the eventual confrontation with the ominous "man from over the seas," who is called "Mr. Viper," stands in for Mephistopheles, and also, of course, in a broader sense, represents Hitler. At the crucial moment of recognition, Marguerite Ida and Helena Annabel exclaims: "No one is one when there are two, look behind you look behind you you are not one you are two" (318), and we see that the man who comes forward across the seas will be Mephistopheles. The specter of geographical movement here is the negative potential of being able to create a series of varying identities en route, identities which here become not only plural but duplicitous.

So then, we might wonder, does the text ask us to consider plural identity as the pact with the devil? In 1938 does wandering become the figure of the moral menace? Marguerite Ida and Helena Annabel falls finally into the arms of the man from across the seas, and the play ends with the little boy and girl singing "he is he and she is she and we are we" (329). The only movement that seems left is for the entire cast to descend to hell. The play ends ominously and none of the characters are exonerated.

Yet within the context of the other texts of that year, whose protagonists are clearly several versions of the same character, the potentially positive readings of this version of subjectivity emerge. In *Ida: A Novel* the grammatical twinning of *Four in America* and the juxtapositions of *Four Saints* merge into a subject who is protean, plural, and on the move from place to place, the ethical self as purposefully adrift from the encumbrances of location. Yet she is also, by the end, a hero, whom Stein meant to be a great fictional figure like Dorothea Brooks or Isabel Archer. The first several sentences seem to introduce a very specific character who belongs to a clearly defined traditional family community – much as in the opening pages of *The Making of Americans*. We never learn Ida's last name, but Stein introduces her by describing how her mother gave birth to her, and telling her family history. She also immediately establishes the theme of multiplicity by telling us that Ida was born a twin: "When the time came Ida came. And as Ida came, with her came her twin, so there she was Ida-Ida."[93] Not only is Ida a twin but that fact itself refers back to twins to whom, we learn, her great-aunt gave birth as the result of being raped by a soldier: "Then the great-aunt had had little twins born to her and then she had quietly, the twins were dead then, born so, she had buried them under a pear tree and nobody knew" (7). The potential for disaster raised by this reference becomes fulfilled by the second page, where Ida's parents go off, never to return (8). She lives with the great-aunt, thus becoming another version of those long-lost twins, and indeed inaugurating a long life of what the novel calls changing places (8), both in terms of identity and in terms of geographical space.

If Irigaray writes of the ethical dimension in the "call to birth for self and other,"[94] which is also a memory of the initial becoming, then this text in both its recursiveness and its doubling of identities – its changing places – enacts that ethics. Ida is both object of this circular identity and creator of her own duality. As in *Doctor Faustus* Stein uses the singular when she refers to Ida-Ida, even though she seems to be speaking of two babies. But once we have become convinced that Ida is a twin, and that we must think of her name as a marker of two distinct but related parts, her twin disappears from the text. Later Ida tells her dog Love about her decision to become a twin: "Yes Love she said to him, you have always had me and now you are going to have two, I am going to have a twin yes I am Love, I am tired of being just one" (10). Ida recreates her twin by fiat, letting her have her own name (Winnie) and her own identity. She writes letters to Winnie. Men fall in love with Winnie, follow her home, and are disappointed to find only Ida. Therefore, Ida and Winnie must be different. Yet they are also the same: those men never find two twins standing on the doorstep to greet them. The categories of Stein's subject can never be resolved into any configuration of the self and the other, either as two separate people or even as contained within the female subject itself.

In fact, after all the discussion of Ida-Ida and twinning in the first sections, the entire concept drops out of this novel. The word "twin," and references to Ida-Ida or Winnie only appear in the first 50 pages of this 150-page book. This novel does not stop with the notion of a dual subject but rather pushes past configurations of two, mentioning multiples of four and five strangers, providing Ida with a seemingly endless series of husbands, and even describing dogs in large numbers. When we arrive at the later sections of the novel, which mainly deal with Ida's many marriages, the same strange play of identities occurs. We read, "Everybody knew that Andrew was one of two. He was so completely one of two that he was two" (87). A few pages later Andrew again appears, with a very cryptic transformation: "Andrew's name changed to Ida and eight changes to four and sixteen changed to twenty-five and they all sat down ... [then] he ... came to be Andrew again and it was Ida" (94–5). Finally Ida marries someone we are told is "Andrew the first" but in the next chapter he is "almost Andrew the first" (111, 115). There is no way to navigate a straight line through this tangled mess of Andrews. Even before we take up the question of all Ida's other husbands, we feel as though Andrew must be a particular man *and* an inscription of the entire community of men whom Ida encounters, turning up everywhere but always slightly different, and therefore always in a varying relation to Ida herself.

Twinning here thus only begins this novel's exploration of the sheer multiplicity of identities and relationships which resolve into narrative coherence only when we stop trying to separate and solidify them. The notion of the self almost ceases to exist outside of the community of relations that construct it, and that community is constantly being revised by Ida's nomadic life. Ida constantly encounters groups of people, from the two mysterious visitors who come to see her great-aunt and then disappear into the house (into her great-aunt? into Ida? [9]), to the family of five "little aunts" who were nobody's aunts but become "the first and last friends she ever had" (13) and the crowds who jostle about her and make her feel "warm being so close to them" (13). Ida gets shuttled from relative to relative, and thinks of herself like a refugee (14). Indeed, in many ways Ida is the late-thirties version of the immigrants in *The Making of Americans*, a displaced person who comes to construct herself and Americanness as one and the same.

In fact, Stein packs so many events and people into her exposition of Ida's life that she clearly wants us to define Ida as a nomadic American Everywoman. Just as she had in *The Making of Americans* Stein employs gerunds to create Ida through the common actions that she repeats over and over, actions which most often refer to traveling:

Was she on a train or an automobile, an airplane or just walking.
Which was it.
Well she was on any of them and everywhere she was just talking. She was saying, yes yes I like to be sitting. Yes I like to be moving. (34)

Each new cycle of travel occasions a new set of relationships, often a new husband, and a new question, whether it be about herself or about the nature of the place in which she finds herself. She turns up in Connecticut and becomes connected with an army officer who defines himself by his unwillingness ever to leave the state – after which of course Ida leaves abruptly (33).

Importantly, Ida wanders in and out of Washington, drawn back there to rest as though she knows that she and the capital city stand together as markers for Americanness. Washington is the only place where she settles, the only place where we might draw her into a traditional community, the place where in the most conventional sense, as well as in metaphorical terms, Ida belongs. Yet her wanderings abroad are important in this novel for they make clear that it is not the place that creates her identity but her nomadic life that makes it possible for her to connect to the place. It is the intersection of wandering and belonging that mark her and demonstrate the extent to which the two have become intertwined in Stein's thought.

Braidotti writes of a "game of dissonant voices moving in between positions in a nomadic quest for alternative representations of female feminist subjectivity."[95] The voices in *Ida*, and the other texts from 1938, play just such a game. Though Braidotti often uses the term "nomadism" in an abstract Deleuzian sense, in *Ida*, as in *The Geographical History of America*, nomadism is specifically engendered by America, but evocative of a cosmopolitan perspective. For one, though Ida seems to stand for America, she also exhibits little parochial loyalty. While she settles for a time in Washington, she is not specifically tied to the *city*, but rather to the possibility that in Washington "some one can do anything" (67), which is here also a definition of politics. In other words, the very American tendency towards doing and going anywhere is part of the character of the capital that attracts Ida. In addition, the function of wandering, or "walking" as she puts it, is a value in and of itself but where she walks makes very little difference. The process is American, the terrain need not be: "Ida did not go directly anywhere. She went all around the world. It did not take her long and everything she saw interested her" (51). So, in *The World is Round* which takes place in the French countryside, the point is *not*, as has often been claimed, that Stein is memorializing the French countryside where she spends her summers, but rather that the roundness of the world, like the lines on the map of America, make wandering a mission. Rose, the hero of *The World is Round*, wanders up a French mountain in order to sit down on the chair she has carried up it and contemplate the different perspective. Travel in these two intertwined narratives evokes the dissonance of the iterative (and plural) "I" who is the same but always seeing from a new perspective.

The narrative process here is also, of course, distinctly non-linear. If Stein wrote of her earlier work as a "marked direction in the direction of being in the present,"[96] *Ida* extends the implications of that present-tense perspective within narrative structure, while introducing it as also a principle of character definition. For Ida and Andrew "there was never any beginning or end, but everyday came before or after another day. Every day did" (133). The novel is about the refusal of the possibility of beginning-middle-end for the subject, "Ida," who speaks her name, her "I," her being, in multiple ways, and in multiple locations, without direction: "Ida never said once upon a time. These words did not mean anything to Ida. This is what Ida said. Ida said yes" (132). She also repeatedly says "I do" and "I am" and "I see" and sometimes just "I, I, I" (127). "Ida" here is necessarily an accumulation of enunciations of identity linked to a variety of places. Although the process of accumulation in a narrative must necessarily proceed one-after-the-other, *Ida* wants to present them all at once, as though she exists spread out before us, like a map of all the places that she visits.

This is the map-based model of experience that predominates in *Ida: A Novel* – a model that can clearly be seen developing throughout Stein's career. It also has obvious affinities with the idea of the play as landscape that Stein herself puts forth. But what of the social implications of this model? Stein's version of a community of the subject – an "I" that is "they" – an intimate caress of the other – must spread itself out across the map, first here, then there, then there and here taken together. If belonging depends upon this movement, so too must the ethics of the being-towards-the-other. Further, while in *Ida* the map is primarily a United States map, this collation of the principles of geography, movement, identity, and belonging, as we have seen, does not restrict itself to the American scene. Indeed, as Rose sits at the top of the mountain, she seems perfectly posed, having traveled (though not far), located herself in the landscape and in relation to her community, yet having remained, like Ida, always ready to move on.

This position represents, I would argue, the narrative inscription of a profoundly subtle form of cosmopolitanism, one which moves beyond the homogenization implied by the idea of an "international style" and beyond Nussbaum's conservative notion of the concentric cosmopolitan perspective. Stein studiously avoids the generalizing perspective attributed to international cosmopolitanism in the twenties because of the primacy she accords geography and the importance of place. Community in her narratives, however, as we have seen, does not arise out of a specific location, or out of any single set of allegiances produced in that location, whether a series of concentric circles or a broadly conceived world citizenship. Rather, it emerges, as it does among many contemporary theorists, out of the combined possibilities of being-towards-the-other and the iterative, expansive self.[97] In this way it is clear that Ida's ethics, if she may be said to have any, are the shifting combinations of Ida-Ida, Ida-Winnie, Ida-Andrew, etc., that begin in America yet can and do move everywhere. Thus if we can speak of the community of subjectivities that make up Ida, the community must be seen to shift and move, to cross borders and ignore loyalties in a way that challenges the dichotomy between community and cosmopolitanism, and that raises the notion of a nomadic cosmopolitanism akin to that of post-colonial theorists like Bhabha.

Or almost. It is a risk of this kind of reading to erase the specific historical and political dimensions of the terminology it uses. Certainly Stein was herself a cosmopolitan – one who, as we recall, thought of herself in her early days as having a nomadic existence. Still, Caren Kaplan is right to point out the tendency of post-modern theory to play fast and loose with the often historically quite specific terms of "exile," "migrant," and "nomad."[98] Stein was certainly *not* nomadic in the sense of being in perpetual movement herself, even if many of her characters are. Nor is her political perspective one that shows much effort to draw common cause with the refugees of the two world wars. Rather she continues to think of *herself* as an exile, yearning for a bit of Americana, or the sound of American speech, even as she refuses to return during the Second World War.[99]

But if we cannot term Stein's exile the same as nomadism, nor her sojourn in France the same as the global wandering made possible by late twentieth-century history or the advent of post-colonial life, we may still describe it as the starting point for some of these later cultural maneuvers. Most contemporary theory wants to describe itself as dramatically new, a tendency it perhaps inherited from the modernists themselves. Yet nomadism as a potentially productive social position does not emerge *sui generis* in the 1960s. Nor does it develop only in those countries that emerge from colonial domination in the second half of the century.[100] Rather, we may say, it finds itself initiated in the earlier versions of exile imagined as transformative and ethically productive. And it finds itself begun in the narrative of iterative subjects, who wander their ways through many modernist texts, like Stein's.[101] Thus, without claiming that Stein's perspective is somehow post-colonial or that there has been no historical change in the period since her death, we can say that Stein's protean narratives begin the project of imagining a nomadic cosmopolitan community.

Stein's attempt to describe America as a specific identity, one grounded in its immigrant history, its geography, and its narration of itself, yet because so grounded still subject to dispersal by the differences of history, geography, and narration, may thus be connected to the cosmopolitan perspectives advanced by Homi Bhabha, Arjun Appadurai, Timothy Brennan, and Bruce Robbins, among others. Her experimentation with a wandering "I," which establishes itself by establishing its relations, also brings Irigaray's ethics of sexual difference to bear on Braidotti's female nomadism. Thus Stein's experimental narratives force us to rethink these theories as post-modernist or post-colonial reactions to a simpler international modernist aesthetic or an easier version of exile – and indeed to challenge their strict divergence from the modern. Her narratives force us to read the full implication of the phrase "America is my country but Paris is my home town" as describing the overlapping webs of experience that surround any Steinian subjectivity, and they force us to see that geography in Stein's work both brings communities into play and makes wandering a mission.

CHAPTER 6

Conclusion

The end of the common world has come when it is seen only under one aspect and is permitted to present itself in only one perspective.
Hannah Arendt, *The Human Condition*, 58[1]

Wandering in Stein's narratives leaves us on the edge of modernist fiction, verging on the ever-elusive migrant meanings that have been attributed instead to post-modernism. The distinction between modern and post-modern writing is everywhere under attack, as critics recognize that what we call "post-modern" literary devices reveal themselves throughout the modernist canon.[2] In the same way, the rigid distinctions between colonial and post-colonial writings may be seen to depend upon perspective, themselves subject to being reinscribed within the discourses of class or gender.[3]

Still it seems important to stop here, to recognize that after the Second World War the social terrain has once again shifted and that, to borrow again from Benjamin, the stories of the past may appear as though from far away, once more in need of translation. While much of what is often called post-modernist also appears in earlier periods, this does not mean that historical changes ought to have no bearing on our reading. Thus while I may claim that Stein's narratives verge on nomadic subjectivity, and are therefore connected to contemporary post-colonial theory, it is also clear that she is irrevocably tied to the early to mid twentieth-century political discourses that surround her. She is not party to the global scene of migrancy and movement available in the year 2000, nor can her exile be equated with the constant displacement occasioned by such movement. In this sense this book attempts to present a historical understanding of the politics of modern-

199

ist fiction, even as it admits to the leaky boundaries between periods and terms of historical change. Further, I want to argue, the politics of connection invoked by these texts is always specifically concerned with its own historical location and engaged with the particular politics of its time. While each of the authors examined here represents vastly divergent ways of understanding both the political and the literary, they represent a common impulse within modernist fiction to engage with the centralization of authority, whether domestic, social, cultural or political, that accompanies the crisis of community in Europe and the United States in the first half of the twentieth century.[4]

If there is any implied movement in this study, then, it is in the growing complexity of the ways that novelists circumvent the drive towards centralized power and unitary community identity that also accompanies the rise of nationalism and totalitarianism in this period. Their work, I would argue, stands as a prominent sign that, despite the way that many histories construe this period and the evidence of the two world wars, many alternative models of community continue to surface in the first half of the century. In other words, not all roads lead to state-based nationalism, and experimental, modernist narrative is often the place where the alternatives may be imagined.

The resistance thus implied in each of these texts may be seen to reside in their different ways of insisting that the dualism between the cosmopolitan and the community fall away. For, in this period, to resist the consolidation of community identity in the form of the patriarchal nation-state, I would argue, is of necessity to posit a certain cosmopolitanism, one not always identical to the simple, elite, world-citizenship so often attached to the modernist use of the term. It is in that dual positioning of community and cosmopolitanism that new realms of non-national affiliation may begin to emerge, those that resist the consolidation of force, take strength on the margins, and insist that a fluctuating being-in-common be the source of any political common being.

But there are many paths to community that emerge here. It has been my purpose to insist on that variety and not to reduce it to a single historical or genealogical trajectory. Thus, this book has argued that questions of community may arise in different ways in the strictures on women's speech in the American popular press, in the political statements of radical French Zionism, in the polemical assertions of British proto-fascist tracts, and the mappings of American cultural geography, and that those same questions of community also often drive the work of

Henry James, Marcel Proust, Virginia Woolf, and Gertrude Stein. Yet the versions of community, as created in the narratives in question here, exist always as discursive performances, acting both in tension and in relation to those around them. They may participate in the polemical discussions I've described, but they very rarely restrict themselves to the specific terms of the political debate.

Thus we arrive back at the question of politics *per se*. To what extent can we see the concern with community in these narratives as political? How can we connect them to current political debate about community or to the legal theory of those like Seyla Benhabib or Drucilla Cornell? It may be argued that these narratives have little to say about global economies, multi-cultural societies, or international human rights, all concerns central to re-working community and democracy in Europe and the United States at the start of the new millennium. Yet, the terms of politics, and more specifically of the politics of community, must not be restricted to these concerns only, as so many are wont to do. For politics clearly inheres in the organization of power that determines the possible ways we may connect with others, whether, for example, in terms of gender relations, ethnic or religious identities, or nationalities. And these political communities are not restricted to those with a name and a recognized status in society. Rather, as this book has argued, modernist fiction often seeks to remind us just how frequently community politics is played out between and among established identities and recognized groups, and in the efforts of subjects to puncture both their borders and their power. In other words, precisely what makes these narratives political is their concern with the repercussions, both individual and social, of the realignments of power that go along with realignments of both subjectivity and community. While the question of politics may sometimes lie submerged beneath seemingly disinterested discussions of identity and affiliation, the implications for political common life are rarely hard to grasp.

The lesson of attending to the politics of community within modernist fiction is therefore the integration of "private" narrative concerns within the realm of public politics, and the concomitant rewriting of community as a web of narrative performances, which are local and always potentially cosmopolitan as well. The failure of so many new communitarian theories lies to a great extent in their failure to see the political community as constantly being reiterated by subjects who also, as Nancy claims, re-make themselves every time they come into connection. Thus, they rarely seem to imagine a political realm where incomplete communication or disagreement over shared values is the norm, and where translation is always fraught with difficulty, or where connection grows stronger precisely because of this lack of an ideal public conversation. Yet this is precisely what we *do* see in many of the narratives of modernism, whether because they emerge out of the concerns of those, like women, homosexuals, and Jews, long considered less-than-ideal participants within that public sphere, or because they begin from a literary need to destabilize the narrative position of public consensus. Community in these narratives can help us see the continuing viability of partial, non-national affiliations within the history of twentieth-century politics. Community in these narratives can demonstrate the limitations of traditional theories of universality and the drive towards ideal consensus, no matter how perspicacious. And community in these narratives can show us how to account for the non-transparency of language and the impossibility of direct translation within the ongoing process of forging new cosmopolitan political bonds.

In asking, "what was modernism?" Raymond Williams questioned the current situation of modernism, after having been tamed and canonized in the middle years of the twentieth century and made mainstream in the subsequent decades. He wondered what an alternative modernism might look like and what the value of its dislocations of meaning might be, were they ever retrieved from the realm of advertising and mass media. In other words, he wondered, along with many others, what is the future of modernism? While it does not propose to answer the question of alternative or future modernisms, or to describe how we might begin to wrest modernist techniques and perspectives back from crass commercialism, this book has attempted to propose a way of reading that addresses Williams's question. The future of modernism, or at least one of modernism's futures, may very well be community.

Notes

1 COSMOPOLITAN COMMUNITIES

1 Raymond Williams, *The Country and the City* (Oxford: Oxford University Press, 1973); Homi Bhabha, *The Location of Culture* (New York: Routledge, 1994); Jean-Luc Nancy, *The Inoperative Community*, ed. Peter Connor (Minneapolis: University of Minnesota Press, 1991).

2 Walter Benjamin, *Illuminations*, trans. Harry Zohn (New York: Schocken Books, 1969), 87, 83, 84.

3 Williams, *The Country and the City*, 165.

4 Ibid., 166.

5 Ibid., 245.

6 The number of stock definitions of modernism is endless, the debate over its identity ongoing. Astradur Eysteinsson provides a concise overview of some of the history of the term in chapter one of *The Concept of Modernism* (Ithaca: Cornell University Press, 1990).

7 Michael Levenson, *Modernism and the Fate of Individuality: Character and Novelistic Form from Conrad to Woolf*, (New York: Cambridge University Press, 1991), xii–xiii.

8 Collected in *The Politics of Modernism: Against the New Conformists*, (New York: Verso, 1989), 35.

9 See, for example, Homi Bhabha's use of the term in "Unpacking My Library ... Again," in Iain Chambers and Lidia Curti, eds, *The Post-Colonial Question: Common Skies, Divided Horizons* (New York: Routledge, 1996), 208. Drawing on Stuart Hall, Bhabha discusses the efforts to posit a "new internationalism" out of those practices that were obscured by the old "international style" of modernism, as though modernism were a monolithic, universalizing practice. It is this too easy conception of modernism that I wish to contest. On the question of international modernism, see also Susan Stanford Friedman, *Mappings: Feminism and the Cultural Geographies of Encounter* (Princeton: Princeton University Press, 1998), 114–20.

10 The re-reading of Joyce along these lines has been immensely productive in recent years. See Robert Spoo, *James Joyce and the Language of History* (New York: Oxford University Press, 1994); Emer Nolan, *James Joyce and National-*

ism (New York: Routledge, 1995); Trevor Williams, *Reading Joyce Politically* (Gainesville: University of Florida Press, 1997). For the concerns of community and cosmopolitanism see, especially, Enda Duffy, *The Subaltern Ulysses* (Minneapolis: University of Minnesota Press, 1994), ch. 1; Joe Valente, "James Joyce and the Cosmopolitan Sublime," in Mark Wollaeger, Victor Luftig, and Robert Spoo, eds., *Joyce and the Subject of History* (Ann Arbor: University of Michigan Press, 1996); Mark Wollaeger, "Posters, Modernism, Cosmopolitanism: *Ulysses* and World War One Recruiting Posters in Ireland," *Yale Journal of Criticism* 6.2 (1993): 87–131.

11 Susan Stanford Friedman, "Woolf, Cultural Parataxis, and Transnational Landscapes of Reading: Toward a Locational Modernist Studies," Plenary Address, The Tenth Annual Conference on Virginia Woolf, June 8, 2000.

12 Michael Tratner, *Modernism and Mass Politics* (Stanford: Stanford University Press, 1995), and James English, *Comic Transactions* (Ithaca: Cornell University Press, 1994).

13 Amitai Etzioni, *The Spirit of Community* (New York: Simon and Schuster, Touchstone, 1993), 1–2.

14 Seyla Benhabib is a notable exception. See *Situating the Self: Gender, Community, and Postmodernism in Contemporary Ethics* (New York: Routledge, 1992).

15 Jurgen Habermas, *Theory of Communicative Action*, trans. Thomas McCarthy (Boston: Beacon Press, 1984), and *The Structural Transformation of the Public Sphere* trans. Thomas Burger and Frederick Lawrence (Cambridge, Mass: MIT Press, 1989).

16 Edward Said, *Culture and Imperialism* (New York: Knopf, 1993), 188–89.

17 John Rawls, *A Theory of Justice* (Cambridge, Mass.: Harvard University Press, 1971); "Justice as Fairness: Political, Not Metaphysical," *Philosophy and Public Affairs* 14.3 (Summer 1985): 223–51; "The Priority of Right and Ideas of the Good," *Philosophy and Public Affairs* 17.4 (Fall 1988): 251–76.

18 See Michael Sandel, *Liberalism and the Limits of Justice* (Cambridge: Cambridge University Press, 1982); Amy Gutmann, "Communitarian Critics of Liberalism," *Philosophy and Public Affairs* 14.3 (Summer 1985): 308–22; Iris Young, *Justice and the Politics of Difference* (Princeton: Princeton University Press, 1990).

19 In fact that is the "official" book store category of Etzioni's 1993 book (see n. 13).

20 Karl Marx, *The German Ideology*, ed. C. J. Arthur (New York: International Publishers, 1972); *The Grundrisse*, trans. David McLellan (New York: Harper and Row, 1971). See also *Pre-Capitalist Economic Formations*, trans. Jack Cohen (London: Lawrence and Wishart, 1964).

21 Karl Marx, *The Civil War in France* (New York: International Publishers, 1988), 59.

22 Ferdinand Tönnies, *Gemeinschaft und Gesellschaft*, trans. Charles Loomis (1957; reprint, New Brunswick, N.J.: Transaction, Inc., 1988), 43–44.

23 Emile Durkheim, *The Division of Labor in Society*, trans. W. D. Halls (New York: The Free Press, 1983), xliii.

24 Ibid., lv.
25 Emile Durkheim, *Le Suicide* (Paris: Presses Universitaires de France, 1967).
26 Robert Redfield, *The Little Community and Peasant Society and Culture* (Chicago: University of Chicago Press, Phoenix Books, 1960), 4, 5.
27 Benedict Anderson, *Imagined Communities: Reflections on the Origin and Spread of Nationalism* (New York: Verso, 1983), 44.
28 Partha Chatterjee also critiques the connection between nation and state in Anderson's theory, arguing that the state is not necessary to the imagination of the nation, as Anderson claims, epecially in colonial India: *The Nation and its Fragments: Colonial and Postcolonial Histories* (Princeton: Princeton University Press, Princeton Studies in Culture/Power/History, 1993), 6–7.
29 Ernest Renan, "What is a Nation?" in Homi K. Bhabha, ed., *Nation and Narration* (New York: Routledge, 1990), 19.
30 George Herbert Mead, "The Social Self," in Andrew J. Reck, ed., *Selected Writings* (Chicago: University of Chicago Press, 1964), 146.
31 Mead, "Natural Rights and the Theory of the Political Institution," in Reck, ed., *Selected Writings*, 159–60.
32 John Dewey, *The Public and its Problems* (Denver: Alan Swallow, 1927). After 1929 Dewey's thought on this subject becomes somewhat less optimistic.
33 John Dewey, *Experience and Nature* (New York: Dover Publications, 1958), 233.
34 John Dewey, "Individualism Old and New," in Jo Ann Boydston, ed., *John Dewey: The Later Works, 1925–1953*, vol. v: *1929–1930* (Carbondale: Southern Illinois University Press, 1984), 80–1.
35 Michael Walzer, *Spheres of Justice* (New York: Basic Books, 1983) and Charles Taylor, K. Anthony Appiah, Jurgen Habermas, Steven C. Rockefeller, Michael Walzer, and Susan Wolf, *Multiculturalism: Examining the Politics of Recognition*, ed. Amy Guttmann (Princeton: Princeton University Press, 1994).
36 Walzer, *Spheres of Justice*, 31–63.
37 Taylor, "The Politics of Recognition," in Taylor *et al.*, *Multiculturalism*, 34.
38 Ibid., 33.
39 See his *Sources of the Self: The Making of Modern Identity* (Cambridge, Mass.: Harvard University Press, 1989).
40 I also see this as similar to the distinction Judith Butler draws between the situated and the constituted self. A situated self is precisely that notion of a subject constrained in advance. See Judith Butler, "For a Careful Reading," in Seyla Benhabib *et al.*, *Feminist Contentions* (New York: Routledge, 1995), 135.
41 See Susan Wolf's critique, in Benhabib *et al.*, *Feminist Contentions*, 85.
42 Rawls, *Theory*, 527; Rawls revises this idea into that of "overlapping consensus" in his later work ("Justice as Fairness") yet the core understanding remains essentially the same.
43 Chantal Mouffe, "Deconstruction, Pragmatism and the Politics of Democracy," in Mouffe, ed., *Deconstruction and Pragmatism* (New York: Routledge,

1996), 6.

44 I here allude to Rorty's use of the "we" in *Contingency, Irony, and Solidarity* (Cambridge: Cambridge University Press, 1989), as well as to Simon Critchley's critique of Rorty in "Deconstruction and Pragmatism – Is Derrida a Private Ironist or a Public Liberal?" in Mouffe, ed., *Deconstruction and Pragmatism.*

45 Young, *Justice*, 227.

46 Benhabib, *Situating the Self*, 6.

47 Ibid., 9.

48 Ibid., 10, 13.

49 Nancy, *The Inoperative Community*, xxxviii. This passage does not appear in the French edition.

50 I resist calling what Woolf writes a "relational subject" for the very reason that the term conjures up a totalizing image of the collectivity contrary to this idea.

51 Nancy Fraser, *Unruly Practices: Power, Discourse, and Gender in Contemporary Social Theory* (Minneapolis: University of Minnesota Press, 1989), 86.

52 Mouffe, "Deconstruction, Pragmatism," 11.

53 Chantal Mouffe, "Democratic Citizenship and the Political Community," in Miami Theory Collective, ed., *Community at Loose Ends* (Minneapolis: University of Minnesota Press, 1991), 78.

54 The history of these notions of cosmopolitanism will be discussed in the chapter that follows.

55 See Martha C. Nussbaum, *Poetic Justice: The Literary Imagination and Public Life* (Boston: Beacon Press, 1995), preface.

56 Martha C. Nussbaum, "Patriotism and Cosmopolitanism," in Nussbaum with Respondants, *For Love of Country: Debating the Limits of Patriotism*, ed. Joshua Cohen (Boston: Beacon Press, 1996), 9.

57 In the sense that K. Anthony Appiah discusses in "Cosmopolitan Patriots," in Nussbaum *et al.*, *For Love of Country*, 21–9.

58 Arjun Appadurai, *Modernity at Large: Cultural Dimensions of Globalization* (Minneapolis: University of Minnesota Press, Public Worlds, 1, 1996), 189.

59 Bruce Robbins, "Introduction Part I: Actually Existing Cosmopolitanism," in Pheng Cheah and Robbins, eds., *Cosmopolitics: Thinking and Feeling Beyond the Nation* (Minneapolis: University of Minnesota Press, Cultural Politics, 14, 1998), 3.

60 James Clifford, "Traveling Cultures," in Lawrence Grossberg, Cary Nelson, Paula Treichler *et al.*, eds., *Cultural Studies* (New York: Routledge, 1992), 103.

61 Bhabha, "Unpacking," 204. For a critique of Bhabha's emphasis on performance as disruption see Sangeeta Ray, "The Nation in Performance: Bhabha, Mukherjee and Kureishi," in Monika Fludernik, ed., *Hybridity and Postcolonialism: Twentieth-Century Indian Literature* (Tubingen: Stauffenburg Verlag, 1998).

62 Homi Bhabha, "DesemiNation: Time, Narrative, and the Margins of the

Modern Nation," in Bhabha, ed., *Nation and Narration*, 291–322.

63 Bhabha uses Salman Rushdie's *Satanic Verses* as the example: "Unpacking," 205.

64 Matei Calinescu, *Five Faces of Modernity* (Durham: Duke University Press, 1987), 279.

65 See, for example, Pamela Caughie, *Virginia Woolf and Postmodernism* (Urbana: University of Illinois Press, 1991), and Brian Richardson, "Remapping the Present: The Master Narrative of Modern Literary History and the Lost Forms of Twentieth Century Fiction," *Twentieth Century Literature* 43.3 (Fall 1997): 291–309.

66 Many of these claims to the modern are collected in Vassiliki Kolocotroni, Jane Goldman, Olga Taxidou, eds., *Modernism: An Anthology of Sources and Documents* (Chicago: University of Chicago Press, 1998).

67 Paul Gilroy, *The Black Atlantic: Modernity and Double Consciousness* (Cambridge, Mass.: Harvard University Press, 1993), 42.

68 Benjamin, *Illuminations*, 83.

69 Ibid., 85.

70 In a different way Homi Bhabha has also insisted upon the importance of "restaging the past" in a specific location. See *The Location of Culture* (New York: Routledge, 1994), especially the introduction.

71 See Benjamin's "The Task of the Translator," in *Illuminations*. Though Bhabha does not make it explicit, he clearly draws on this essay.

72 As Appadurai puts it, "the steady increase in the efforts of the modern nation-state to define all neighborhood under the sign of its forms of allegiance and affiliation": *Modernity at Large*, 189.

73 See Garrett Stewart, "Catching the Stylistic D/Rift: Sound Defects in Woolf's *The Waves*," *ELH* 54.2 (Summer 1987): 421–461.

74 Elizabeth Deeds Ermarth, *Realism and Consensus in the English Novel* (Princeton: Princeton University Press, 1983), 65. It is interesting to note that this idea of disagreement as a question of position is also key to liberal political theory.

75 Ibid., 222.

76 Anderson, *Imagined Communities*, 133.

77 Timothy Brennan, "The National Longing for Form," in Bhabha, ed. *Nation and Narration*, 49.

78 For an alternative model of nation and state, see Chatterjee, *The Nation and its Fragments*.

79 Said's *Culture and Imperialism* sometimes commits this error, though its readings of individual texts are often quite subtle.

80 Susan Suleiman's *Authoritarian Fictions: The Ideological Novel as a Literary Genre* is instructive on this point, (New York: Columbia University Press, 1983).

81 Virginia Woolf, *Three Guineas* (New York: Harcourt Brace and Company, 1938), 109.

82 The term is Benhabib's although the concept emerges in several different writers' work. See for example Naomi Schor, "French Feminism is a

Universal," in *Differences* 7.1 (1995): 15–47. The entire issue is devoted to debate on this topic.

83 Benhabib, *Situating the Self*, 3.

84 Drucilla Cornell, "Enlightening the Enlightenment: A Response to John Brenkman," *Critical Inquiry* 26 (Autumn, 1999): 136.

85 Ibid., 137.

86 Ibid., 136.

87 As Susan Stanford Friedman describes it, this is the challenge of "locational feminism": *Mappings*, 5.

88 See Sara Ruddick, *Maternal Thinking: Toward a Politics of Peace* (Boston: Beacon Press, 1995), on the ethics of care, and Bonnie Kime Scott, *Refiguring Modernism*, vol. 1: *The Women of 1928* (Bloomington: University of Illinois Press, 1995), for critical use of the figure of the web.

89 On this issue see the Kohlberg/Gilligan debate, as well as many more recent reflections on Gilligan's work (see Benhabib, *Situating the Self*). See also Habermas's espousal of Kohlberg's perspective on the ideal realm of justice.

90 Of course the dismantling of gendered discourses is predicated on the dismantling of the unitary subject, another exemplary myth of modern western culture.

91 The recent anthology edited by Kolocotroni *et al.*, *Modernism: An Anthology of Sources and Documents*, makes this especially clear.

92 Woolf, "Character in Fiction," in *Collected Essays* (London: Hogarth Press, 1967).

93 Andreas Huyssen, *After the Great Divide: Modernism, Mass Culture, Postmodernism* (Bloomington: Indiana University Press, 1986), vii.

94 On the question of cultural studies and the high/low culture divide, see Michèle Barrett, *Imagination in Theory: Culture, Writing, Words, and Things* (New York: New York University Press, 1999), 5.

95 Huyssen, *After the Great Divide*, 56. This is, of course, the same universalizing account that prompts Raymond Williams to look for community at the margins of modernism.

96 In using the term "modernist" or "high modernist" I restrict myself to the varieties of literary modernism practiced between 1880 and the Second World War. I am therefore not referring to the common use of the term "modernism" in philosophy to designate the period dating variably from the writings of Kant, Descartes, or Rousseau, and categorized by a particular sense of individual identity, among other dimensions. This is especially important when considering Habermas whose use of "modern" is philosophical.

97 When we define modernism as, for example, focused on the dislocation of language from referentiality, the concern with images, symbols, and mythic archetypes, and the pursuit of a reality and narrative structure true to inner subjective or collective unconscious experience, as does David Lodge (*The Modes of Modern Writing: Metaphor, Metonymy, and the Typology of Modern*

Literature [Chicago: University of Chicago Press, 1977]), or even when we speak in terms of its intellectual genealogy, as does Michael Levenson (*The Genealogy of Modernism* [Cambridge: Cambridge University Press, 1984]), we do not speak of specific historical events or concerns, cultural identities, or gendered discourse.

98 K. Anthony Appiah, "Against National Culture" (paper delivered at the conference on Text and Nation, Georgetown University, Washington, D.C., 21 April, 1995). Appiah uses the Stein remark as an example. It appears in Nussbaum *et al.*, *For Love of Country*, 21–9.

2 HENRY JAMES

1 Between 1885 and 1890 over 1,000 new magazines were launched: Frank Luther Mott, *A History of American Magazines*, vol. IV: *1885–1905* (Cambridge, Mass.: Harvard University Press, 1957), 11.

2 See John Higham, "The Transformation of the Statue of Liberty," in *Send These to Me: Immigrants in Urban America*, rev. edn. (Baltimore: Johns Hopkins University Press, 1984).

3 "Topics of the Times – 'The Century' a National Magazine," *Century Magazine* 42 (1891): 950.

4 In 1890 seven-eighths of magazine subscribers were female, quoted in Mott, *American Magazines*, 353.

5 According to Mott, "By the end of 1892, the *Cosmopolitan* had reached a place among the country's leading illustrated magazines" (Ibid., 484). Schneirov claims that *Cosmopolitan* was one of the three most significant magazines of the end of the nineteenth century: Matthew Schneirov, *The Dream of a New Social Order: Popular Magazines in America, 1893–1914* (New York: Columbia University Press, 1994), 13.

6 Ibid., 13.

7 See, for example, Edward Everett Hale, "Social Problems: Emigration and Immigration," *Cosmopolitan Vol* 9 (1890): 254–5.

8 Eleanor Waddle, "Side Glances at American Beauty," *Cosmopolitan* 9 (1890): 193–202; F. Leslie Baker, "Transplanted American Beauty," *Cosmopolitan* 9 (1890): 517–32; Olive Shreiner, "The Woman Question," *Cosmopolitan* 28 (1899): 45–54.

9 See Richard Ohmann, *Selling Culture: Magazines, Markets, and Class at the Turn of the Century* (London: Verso, 1990).

10 David J. Hill, "The Emancipation of Women," *Cosmopolitan* 1 (1886): 96.

11 Ann Douglas, *The Feminization of American Culture* (New York: Avon, 1977).

12 Waddle, "Side Glances," 202.

13 Baker, "Transplanted," 517.

14 "The Making of An Illustrated Magazine," *Cosmopolitan* 14 (1893): 262.

15 Involving between 10 and 100,000 people: Aristotle, *Ethics*, trans. J. A. K. Thompson (New York: Penguin, 1976), Book IX, x.

16 Ibid., Book VIII, i.

17 Ibid., ix.
18 See Derek Heater, *World Citizenship and Government: Cosmopolitan Ideas in the History of Western Political Thought* (New York: St Martin's Press), 1996; Jonathan Barnes, "Introduction," Aristotle, *Ethics*, 13.
19 Plutarch, "On the Fortune or Virtue of Alexander," in *Moralia*, vol. IV, quoted in Heater, *World Citizenship*, 13.
20 Marcus Aurelius, *The Communings with Himself*, quoted in Heater, *World Citizenship*, 19.
21 Seneca, "On the Happy Life," in *Moral Essays*, vol. II, quoted in Heater, *World Citizenship*, 18.
22 See Julia Kristeva on Montesquieu and Diderot, *Nations Without Nationalism* (New York: Columbia University Press, 1993), 27–8; 54–5; and Pheng Cheah, "Introduction Part II: The Cosmopolitical Today," in Pheng Cheah and Bruce Robbins, eds., *Cosmopolitics: Thinking and Feeling Beyond the Nation* (Minneapolis: University of Minnesota Press, Cultural Politics, 14, 1998), 22.
23 Kant, "The Idea for a Universal History from a Cosmopolitan Point of View," in Kant, *On History*, ed. Lewis White Beck (Indianapolis: Bobbs-Merrill, The Library of Liberal Arts, 1963), 20.
24 Ibid., 16.
25 Lewis White Beck, "Editor's Introduction," in Kant, *On History*, x.
26 Kant, "Perpetual Peace," in Kant, *On History*, 87, 88, 93.
27 Ibid., 105.
28 Cheah, "The Cosmopolitical," 23.
29 Ibid.
30 Benedict Anderson, *Imagined Communities: Reflections on the Origin and Spread of Nationalism* (New York: Verso, 1983), 49, 102.
31 E. J. Hobsbawm, *Nations and Nationalism Since 1780* (Cambridge: Cambridge University Press, Canto, 1990), 18.
32 Karl Marx and Friedrich Engels, *The Communist Manifesto* (New York: Signet, 1998), 54.
33 *Oxford English Dictionary*, compact edn. (Oxford: Oxford University Press, 1971), "Cosmopolitan," 1032.
34 See Timothy Brennan on the connection between national development and theories of cosmopolitanism: Timothy Brennan, "The National Longing for Form," in Homi K. Bhabha, ed., *Nation and Narration* (New York: Routledge, 1990), and *At Home in the World: Cosmopolitanism Now* (Cambridge, Mass.: Harvard University Press, 1997), Introduction.
35 Ibid., 248.
36 Ibid.
37 *OED*, "Cosmopolitan," 1032.
38 Journal entry, September ?, 1846, in Stephen E. Wicher, ed., *Selections from Ralph Waldo Emerson* (Boston: Houghton Mifflin, Riverside Edition, 1957), 309.

39 See, for example, the international basis of appeals for an eight-hour work-day (Mott, *American Magazines*, 219).

40 Robbins, "Introduction Part I: Actually Existing Cosmopolitanism," in Pheng Cheah and Bruce Robbins, eds., *Cosmopolitics*, 1–2.

41 Martha C. Nussbaum *et al.*, *For Love of Country: Debating the Limits of Patriotism* (Boston: Beacon Press, 1996), 9.

42 John Tebbel and Mary Ellen Zuckerman, *The Magazine in America: 1741–1990* (New York: Oxford University Press, 1991), 57.

43 See Ohmann, *Selling Culture*.

44 Frank Luther Mott, *A History of American Magazines*, vol. III: *1865–1885* (Cambridge Mass.: Harvard University Press, 1938), 249.

45 Thomas Peyser, *Utopia and Cosmopolis: Globalization in the Era of American Literary Realism* (Durham: Duke University Press, 1998).

46 This series ran in *Century*, 45 in 1892–3.

47 Mrs A. G. Lewis, "Educating Our Daughters Abroad," *Ladies Home Journal* (September, 1891): 2; Varina Anne Davis, "The American Girl who Studies Abroad," *Ladies Home Journal* (February, 1892), 9.

48 See Maureen Montgomery, *"Gilded Prostitution": Status, Money, and Transatlantic Marriages, 1870–1914* (New York: Routledge, 1989).

49 Peyser, *Utopia and Cosmopolis*.

50 See Ohmann, *Selling Culture*.

51 Howells's letter to James makes clear his intention that "The Cosmoptn [*sic*] will at once lead all N.Y. magazines in literary quality": Howells to James, February 23, 1892, in Mitchell Anesko, ed., *Letters, Fictions, Lives: Henry James and William Dean Howells* (New York: Oxford University Press, 1997), 288.

52 All references are to the contents of *Cosmopolitan* 13 (May–Oct., 1892), and 14 (Nov.–April, 1893).

53 A notable exception is Franz Boas's "Ethnology at the Exhibition," *Cosmopolitan* 14 (1893): 607–9.

54 J. M. Hager, quoted in Carol Wald, *Myth America: Picturing Women 1865–1945* (New York: Pantheon, 1975), 156.

55 Annette Kolodny, *The Lay of the Land* (Chapel Hill: University of North Carolina Press, 1975), 6, 8–9. See also Lauren Berlant, *The Anatomy of National Fantasy: Hawthorne, Utopia, and Everyday Life* (Chicago: University of Chicago Press, 1991), 28.

56 The classic formulations of this myth appear in Barbara Welter, "Cult of True Womanhood," *American Quarterly* 18 (Summer, 1966): 151–74, and *Dimity Convictions* (Athens, Ohio: Ohio University Press, 1976). While this mythology has been much debated, I remain convinced that "true womanhood" held significant sway on the popular imagination. See also Nancy Cott, *The Bonds of Womanhood: "Woman's Sphere" in New England, 1780–1835* (New Haven: Yale University Press, 1977); Linda Gordon, *Women's Body, Women's Right: A Social History of Birth Control* (New York: Grossman, 1976);

Paula Baker, "The Domestication of Politics: Women and American Political Society, 1780–1920," *American Historical Review* 89 (1984): 620–47; Gwendolyn Mink, "The Lady and the Tramp: Gender, Race and the Origins of
the American Welfare State," in Linda Gorden, ed., *Women, the State and
Welfare* (Madison: University of Wisconsin Press, 1990); Carole R. McCann,
Birth Control Politics in the United States, 1916–1945 (Ithaca: Cornell University
Press, 1994).

57 Cott, *Bonds*, 2.
58 See Baker, "Domestication."
59 In 1910 girls made up 56.45% of high school enrollments and took 41.1% of
the A/B degrees granted. For Earl Barnes, writing in 1912, the influx of
women into higher education was a key indicator of what he called "The
Feminizing of Culture": Barnes, *Woman in Modern Society* (New York:
Huebsch, 1912), 91.
60 Nina Baym, *Feminism in American Literary History* (New Brunswick: Rutgers
University Press, 1992), 121.
61 Baker, "Domestication," 631.
62 "The Marriage Rate Among College Educated Women," *Century* 50 (1895);
"Notes on the Health of Women Students," *Century* 42 (1891): 294–5;
"Women Clerks in New York," *Cosmopolitan* 10 (1891); "Avocations Open to
Women," *Ladies Home Journal* 8 (1891); "When Lady, When Woman?"
Ladies Home Journal 12 (1895) .
63 "The Invasion of Women," *Harper's Bazar* 21 (1888): 710; "The Sisterhood
of Women," *Harper's Bazar* 31 (1898): 66.
64 "Editorial," *Harper's Bazar* 31 (May, 1898): 390.
65 Grace N. Kimball, MD, "Women and War," *Harper's Bazar* 31 (May, 1898):
438.
66 Quoted in "Editorial," *Harper's Bazar* 31 (May, 1898): 390.
67 William Safire, *New Political Dictionary* (New York: Random House, 1993),
379.
68 "Editorial," *Harper's Bazar* 31 (May, 1898): 390.
69 Ibid.
70 Amelia E. Barr, "Have Women Found New Weapons?" *Ladies Home Journal*
11 (1894): 4.
71 Carol Levander, *Voices of the Nation: Women and Public Speech in Nineteenth-
Century American Literature and Culture* (Cambridge: Cambridge University
Press, 1998).
72 Ohmann, *Selling Culture*, 23–4.
73 Ibid., 223, 244–5.
74 Ibid., 245.
75 Gillian Brown, *Domestic Individualism: Imagining Self in Nineteenth-Century America* (Berkeley: University of California Press, 1990), 197.
76 Henry James, *The Bostonians* (New York: Penguin, 1984), 326. Further
references will be cited in the text.
77 *Henry James Letters*, vol. III: *1883–1895*, ed. Leon Edel (Cambridge, Mass.:

Harvard University Press, Belknap Press, 1980), 106. See also the entry on *The Bostonians* in Leon Edel and Lyall Powers, eds., *The Complete Notebooks of Henry James* (New York: Oxford University Press, 1987); Marcia Jacobson, *Henry James and the Mass Market* (University, Ala.: University of Alabama Press, 1983), 20.

78 It is precisely this claim that I here seek to re-examine, by situating James within the context of American popular discourse about cosmopolitanism in the 1890s.

79 Tintner, *The Cosmopolitan World of Henry James: An Intertextual Study* (Baton Rouge: Louisiana State University Press, 1991), 2.

80 Ibid., xiii.

81 There are clearly real-life sources for this fictional anxiety about publication in this period, when opportunities to make money from his fiction were slim.

82 See "Henry James: The Americano-European Legend," *University of Toronto Quarterly* 4 (July, 1967): 321–4, which is reprinted in the Norton Critical edition of *The Tales of Henry James*, ed. Christof Wegelin (New York: Norton, 1984).

83 "Occasional Paris," in *Collected Travel Writings: The Continent* (New York: The Library of America, 1993), 721. Further references will be cited in the text.

84 In this sense I want to argue that nineteenth-century cosmopolitanism was *not* synonymous with travel as some contemporary theorists claim. See for example James Clifford's "Traveling Cultures," in Lawrence Grossberg *et al.*, eds., *Cultural Studies* (New York: Routledge, 1992), 103, and Caren Kaplan, *Questions of Travel: Postmodern Discourses of Displacement* (Durham: Duke University Press, Post-Contemporary Interventions, 1996), 101–42.

85 All stories cited from *Henry James: Complete Stories 1892–1898* and *1898–1910* (New York: The Library of America, 1996).

86 Tintner, *Cosmopolitan World*, 124.

87 In a second letter he also specifically criticizes Bourget for displaying a character's underclothing (*ibid.*, 183–5).

88 Julia Prewitt Brown, *Cosmopolitan Criticism: Oscar Wilde's Philosophy of Art* (Charlottesville: University Press of Virginia, 1997), 25.

89 Oscar Wilde, "The Critic As Artist: Part II," in Richard Ellmann, ed., *The Artist as Critic: Critical Writings of Oscar Wilde* (Chicago: University of Chicago Press, 1982).

90 While James was lodged at the Cosmopolitan Club in Washington, D.C.

91 Leon Edel, *Henry James: The Middle Years* (Philadelphia: Lippincott, 1962), 31.

92 Oscar Wilde, "The Critic As Artist: Part II," 372–3.

93 See Tintner, *Cosmopolitan World*, 190. My reading of Bourget here is indebted to Tintner's analysis.

94 Kaplan, *Questions of Travel*, 309.

95 Paul Bourget, *Némésis* (Paris: Librairie Plon, 1918), 104. The description of Daisy's marriage at a young age to a man who turns out to have been the

lover of her mother's good friend (197) also points clearly to Bourget's use of *The Portrait of a Lady* as material for this novel.

96 Tintner, *Cosmopolitan World*, 6.

97 Given by the same Gloriani who appears in *The Ambassadors*.

98 James to W. E. Norris, February 4, 1896, in Edel, ed., *Henry James Letters*, vol. IV:*1895–1916*, ed. Leon Edel (Cambridge, Mass.: Harvard University Press, The Belknap Press, 1984), 27.

99 James to William James, April 20, 1898, in Edel, ed., *Henry James Letters*, IV: 72.

100 Kwame Anthony Appiah, "Cosmopolitan Patriots," in Nussbaum *et al.*, *For Love of Country*, 22–3.

101 James, *The Speech and Manners of American Women*, 1906–7, ed. E. S. Riggs, (Lancaster, Pa.: Lancaster, 1973). Further references will be cited in the text.

102 Henry James, *The Question of Our Speech; The Lesson of Balzac*. 1906 (Folcroft, Pa.: Folcroft Press, 1974), 10. Further references will be cited in the text.

103 Homi K. Bhabha, "DesemiNation: Time, Narrative, and the Margins of the Modern Nation," in Bhabha, ed., *Nation and Narration* (New York: Routledge, 1990).

104 Kenneth B. Warren, *Black and White Strangers* (Chicago: University of Chicago Press, 1993), 116.

105 Virginia Fowler also makes this claim: *Henry James's American Girl: The Embroidery on the Canvas* (Madison: University of Wisconsin Press, 1984), 39.

106 See Elsa Nettels, *Language and Gender in American Fiction: Howells, James, Wharton, Cather* (Charlottesville: University Press of Virginia, 1997), 6.

107 See John Higham, *Strangers in the Land: Patterns of American Nativism, 1860–1925* (New Brunswick: Rutgers University Press, 1988). Though they present the case with subtlety, both Alex Zwerdling (*Improvised Europeans: American Expatriates and the Siege of London* [New York: Basic Books, 1998]) and Sara Blair (*Henry James and the Writing of Race and Nation* [Cambridge: Cambridge University Press, 1996]) also share the view that *The American Scene* relies on nativist assumptions.

108 See William Ernest Castle, *Heredity and Eugenics: A Course of Lectures* (Chicago: University of Chicago Press, 1912); Edward East, *Mankind at the Crossroads* (New York: Scribner's, 1923; reprt. New York: Arno, 1977); and Daniel Kevles, *In the Name of Eugenics: Genetics and the Uses of Human Heredity* (New York: Knopf, 1985). When James writes, this movement is not yet at its peak.

109 Warren, *Black and White*, 38. I have not here rehearsed arguments about James's portrayal of black Americans that Warren treats so well in this volume. Although Warren makes clear that James's writings from the early 1880s on concern themselves with the "black social presence" (20), it is also true that discussions of race and nationality within these texts often focus on racial differences among whites of European descent.

110 Mink, "The Lady and the Tramp," 97.

111 For a a different perspective see Walter Benn Michaels, "American Modernism and the Poetics of Identity," *Modernism/Modernity* 1. 1 (January, 1994): 38–56.
112 Blair, *Henry James and the Writing of Race and Nation*, 162.
113 Zwerdling, *Improvised Europeans*, 200.
114 Beverly Haviland, *Henry James's Last Romance: Making Sense of the Past and The American Scene* (Cambridge: Cambridge University Press, 1997), xiii.
115 Henry James, *The American Scene*, first published, 1907, in *Collected Travel Writings: Great Britain and America* (New York: The Library of America, 1993), 372. Further references will be cited in the text.
116 Fowler, *James's American Girl*, 13.
117 See Elizabeth Allen, *A Woman's Place in the Novels of Henry James* (New York: St. Martin's, 1984), 19.
118 See Lynn Wardley, "Woman's Voice, Democracy's Body, and *The Bostonians*," *ELH* 56 (1989): 641.
119 "The New Woman," *Good Housekeeping* 40 (1905): 700.
120 Anglo-American eugenicists also shared James's antipathy to the "economic top of modern society" and to business in general (Kevles, *In the Name of Eugenics* 77). See ch. 1 in Warren's *Black and White* for the implications of the term "social equality" in the reconstruction era.
121 This was a charge that had also been leveled against immigrants (H. L. Wayland quoted in Mink, "The Lady and the Tramp," 100). I am indebted to Carole R. McCann for pointing out this connection.
122 Higham, *Strangers*, 33.
123 Charles Alexander, *Here the Country Lies: Nationalism and the Arts in Twentieth-Century America* (Bloomington: Indiana University Press), 8–9.
124 Higham, *Strangers*, 33.
125 Alexander, *Here the Country Lies*, 9.
126 Ernst Renan, "What is a Nation," in Bhabha, ed., *Nation and Narration*, 15.
127 Higham, *Strangers*, 33. See also George W. Stocking, Jr., "The Turn-of-the-Century Concept of Race," *Modernism/Modernity* 1.1 (January 1994): 4–16; Kevles, 71; Mink, *In the Name of Eugenics*, "The Lady and the Tramp," 95–6.
128 *Henry James Letters*, vol. 1: *1843–75*, ed. Leon Edel (Cambridge, Mass.: Harvard University Press, The Belknap Press, 1974), 77.
129 "The American Wife in Europe," *Cosmopolitan* 38 (1905): 371–82. Clearly, the new Southern European immigrants had yet to appear within the elite ranks of the "nicest ... American women" described here.
130 See Charles Caramello, "The Duality of the American Scene," in Daniel Mark Fogel, *Companion to Henry James Studies* (Westport, Conn.: Greenwood Press, 1993), 467; Richard Brodhead, "Strangers on a Train: The Double Dream of Italy in the American Gilded Age," *Modernism/Modernity* 1. 2 (April, 1994): 1–19.
131 Mink, "The Lady and the Tramp," 103–4; McCann, *Birth Control Politics*, ch. 4.

132 See Sander Gilman, *The Jew's Body* (New York: Routledge, 1991), and "Sexology, Psychoanalysis, and Degeneration: From a Theory of Race to a Race for Theory," in *Degeneration* (New York: Columbia University Press, 1985). Yet it is important to note that James was a proclaimed Dreyfusard and broke with Bourget in part over his anti-Semitic views (see Kaplan, *Questions of Travel*, 435–6; Tintner, *Cosmopolitan World*, 2–3).

133 Sara Blair describes the train and its scene of performance as one of the key figures of *The American Scene*. See *Henry James and the Writing of Race and Nation*, 190–210.

134 Fowler, *James's American Girl*, 17; *American Scene*, 500.

135 John Carlos Rowe, *The Theoretical Dimensions of Henry James* (Madison: University of Wisconsin Press, 1984), 201.

136 See William Veeder, "Henry James and the Uses of the Feminine," in Laura Claridge and Elizabeth Langland, eds., *Out of Bounds: Male Writers and Gender(ed) Criticism* (Amherst: University of Massachusetts Press, 1990), 226.

137 Henry James, *The Ambassadors* (Oxford: Oxford University Press, 1985), 231. Further references will be cited in the text.

138 Henry James, *The Golden Bowl* (New York: Doubleday, n.d.), 440. Further references will be cited in the text.

139 I do not agree with Priscilla Walton that Maggie's perspective is polysemous or that James "privileges her writing over the realist referential text": Priscilla Walton, *The Disruption of the Feminine in Henry James* (Toronto: University of Toronto Press, 1992), 145.

140 Michaels, "American Modernism," 41.

141 Ibid., 53.

142 Mink, "The Lady and the Tramp," 98.

143 Bhabha, *Nation and Narration*, 297.

3 MARCEL PROUST

1 Lazare, *Le Fumier de Job* (Strasbourg: Circé Editeur, 1990), my translation; Kristeva, *Time and Sense: Proust and the Experience of Literature*, trans. Ross Guberman (New York: Columbia University Press, 1996).

2 *Correspondance de Marcel Proust*, vol. III: *1902–1903*, ed. Philip Kolb (Paris: Librairie Plon, 1976), 71; George Painter, *Marcel Proust: A Biography*, 2 vols. (New York: Vintage, 1978), I: 223; Kristeva, *Time and Sense*, 144.

3 Michael R. Marrus, *The Politics of Assimilation: The French Jewish Community at the Time of the Dreyfus Affair* (Oxford: Clarendon Press, 1971), 164.

4 Péguy specifically calls Lazare a prophet: "Péguy's Portrait of Bernard-Lazare" from *Notre Jeunesse*, in Annette Aronowicz, *Jews and Christians on Time and Eternity: Charles Péguy's Portrait of Bernard-Lazare* (Stanford: Stanford University Press, 1998), 59.

5 Marcel Proust, *Remembrance of Things Past*, trans. C. K. Scott Moncrieff and Terence Kilmartin (New York: Random House, 1981), III: 237. Further

references will be to this translation and will be cited in the text. See also Michael Sprinker, *History and Ideology in Proust* (Cambridge: Cambridge University Press, 1994).

6 Proust's father was a supporter of the government's position (Painter, *Proust*, 1:223).

7 My use of this term derives from Bernard Lazare's *Le Fumier de Job*, and from Hannah Arendt's elaboration on it in *The Origins of Totalitarianism* (New York: Harcourt Brace Jovanovich, Publishers, A Harvest/HBJ Book, 1973), and Ron H. Feldman, ed., *The Jew as Pariah: Jewish Identity and Politics in the Modern Age* (New York: Grove Press, Inc., 1978). Arendt's formulation of pariahdom clearly also derives from Max Weber: *Ancient Judaism* (New York: The Free Press), 1952.

8 David Lloyd, *Nationalism and Minor Literature: James Clarence Mangan and the Emergence of Irish Cultural Nationalism*, (Berkeley: University of California Press, The New Historicism: Studies in Cultural Poetics, 1987), 24.

9 See Arendt, "We Refugees," in Feldman, ed., *The Jew as Pariah*.

10 Arendt, "The Jew as Pariah: A Hidden Tradition," in Feldman, ed., *The Jew and Pariah*, 68. The same kind of tradition is crucial to Isaiah Berlin's "The Life and Opinions of Moses Hess," and "Benjamin Disraeli, Karl Marx and the Search for Identity," in *Against the Current* (New York: Viking, 1980).

11 Péguy, "Portrait," 59.

12 Kristeva describes this same movement as a "fugue" (*Time and Sense*, 154).

13 See, for example, Paula Hyman, "French Jewish Historiography since 1870," in Frances Malino and Bernard Wasserstein, eds, *The Jews in Modern France* (Hanover: University Press of New England for Brandeis University Press, 1985).

14 See Benhabib, "The Pariah and Her Shadow: Hannah Arendt's Biography of Rahel Varnhagen," in Bonnie Honig, ed., *Feminist Interpretations of Hannah Arendt* (University Park, Pa.: Pennsylvania State University Press, 1995).

15 To Arendt action and contemplation are opposed terms: see *The Human Condition* (Chicago: University of Chicago Press, 1958), and Melvyn Hill, ed., *Hannah Arendt and the Recovery of the Public World* (New York: St. Martin's, 1979), 304.

16 Proust was born right after the Paris Commune. See Ronald Hayman, *Marcel Proust: A Biography* (New York: HarperCollins Publishers, An Edward Burlingame Book, 1990), and Kristen Ross, *The Emergence of Social Space: Rimbaud and the Paris Commune* (Minneapolis: University of Minnesota Press, Theory and History of Literature, 60, 1988), 42.

17 Arendt, *The Origins of Totalitarianism*, 67.

18 Eugen Weber, *Peasants into Frenchmen: The Modernization of Rural France, 1870–1914* (Stanford: Stanford University Press, 1976), 221n.

19 Ibid., 67.

20 Ibid., 156, 140–1.

21 Ibid., 96.

22 Ibid., 112.
23 Hyman, "French Jewish Historiography since 1870," 331.
24 Quoted in Wladimir Rabi, "Ecrivains juifs face à l'affaire Dreyfus: étude des comportements," in Géraldi Leroy, ed., *Les Ecrivains et L'Affaire Dreyfus* (Paris: Presses Universitaires de France, Collection Université d'Orléans, 1983), 18. My translation.
25 Arendt, *The Origins of Totalitarianism*, 62–4.
26 Bernard Lazare, "Juifs et Israélites," *Les Entretiens politiques et littéraires*, 1, (Sept., 1890): 174–9.
27 Marrus, *The Politics of Assimilation*, 32–3.
28 *Archives Israélites de France* (4 January, 1894). My translation.
29 Marrus, *The Politics of Assimilation*, 32–33.
30 The annual *Bulletin de l'Alliance Israélite Universelle* consistently re-iterates this claim in this period.
31 See for example Zadoc Kahn, *Sermons and Allocutions*, vol. II (Paris, 1903), 208.
32 See Marrus, *The Politics of Assimilation*, 161.
33 Simon Levitte, *Le Sionisme: quelques pages de son histoire* (Paris: Editions des Cahiers Juifs, 1936), 42.
34 Here I take issue with Marrus, *The Politics of Assimilation*, 196. For many, the Dreyfus Affair sparked a re-affirmation of allegiance to the Jewish community.
35 Despite Tadié's claim that Proust was not Jewish (Jean-Yves Tadié, *Marcel Proust: Biographie* [Paris: Gallimard, 1996], 34), I read the novel and the correspondence as indicating a movement towards that heritage.
36 Theodor Herzl, *A Jewish State: An Attempt at a Modern Solution of the Jewish Question*, trans. Sylvia D'Avigdor (New York: Federation of American Zionists, 1917), 4n.
37 Theodor Herzl, "First Congress Address – Basle, Aug. 29," in *The Congress Addresses of Theodor Herzl*, trans. Nellie Straus (New York: Federation of American Zionists, 1917), 5.
38 Nelly Wilson, *Bernard Lazare: Antisemitism and the Problem of Jewish Identity in Late Nineteenth-Century France* (Cambridge: Cambridge University Press, 1978), 241–3.
39 Both Mallarmé and Leconte de Lisle subscribed to the anarchist journal *La Révolte*, Richard D. Sonn, *Anarchism and Cultural Politics in Fin de Siècle France* (Lincoln: University of Nebraska Press, 1989), 5.
40 Ibid., 3.
41 Ibid., 7.
42 Arendt misses this art/action connection.
43 Sonn, *Anarchism and Cultural Politics*, 7.
44 In "Juifs et Israélites" Lazare defines the terms that apply so well to assimilationist sentiment among both Jews and the broader French populace in this period.
45 Ibid., 177. My translation.

46 Ibid., 178.
47 In this way Lazare's conception of the *Juif* clearly resembles that in Marx's *On the Jewish Question*, in *Collected Works*, vol. I, trans. Richard Dixon *et al.* (New York: International Publishers, 1975).
48 Bernard Lazare, "La Solidarité juive," *Les Entretiens politiques et littéraires* 7 (October 1890): 230. My translation.
49 Bernard Lazare, *Antisemitism: Its History and Its Causes* (Lincoln: University of Nebraska Press, Bison Books, 1995), 64. This is a common version of Jewish self-hatred: see Sander Gilman, *Jewish Self-Hatred: Anti-Semitism and the Hidden Language of the Jews* (Baltimore: Johns Hopkins University Press, 1986).
50 See Wilson, *Bernard Lazare*, 222–52. Lazare was memorialized by Péguy in *Par ce demi-clair matin* (Paris: Gallimard, 1952).
51 Lazare, "Juifs et Israélites," 177. Note the connection between this way of thinking and Jean-François Lyotard's writings on "the jews," *Heidegger et "les juifs"* (Paris: Editions Galilée, 1988).
52 Lazare, *Antisemitism*, 175. Translation adjusted.
53 Marrus, *The Politics of Assimilation*, 18–20.
54 Tzvetan Todorov, *Nous et les autres: la réflexion française sur la diversité humaine* (Paris: Editions du Seuil, La Couleur des idées, 1989), 179.
55 See Hippolyte Taine, *Histoire de la littérature anglaise* (Paris: 1864), and Ernest Renan, *De l'origine du langage*, in *Oeuvres complètes*, vol. VIII (Paris: Calmann-Lévy, 1947–61).
56 See the change from Renan, *Histoire générale et Système comparé des langues sémitiques* (1855) (*Oeuvres complètes*, vol. VIII) to "Le Judaïsme comme race et comme religion" (*Oeuvres complètes*, vol. I, originally published 1883).
57 This is why some critics call the distinction between race and culture false. For example, see Walter Benn Michaels, "Race into Culture: A Critical Genealogy of Cultural Identity," *Critical Inquiry* 18 (Summer, 1992): 683.
58 Lazare, *Le Fumier de Job*, 25. My translation.
59 Quoted in Wilson, *Bernard Lazare*, 144. My translation.
60 Ibid., 38.
61 Bernard Lazare, "Le Nationalisme juif," in *Le Fumier de Job*, 108. My translation.
62 Weber also links the position of the prophet to the success of the pariah community in exile. See *Ancient Judaism*, 364.
63 Arendt, *The Human Condition*, 41, and Bonnie Honig's "Toward an Agonistic Feminism: Hannah Arendt and the Politics of Identity," in Honig, ed., *Feminist Interpretations*.
64 For an alternative reading of Arendt, see Benhabib, "The Pariah and Her Shadow."
65 Emmanuel Levinas, "Judaism and the Present," in Sean Hand, trans., *Difficult Freedom: Essays on Judaism* (Baltimore: Johns Hopkins University Press, 1990), 213.
66 Ibid., 293.

67 Georg Simmel, "The Stranger," in *The Sociology of Georg Simmel*, trans. Kurt Wolff (New York: The Free Press, Macmillan Publishing Co., Inc., 1950), 402.
68 See Wilson, *Bernard Lazare*, 222–52.
69 Wilson, *Bernard Lazare*, 229–30.
70 Lazare, *Le Fumier de Job*, 85. My translation.
71 This text was published posthumously in two different versions and is considered incomplete.
72 Gilles Deleuze and Felix Guattari, *Kafka: Toward a Minor Literature*, trans. Dana Polan (Minneapolis: University of Minnesota Press, Theory and History of Literature, 30, 1986), 18.
73 Lazare, *Le Fumier de Job*, 19. My translation.
74 Deleuze and Guattari, *Kafka*, 18.
75 Ibid., 17.
76 Ibid.
77 Lazare, *Le Fumier de Job*, 89. My translation.
78 Edmund Wilson, *Axel's Castle: A Study in the Imaginative Literature of 1870–1930* (New York: W. W. Norton, 1984).
79 *A la recherche*'s precursor *Jean Santeuil* (Paris: Editions Gallimard, 1952) makes its connection with Jewish issues and the Dreyfus Affair much more obvious. I find the treatment of Jewish issues in *A la recherche* far more subtle.
80 See Gilles Deleuze's classic analysis in *Marcel Proust et les signes* (Paris: Presses Universitaires de France, 1964).
81 I take issue with Arendt's reductive reading of Proust as *parvenu: The Origins of Totalitarianism*, 80.
82 See Levinas, "Judaism and the Present."
83 See Genette's classic discussion of prolepse and analepse in this connection: Gérard Genette, *Figures III* (Paris: Editions du Seuil), 1972).
84 See Antoine Compagnon, *Proust Between Two Centuries*, trans. Richard E. Goodkin (New York: Columbia University Press, 1992).
85 See Genette, *Figures III*; Hans-Robert Jauss, *Zeit und Erinnerung in Marcel Prousts A la recherche du temps perdu* (Heidelberg: Carl Winter, 1970).
86 III: 996. Translation modified.
87 See for example Kristeva, *Time and Sense*, 154
88 Marrus, *The Politics of Assimilation*, 25; Morris Kaplan, "Refiguring the Jewish Question: Arendt, Proust and the Politics of Sexuality," in Honig, ed., *Feminist Interpretations*.
89 This is an inversion of Sander Gilman's contention that "the Other's pathology is revealed in anatomy". "Black Bodies, White Bodies: Toward an Iconography of Female Sexuality in Late Ninteenth-Century Art, Medicine, and Literature," in H. L. Gates, Jr., *Race, Writing and Difference* (Chicago: University of Chicago Press, 1985), 256.
90 A notable exception is the dinner scene at Bloch's house (II: 413–25).
91 Mieke Bal, *The Mottled Screen: Reading Proust Visually*, trans. Anna-Louise Milne (Stanford: Stanford University Press, 1997), 222.

92 For a more charitable reading, see Angela Moorjani, *The Aesthetics of Loss and Lessness* (New York: St. Martin's Press, 1992), 169.

93 Compagnon, *Proust Between Two Centuries*, 149–50.

94 Moorjani, personal communication.

95 I use the term tragic here despite the fact that Lucien Goldmann considers Racine's last plays to be opposed to the Jansenist tragedy of his earlier work: *Le Dieu caché* (Paris: Gallimard, 1959), 440.

96 See also Kristeva, *Time and Sense*, 150–1, and Compagnon, *Proust Between Two Centuries*, 52–92.

97 See Georges Poulet, *Les Métamorphoses du cercle* (Paris: Plon, 1961), for the classic discussion of the *cercle*.

98 For in-depth discussion of the figure of the prophet, including his relation to poetic inspiration, see Abraham Joshua Heschel, *The Prophets* (New York: Harper and Row, 1963). I here rely on the aspects of prophetic vision, transcendence, and connection to two worlds at once rather than the role of divine inspiration.

99 This is what Kristeva refers to as a Jewish "stench" (*Time and Sense*, 156).

100 Sander Gilman, *The Jew's Body* (New York: Routledge, 1991), 39.

101 Sander Gilman, "Sexology, Psychoanalysis, and Degeneration: From a Theory of Race to a Race for Theory," in *Degeneration* (New York: Columbia University Press, 1985), 87.

102 Albert Sonnenfeld, "Marcel Proust: Antisemite?" in Mary Ann Caws and Eugène Nicole, eds., *Reading Proust Now* (New York: Peter Lang, 1990), 249.

103 Ibid., 246.

104 See, also, Margaret Mein, *Thèmes proustiens* (Paris: Editions A. G. Nizet, 1979), 144.

105 Marcel Proust, *Proust Correspondance II, 1896–1901*, ed. Philip Kolb (Paris: Librarie Plon, 1976), no. 20, May 19, 1896? 66. My translation.

106 Ibid., no. 175, November 26 or 27 1898, 268. My translation.

107 *Correspondance de Marcel Proust*, vol. v: *1905*, ed. Philip Kolb (Paris: Librairie Plan, 1979), 180–1.

108 Although Mme. Arman de Caillavet converted when she married, her Jewishness remained a factor in the constitution of her salon, see Jean-Jacques Brousson, *Les Vêpres de l'Avenue Hoche* (Paris: Editions du Cadran, 1932), 24.

109 It was at Mme. Straus's in 1892 that Proust founded *Le Banquet*, his first "professional" review.

110 Benhabib, "The Pariah and Her Shadow," 97.

111 The list of those who could be found at Mme. Arman de Caillavet's before the Affair includes Barrès, Maurras, Lemaître, and Loti as well as Zola, Renan, and Mirabeau: George Andrieux, ed., *Livres–Manuscrits–Dessins provenant des bibliothèques de Madame Arman de Caillavet et de Madame Gaston de Caillavet, Manuscrits et Lettres d'Anatole France* (Paris, 1932).

112 Wolitz, *The Proustian Community*, 153.

113 Robert Dreyfus, "Madame Straus et Marcel Proust," *Revue de Paris* 5. 43

(1936): 816.
114 William Sansom, *Proust and his World* (London: Thames and Hudson, 1973), 14.
115 Levinas, "Judaism and the Present," 213.
116 Edmund Wilson even goes so far as to link the narrator to this kind of prophetic stance: *Axel's Castle*, 144.
117 Swann also utters what the narrator refers to as "a prophetic warning" (II: 606).
118 Seth Wolitz, *The Proustian Community* (New York: New York University Press, 1971).
119 Goldmann, *Le Dieu caché*, 180.
120 Ibid., 445.
121 See Kristeva, "Questions of Identity," 141–63; and Georges Bataille, *Literature and Evil* (London: Calder Boyars Ltd.), 1973.
122 Samuel Beckett, *Proust*, in *The Collected Works of Samuel Beckett* (New York: Grove, 1970), 49.
123 The name "Morel" alludes to Dr. Benedict Morel, author of the *Traité des dégénérescences physiques, intellectuelles et morales de l'espèce humaine et des causes qui produisent ces variétés maladives* (Paris: J. B. Baillière, 1857).
124 Kristeva, "Questions of Identity," 95.
125 Barrès always considered the Jews to be *déracinés*. See Paula Hyman, *From Dreyfus to Vichy* (New York: Columbia University Press, 1979), 15.
126 Emmanuel Levinas, "L'Autre dans Proust," *Deucalion* 2 (1947): 122–3. My translation.

4 VIRGINIA WOOLF

1 Virginia Woolf, *Orlando* (New York: Harcourt, 1928, 1956); Letter to Ethel Smyth, in *The Letters of Virginia Woolf*, vol. IV, ed. Nigel Nicolson and Joanne Trautman (New York: Harcourt, 1978); *The Waves* (New York: Harcourt, 1931); George Bataille, "The Sorcerer's Apprentice," in Allan Stoekl, ed. and trans., *Visions of Excess: Selected Writings, 1927–1939* (Minneapolis: University of Minnesota Press, Theory and History of Literature, 14, 1985).
2 Oswald Mosley, "Crisis," in *Action* 1.1 (1931): 1.
3 Ibid.
4 Virginia Woolf, *Three Guineas* (New York: Harcourt, 1938,) 109. Further references will be cited in the text.
5 See, among many others, Natania Rosenfeld, *Outsiders Together: Virginia and Leonard Woolf* (Princeton: Princeton University Press, 2000); Karen Levenback, *Virginia Woolf and the Great War* (Syracuse: Syracuse University Press, 1999); Michael Tratner, *Modernism and Mass Politics: Joyce, Woolf, Eliot, Yeats* (Stanford: Stanford University Press 1995); James F. English, *Comic Transactions: Literature, Humor, and the Politics of Community in Twentieth-Century Britain* (Ithaca: Cornell University Press, 1994); Melba Cuddy-Keane,

"The Politics of Comic Modes in Virginia Woolf's *Between the Acts*," (*PMLA* 105 (March, 1990): 273–85; the collection of essays edited by Mark Hussey, *Virgina Woolf and War: Fiction, Reality, and Myth* (Syracuse: Syracuse University Press, Syracuse Studies on Peace and Conflict Resolution, 1991); Jane Marcus's several collections of feminist essays, and her article "Britannia Rules *The Waves*," in Karen R. Lawrence, ed., *Decolonizing Tradition: New Views of Twentieth-Century "British" Literary Canons* (Urbana: University of Illinois Press, 1992); the work of Gillian Beer, most recently in *Virginia Woolf: The Common Ground* (Ann Arbor: University of Michigan Press, 1997); as well as Alex Zwerdling's now classic *Virginia Woolf and the Real World* (Berkeley: University of California Press, 1986).

6 Leonard Woolf, *Downhill All the Way: An Autobiography of the Years 1919–1939* (New York: Harcourt, 1967), 27.

7 I thus disagree with Michèle Barrett and others who claim that she turned to a "new type of fiction and a new political identity" though I agree that as the decade progresses "her feminism became more pronounced and overt, her concern with the rise of fascism more and more profound, and her conviction that women had a particular role to play in combating what she saw as a masculine tendency towards militarism more readily argued": Barrett, *Imagination in Theory: Culture, Writing, Words, and Things* (New York: New York University Press, 1999), 48.

8 "Other Books: Virginia Woolf," *Action* 1.1 (October 8, 1931): 6.

9 Mosley, "Crisis," 1.

10 Virginia Woolf, "Introductory Letter," Margaret Llewelyn Davies, ed., *Life As We Have Known It* (New York: Norton, 1975), xvii–xix.

11 Leonard Woolf makes a similar point in his 1913 article about the WCG, quoted in Sybil Oldfield, "Margaret Llewelyn Davies and Leonard Woolf," in Wayne Chapman and Janet Manson, eds., *Women in the Milieu of Leonard and Virginia Woolf: Peace, Politics and Education* (New York: Pace University Press, 1998), 6.

12 For a different reading see Jane Lillienfeld, "'The Gift of the China Inkpot': Violet Dickinson, Virginia Woolf, Elizabeth Gaskell, Charlotte Brontë, and the Love of Women in Writing," in Eileen Barrett and Patricia Cramer, eds., *Virginia Woolf: Lesbian Readings* (New York: New York University Press, 1997).

13 "Introductory Letter," xx–xxi.

14 Ibid., xxviii.

15 See Laura Doyle, *Bordering on the Body* (New York: Oxford University Press, 1994), and Gillian Beer, "The Body of the People: *Mrs. Dalloway* to *The Waves*," in Sue Roe, ed., *Women Reading Women's Writing* (New York: St. Martin's, 1987).

16 "Introductory Letter," xxviii.

17 Virginia Woolf, *The Diary of Virginia Woolf*, vol. II: *1920–24*, ed. Anne Olivier Bell, assisted by Andrew McNeillie (New York: Harcourt Brace Jovanovich, 1977), 20. Woolf was nevertheless at this time a member of the

Fabian Society.

18 A sizeable body of work on *Between the* Acts exists, most notably Brenda Silver's "Virginia Woolf and the Concept of Community: The Elizabethan Playhouse," *Woman's Studies* 4 (1977): 291–8; English, *Comic Transactions*; Cuddy-Keane, "Comic Modes"; Rachel Blau DuPlessis, *Writing Beyond the Ending* (Bloomington: Indiana University Press, 1985). On the presence of this dynamic in Woolf's earlier writing, see Gillian Beer's "The Body of the People," as well as her "*The Waves*: 'The Life of Anybody,'" both reprinted in *Virginia Woolf: The Common Ground.*

19 Jane Goldman connects *The Waves* and Woolf's "Introductory Letter": *The Feminist Aesthetics of Virginia Woolf: Modernism, Post-Impressionism and the Politics of the Visual* (Cambridge: Cambridge University Press, 1998), 186.

20 Gillian Beer's "The Body of the People" comes closest to connecting these aspects throughout Woolf's career. Mark Hussey, in "'"I" Rejected; "We" Substituted': Self and Society in *Between the Acts*," in Bege K. Bowers and Barbara Brothers, eds., *Reading and Writing Women's Lives: A Study of the Novel of Manners* (Ann Arbor: UMI Research Press, 1990), highlights communal issues in Woolf.

21 Jean-Luc Nancy. *The Inoperative Community*, ed. Peter Connor (Minneapolis: University of Minnesota Press, Theory and History of Literature, 76, 1956).

22 *Diary* II: 313–14.

23 *Diary* II: 314.

24 From "co-appear" or the French "com-paraît."

25 *Collected Essays*, ed. Leonard Woolf (London: The Hogarth Press, 1967), IV: 198. Thanks to Ellen Tremper, *Who Lived at Alfoxten?: Virginia Woolf and English Romanticism* (Lewisburg: Bucknell University Press, 1998), 196, for pointing out this connection.

26 Nancy, *Inoperative Community*, xxxix–xl.

27 Leonard Woolf was working on community in the late twenties, see *After the Deluge: A Study in Communal Psychology* (London: The Hogarth Press), 1931.

28 *The Essays of Virginia Woolf*, vol. II, ed. Andrew McNeillie (New York: Harcourt, 1987), 50.

29 Susan Squier, *Virginia Woolf and London: The Sexual Politics of the City* (Chapel Hill: University of North Carolina Press, 1985), 11.

30 Gillian Beer, "The Body of the People," 91–2. For the role of war in *Mrs. Dalloway* see Levenback, *Woolf and the Great War*, ch. 2.

31 Nancy, *Inoperative Community*, 15.

32 They were "wholly lacking in the nostalgia for rural or simpler forms of community": Stanley Pierson, *British Socialists: The Journey from Fantasy to Politics* (Cambridge, Mass: Harvard University Press, 1979), 115.

33 Peter Beiharz, *Labour's Utopias: Bolshevism, Fabianism, Social Democracy* (New York: Routledge, 1992), 54.

34 Sidney Webb, "Socialism: True and False," Fabian Tract no. 51, in *Fabian Tracts*, nos. 1–188, *1884–1919* (London: Fabian Society, n.d.), 4.

35 Sidney Webb, "The Difficulties of Individualism," Fabian Tract 69, in *Fabian Tracts*, 5.
36 Virginia Woolf, *The Diary of Virginia Woolf*, vol. IV, ed. Anne Olivier Bell, assisted by Andrew McNeillie (New York: Harcourt, 1982), 345.
37 "Introductory Letter", xxviii.
38 "Basis of the Fabian Society," in *Fabian Tracts*, 19.
39 On the limitations of Fabian socialism see Peter Beiharz, Stanley Pierson, and Peter Gurney, *Co-operative Culture and the Politics of Consumption in England, 1870–1930* (New York: Manchester University Press, 1996).
40 Quoted by Frederic Spotts in *Letters of Leonard Woolf*, ed. Spotts (San Diego: Harcourt Brace Jovanovich, 1989), 377.
41 L. Woolf, *Downhill*, 221.
42 As Beiharz claims, "Co-operation was the natural value of English socialism from Robert Owen onwards": *Labour's Utopias*, 55. For the history of the Co-operative Movement see, Beatrice (Potter) Webb, *The Co-operative Movement in Great Britain* (n.p., 1891); Leonard Woolf, *Co-operation and the Future of Industry* (London: G. Allen and Unwin, 1918), *Socialism and Co-operation* (London: Leonard Parsons, 1921), and L. Woolf, ed., *Fabian Essays on Co-operation* (London: Fabian Society, 1923); and, more recently, Gurney, *Co-operative Culture.*
43 *The Rise of the Labour Party* ([London?]: The Labour Party, Labour Discussion Series, 1, 1946), 6.
44 Naomi Black, "Virginia Woolf and the Women's Movement," in Jane Marcus, ed., *Virginia Woolf: A Feminist Slant* (Lincoln: University of Nebraska Press, 1983), 185.
45 A 1932 official pamphlet lists "International Brotherhood [*sic*] and Opposition to Militarism" as one of the main reforms advocated by the Guild: *The Women's Co-operative Guild: Notes on its History, Organisation, and Work*. (Manchester: The Co-operative Wholesale Society's Printing Works[?], 1932), 14. See also Black, "Woolf and the Women's Movement," 187.
46 Sybil Oldfield points to the difficult consequences of the democratic character of the WCG, which voted against Margaret Llewelyn Davies's resolution for a more temperate peace treaty in 1918: Oldfield, "Davies and Leonard Woolf," 19.
47 *Women's Co-operative Guild*, 5.
48 Gurney, *Co-operative Culture*, 232.
49 *Three Guineas*, 110.
50 See L. Woolf, *Downhill.*
51 Editorial, *Co-operative News* (August 30, 1913), quoted in Gurney, *Co-operative Culture*, 88.
52 Gurney, *Co-operative Culture*, 93.
53 *Co-operative News* (July 6, 1929): 9.
54 As it had in 1918. Gurney, *Co-operative Culture*, 105.
55 *Co-operative News* (July 6, 1929): 9.
56 Ibid., 16.

57 *Diary of Virginia Woolf*, vol. III: *1925–1930*, ed. Anne Olivier Bell (New York: Harcourt, Brace, Jovanovich, 1980), 77–8, 85; Kate Flint, "Virginia Woolf and the General Strike," *Essays in Criticism* 31.4 (October 1986), 322–3.

58 For example, Labour leader C. R. Atlee states that the "Trade Union movement is predominantly representative of men's interests … while the Co-operative movement is an expression of the interests of the woman in the home": *The Labour Party in Perspective – and Twelve Years Later* (London: Gollancz, 1949), 70.

59 *Women's Co-operative Guild*, 12.

60 Llewellyn Davies, ed., *Life As We Have Known It*, ix.

61 See, for example, IV: 333.

62 See Beer, "Body of the People"; Hussey, "'I' Rejected"; M. Keith Brooker, "Tradition, Authority and Subjectivity: Narrative Constitution of the Self in *The Waves*," *LIT* 3 (1991): 33–55.

63 Rachel Blau DuPlessis, *Writing Beyond the Ending*, 163. Surprisingly, DuPlessis barely mentions *The Waves*.

64 Bette London, *The Appropriated Voice: Narrative Authority in Conrad, Forster, and Woolf* (Ann Arbor: University of Michigan Press, 1990), 132–3.

65 Woolf, *Orlando*, 294. Further references will be cited in the text.

66 Raymond Williams's *The Country and the City* (New York: Oxford University Press, 1973), is still the best examination of this kind of nostalgia.

67 Virginia Woolf, "Character in Fiction," in *The Essays of Virginia Woolf*, vol. III: *1919–1924*, ed. Andrew McNeillie (New York: Harcourt Brace Javanovich, 1985), 425. Further references will be cited in the text.

68 Tzvetan Todorov, *The Fantastic: A Structural Approach to a Literary Genre*, trans. Richard Howard (Ithaca: Cornell University Press, 1975), 116.

69 Beer, *Virginia Woolf: The Common Ground*, 64.

70 See Joan Stambaugh, *The Finitude of Being* (Albany: State University of New York Press, 1992); Jacques Taminiaux, *Dialectic and Difference: Finitude in Modern Thought* (Atlantic Highlands, N.J.: Humanities Press, 1985). Nancy defines finitude as "infinite lack of infinite identity" (*Inoperative Community*, xxxviii).

71 Lytton Strachey, *Eminent Victorians* (New York: Harcourt Brace Jovanovich, 1918), vii.

72 Harold Nicolson, *The Development of English Biography* (New York: Harcourt, 1928), 13.

73 Virginia Woolf, "Modern Fiction," in *The Common Reader: First Series* (New York: Harcourt, Brace and World, 1925), 156.

74 Alice Kaplan, *Reproductions of Banality* (Minneapolis: University of Minnesota Press, Theory and History of Literature, 36, 1986), 13.

75 Walter Benjamin, "The Work of Art in the Age of Mechanical Reproduction," in *Illuminations*, trans. Harry Zorn (New York: Schocken, 1969), 241.

76 Kaplan, *Reproductions*, 32.

77 Russell A. Berman, "Modernism, Fascism, and the Institution of Litera-

ture," in Monique Chefdor, Ricardo Quinones, and Albert Wachhel, eds., *Modernism: Challenges and Perspectives* (Urbana: University of Illinois Press, 1986), 95.

78 *The Waves*, 16; further references will be cited in the text.

79 See, most recently, Hermione Lee, *Virginia Woolf* (New York: Knopf, 1998), 569.

80 See Russell Berman, "The Aestheticization of Politics: Walter Benjamin on Fascism and the Avant-Garde," *Stanford Italian Review* 8:2–3 (1990): 35–52.

81 Kaplan, *Reproductions*, 32.

82 Marcus, "Britannia," 145.

83 Klaus Theweleit, *Male Fantasies*, vol. 1, trans. Stephen Conway (Minneapolis: University of Minnesota Press, Theory and History of Literature, 22, 1987), 230.

84 On German fascism see George Mosse, *Nationalism and Sexuality: Middleclass Morality and Sexual Norms in Modern Europe* (Madison: University of Wisconsin Press, 1985), especially chapters 5 and 8.

85 See Richard Thurlow, *Fascism in Britain* (London: Basil Blackwell, 1987), 92–118.

86 Zeev Sternhell, "Fascist Ideology," in Walter Laqueur, ed., *Fascism: A Reader's Guide* (Berkeley: University of California Press, 1976), 320.

87 Sternhell makes this argument about France and only by passing allusion about England, *Neither Right Nor Left: Fascist Ideology in France*, trans. David Meisel (Princeton: Princeton University Press, 1986).

88 By December 1930 there were over $2\frac{1}{2}$ million unemployed: Robert Benewick, *The Fascist Movement in Britain* rev. 1st. edn. (London: Allen Lane, The Penguin Press, 1972), 60.

89 See D. S. Lewis, *Illusions of Grandeur: Mosley Fascism and British Society, 1931–81* (Manchester: Manchester University Press , 1987), 13.

90 For example, John Strachey and Allan Young. *Action* sold 160,000 copies of its initial issue: Benewick, *The Fascist Movement*, 76.

91 Oswald Mosley, *The Greater Britain* (London: British Union of Fascists, 1932, 1934), 20.

92 Ibid., 34.

93 *Action* 1.2 (October 15, 1931): 3.

94 Kaplan, *Reproductions*, 23.

95 *Action* 1.2, 3.

96 *Action* 1.1 (October 8, 1931): 29.

97 *Letters*, IV: 333; Kathy J. Phillips, *Virginia Woolf Against Empire* (Knoxville: University of Tennessee Press, 1994).

98 Marcus, "Britannia."

99 R. K. Webb, *Modern England*, 2nd edn. (New York: Harper, 1980), 528. Unemployment went from 2.1% in 1919 to 21.3% in 1931 and still higher in 1932: A. H. Halsey, ed., *British Social Trends Since 1900*, 2nd edn. (London: Macmillan, 1988), 174. See also Philip Williamson, *National Crisis and*

National Government: British Politics, the Economy and Empire, 1926–1932 (New York: Cambridge University Press, 1992), especially ch. 2, "Economic and Imperial Troubles," 58–91.

100 *Diary.* IV: 47.
101 Beer, "Body," 110.
102 Ibid.
103 Ibid., 111.
104 Labour Party, *Labour and the Nation* (London?: Transport House, 1928).
105 *Action* 1.2, 3.
106 *Action* 1.9 (December 3, 1931): 1.
107 Theweleit, *Male Fantasies,* I: 195–6.
108 See also Mosse, *Nationalism and Sociality,* 160.
109 Melba Cuddy-Keane, "The Politics of Comic Modes in Virginia Woolf's *Between the Acts,*" 273. I am greatly indebted to this article.
110 See ch. 1.
111 Garrett Stewart, "Catching the Stylistic D/Rift: Sound Defects in Woolf's *The Waves, ELH* 54.2 (Summer, 1987): 424. I am greatly indebted to this article.
112 Ibid., 428.
113 See also Goldman, *Feminist Aesthetics,* 186–206.
114 *Action* 1.9, 1.
115 Ibid.
116 Ibid.
117 *Harold Nicolson Diaries and Letters,* vol. I: *1930–39,* ed. Nigel Nicolson (New York: Athenaeum, 1966), 107. The Woolfs published Mussolini in 1933: J. Howard Woolmer, *A Checklist of the Hogarth Press, 1917–1946* (Revere, Pa.: Woolmer/Brotherson Ltd., 1986), 114.
118 Ibid., 97.
119 Ibid., 91.
120 *Action* 1.1, 10.
121 Nicholas Mosley, *The Rules of the Game: Sir Oswald and Lady Cynthia Mosley, 1896–1933* (London: Secker and Warburg, 1982), 160.
122 Ibid., 185.
123 Nicolson, *Diaries and Letters,* 68.
124 Ibid., 205. See also Mosley, *The Rules of the Game.*

5 GERTRUDE STEIN

1 Stein, *The Geographical History of America, Or, The Relation of Human Nature to the Human Mind* (Baltimore: Johns Hopkins University Press, 1995), further references will be cited in the text; Stein, *Four in America* (Freeport, N.Y.: Books for Libraries Press, 1969), further references will be cited in the text; Williams, *Imaginations* (New York: New Directions Books, 1970).
2 Linda Wagner-Martin, *"Favored Strangers": Gertrude Stein and Her Family* (New Brunswick, N.J.: Rutgers University Press, 1995), 62.

3 Ibid., 63.
4 Lisa Ruddick, *Reading Gertrude Stein: Body, Text, Gnosis* (Ithaca: Cornell University Press, 1990), 18. See also Ellen Berry, *Curved Thought and Textual Wandering: Gertrude Stein's Postmodernism* (Ann Arbor: University of Michigan Press, 1992).
5 On Stein's wanderings in Baltimore, see Carla L. Peterson, "The Remaking of Americans: Gertrude Stein's 'Melanctha,' and African-American Musical Traditions," in Henry B. Wonham, ed., *Criticism and the Color Line: Desegregating American Literary Studies* (New Brunswick, N.J.: Rutgers University Press, 1996). See, more generally, Sara Blair, "Cultural Geography and the Place of the Literary," *American Literary History* 10.3 (Fall, 1998): 544–67.
6 William Davis, "The Essential in Geography," 1903 address to American Association for the Advancement of Science, *American Geographical Society of New York Bulletin* 36.8 (1904): 470.
7 See Ellen Churchill Semple, *Influences of Geographic Environment* (New York: Henry Holt, 1911).
8 Anne Buttimer, "Integration in Geography: Hydra or Chimera" in Leonard Guelke, ed., *Department of Waterloo Lectures in Geography*, vol. ii: *Geography and Humanistic Knowledge* (Waterloo, Ontario[?]: University of Waterloo Dept. of Geography Publication Series, 25, 1986), 45–67, and Peter Nash, "The Making of a Humanist Geographer: A Circuitous Journey," in Guelke, *Geography*, 4.
9 On this distinction see Wilbur Zelinsky, *Nation into State: The Shifting Symbolic Foundations of American Nationalism* (Chapel Hill: University of North Carolina Press, 1988), 4.
10 Rosi Braidotti, *Nomadic Subjects: Embodiment and Sexual Difference in Contemporary Feminist Theory* (New York: Columbia University Press, 1994).
11 Rosi Braidotti, "Comment on Felski's 'The Doxa of Difference': Working Through Sexual Difference," *Signs* 23.1 (1997), 39.
12 Homi Bhabha, "Unpacking My Library . . . Again," in Iain Chambers and Lidia Curti, eds., *The Post-Colonial Question: Common Skies, Divided Horizons* (New York: Routledge, 1996), 200.
13 J. Scott Keltie and O. J. R. Howarth, *History of Geography* (New York: G. P. Putnam, 1913), 183.
14 Ibid.
15 William Davis, "The Essential in Geography," *American Geographical Society of New York. Bulletin* 36.8 (1904), 470.
16 Marion I. Newbigin, *Modern Geography* (London: Williams and Norgate, [1911?]), 13.
17 Five vols., published between 1845 and 1862. See, also, Richard Hartshorne, *Perspective on the Nature of Geography* (Chicago: RandMcNally, for the American Society of Geographers, 1959), 48.
18 Robert H. Fuson, *A Geography of Geography: Origins and Development of the Discipline* (Dubuque, Iowa: Wm. C. Brown Company, 1969), 96.
19 Newbigin, *Modern Geography*, 11.

20 W. B. Morgan and R. P. Moss, "Geography and Ecology: The Concept of the Community and its Relation to Environment," in Fred E. Dohrs and Lawrence M. Sommers, eds., *Cultural Geography: Selected Readings* (New York: Thomas Y. Crowell, 1967), 61.

21 Martin Ira Glassner, *Political Geography*, 2nd. edn. (New York: John Wiley, 1996), 332–3.

22 Ratzel never uses the term "geopolitics" which is distinct from the discipline of political geography – see George Kiss, "Political Geography Into Geopolitics: Recent Trends in Germany," *Geographical Review* 32.4 (1942): 632–45.

23 His influence in France is less pronounced.

24 Friedrich Ratzel, *Politische Geographie* (Munich: R. Oldenbourg, 1897); *Anthropogeographie*, 2 vols. (Stuttgart: J. Englehorn, 1899).

25 Friedrich Ratzel, *The History of Mankind*, 3 vols., trans. A. J. Butler (London: Macmillan, 1896).

26 Ellen Churchill Semple, *Influences of Geographic Environment: On the Basis of Ratzel's System of Anthro-Geography* (1911; reprt. New York: Russell and Sage, 1968), 18.

27 Matti Bunzl, "Franz Boas and the Humboldtian Tradition: From *Volksgeist* and *Nationalcharakter* to an Anthropological Concept of Culture," in George W. Stocking, Jr., ed., Volksgeist *as Method and Ethic: Essays on Boasian Ethnography and the German Anthropological Tradition* (Madison: University of Wisconsin Press, History of Anthropology, 8, 1996,), 43. Boas began his career as a geographer.

28 Harriet Wanklyn, *Friedrich Ratzel: A Biographical Memoir* (Cambridge: Cambridge University Press, 1961), 23.

29 George Kiss, "Political Geography into Geopolitics," 635.

30 See, for example, Isaiah Bowman, "Geography vs. Geopolitics," *Geographical Review* 32.4 (1942): 646–58, and, more recently, Gearóid Tuathail, "Thinking Critically about Geopolitics," in Gearóid Ó Tuathail, Simon Dalby, and Paul Routledge, eds., *The Geopolitics Reader* (New York: Routledge, 1998), 4–5.

31 Wanklyn, *Ratzel*, 23.

32 Frederick Jackson Turner, "The Significance of the Frontier in American History," in *The Frontier in American History* (Tucson: University of Arizona Press), 1986.

33 Ibid., 37.

34 She was Ratzel's only woman student and was forced to listen to his lectures from behind a partially closed door in an adjacent room (Wanklyn, *Ratzel*, 31). The parallels between Semple's experience with Ratzel and Stein's experience as a "special student" of William James at the Harvard Annex for women would make an interesting study.

35 W. W. Atwood, quoted in *Dictionary of American Biography* (New York: Scribner, 1997), 583.

36 Semple, *Influences*, vii.

37 These were in any case more present in the earlier *Völkerkunde* than in the *Anthropogeographie*.
38 Semple, *Influences*, vii.
39 Ibid., 1.
40 This she attributes to Spencer's influence: ibid., vi.
41 Ibid., vii.
42 Ibid., 2.
43 For a similar reading see Laura Doyle, "The Flat, the Round, and Gertrude Stein: Race and the Shape of Modern(ist) History," *Modernism/Modernity* 7.2 (April, 2000): 249–71.
44 *Influences*, 112.
45 DeKoven, *Rich and Strange* (Princeton: Princeton University Press, 1991), 71. See also Doyle, "The Flat, the Round."
46 Gertrude Stein, *Three Lives* (New York: Random House, 1909), 86. Cited hereafter in the text.
47 See Doyle, "The Flat, the Round," 263–64.
48 DeKoven, *Rich and Strange*, 72. See also Michael North, *The Dialect of Modernism: Race, Language, and Twentieth-Century Literature* (New York: Oxford University Press, 1994), and Jaime Hovey, "Sapphic Primitivism in Gertrude Stein's *QED*," *MFS* 42.3 (Fall, 1996), 548.
49 Peterson, "The Remaking of Americans," 151.
50 Stein, *The Making of Americans: Being the History of a Family's Progress* (New York: Something Else Press, 1966), 63. Further references will be cited in the text.
51 In this way Stein, like James, serves to complicate Walter Benn Michaels's description of the changing notions of Americanization in the first decades of the twentieth century. See *Our America* (Durham: Duke University Press, 1995), in particular 136–7.
52 On Stein and Weiniger, see Leon Katz, "The First Making of the Making of Americans" (Ph.D. diss., Columbia University, 1963); Jayne Walker, *The Making of a Modernist: Gertrude Stein from Three Lives to Tender Buttons* (Amherst: University of Massachusetts Press, 1984); Priscilla Wald, *Constituting Americans: Cultural Anxiety and Narrative Form* (Durham: Duke University Press, 1995), 274–5; Doyle, "The Flat, the Round."
53 Stein makes clear in "The Gradual Making..." that this concept of Bottom natures predates the writing of *The Making of Americans*, going as far back as her Radcliffe days: *Writings 1932–1946* (New York: Library of America, 1998), 271.
54 These characters also evoke May Bookstaver and her lover Mabel Haynes, Stein's rival for May's affections.
55 See Ruddick, *Reading Gertrude Stein*, 68.
56 See Sandra Gilbert and Susan Gubar, *No Man's Land: The Place of the Woman Writer in the Twentieth Century*, vol. II (New Haven: Yale University Press, 1988–94), 240.
57 I am using this term as I understand Longinus to have meant it. See "On

the Sublime," trans. W. R. Roberts, in Hazard Adams, ed., *Critical Theory Since Plato* (New York: Harcourt Brace Jovanovich, Inc., 1971), 84–5.

58 On the other hand Susan Stanford Friedman's *Mappings* hardly mentions Stein. Nonethless I think Stein would fit very well into Friedman's conception of feminism as a "geopolitics of identity within differing communal spaces": *Mappings: Feminism and the Cultural Geographies of Encounter* (Princeton: Princeton University Press, 1998), 3.

59 "Composition as Explanation," in Stein, *Writings, 1903–1932* (New York: Library of America, 1998).

60 Quoted in Wagner-Martin, *"Favored Strangers"*, 216.

61 Stein, *Four in America*, 31.

62 Introduction to proposed American edition of Marshal Pétain, *Paroles aux Français, Messages et écrits, 1934–1941.* See Wagner-Martin, *"Favored Strangers"*, 247.

63 Wagner-Martin, *"Favored Strangers"*, 247.

64 See *Doctor Faustus Lights the Lights*, in *Writings, 1932–1946*.

65 Judy Grahn, "Exiled to the Center of the World," in Grahn, ed., *Really Reading Gertrude Stein* (Freedom, Calif.: The Crossing Press, 1989), 141.

66 John Whittier-Ferguson, "Stein in Time: History, Manuscripts, and Memory," *Modernism/Modernity* 6.1 (1999), 119.

67 Claudia Koonz, "The Competition for a Woman's *Lebensraum*, 1928–34," in Renate Bridenthal, Atina Grossman, and Marion Kaplan, eds., *When Biology Became Destiny: Women in Weimar and Nazi Germany* (New York: Monthly Review Press, 1984), 200.

68 Ibid.

69 Gertrude Stein, *Stanzas in Meditation* (Los Angeles: Sun and Moon Press, 1994), PART V, Stanza xxxv, 179. Further references will be cited in the text.

70 Schmitz, "The Difference of her Likeness," 134. On the "collaborative" voice in Stein see "'She Meant What I Said': Lesbian Double Talk," in Gilbert and Gubar, *No Man's Land*, especially 238–57.

71 Ulla Dydo, *"Stanzas in Meditation*: The Other Autobiography," *Chicago Review* 35.2 (1985): 4–20, and Douglass Messerli, preface to *Stanzas in Meditation*.

72 Lisa Ruddick, "Stein and Cultural Criticism in the Nineties," *MFS* 42.3 (Fall, 1996), 647.

73 Ibid., 648.

74 Emmanuel Levinas, *Otherwise Than Being or Beyond Essence*, trans. Alphonso Lingis (Dordrecht: Kluwer Academic Publishers, 1991), 18.

75 See Jill Robbins, *Altered Readings: Levinas and Literature* (Chicago: University of Chicago Press, 1999). Thanks to Christopher Devenney for pointing out this connection.

76 Levinas, *Otherwise*, 48.

77 Ibid., 49.

78 Levinas, *Totality and Infinity*, trans. Alphonso Lingis (Pittsburgh: Duquesne

University Press, 1969), 194.

79 Ibid., 278.
80 Ibid., 279.
81 Ibid., 265.
82 Ibid., 264.
83 Ibid., 266.
84 Ibid., 267.
85 Luce Irigaray, quoted in Gayatri Chakravorty Spivak, "French Feminism Revisited," in Judith Butler and Joan W. Scott, eds., *Feminists Theorize the Political* (New York: Routledge, 1992), 75, and "The Fecundity of the Caress," trans. Carolyn Burke, in Richard A. Cohen, ed., *Face to Face with Levinas* (Albany: SUNY Press, 1985); the latter was reprinted in Luce Irigaray, *An Ethics of Sexual Difference* (Ithaca, New York: Cornell University Press, 1984), 185–217. See also Irigaray's "Questions to Emmanuel Levinas," trans. Margaret Whitford, in Robert Bersanconi and Simon Critchley, eds., *Rereading Levinas* (Bloomington: Indiana University Press, 1991); also reprinted in Margaret Whitford, ed., *The Irigaray Reader* (Oxford: Basil Blackwell, 1991).
86 Spivak, "French Feminism," 76.
87 Ibid., 78. For several astute recent assessments of Irigaray, see Carolyn Burke, Naomi Chor, and Margaret Whitford, eds., *Engaging with Irigaray* (New York: Columbia University Press, 1994).
88 Tina Chanter, *Ethics of Eros: Irigaray's Rewriting of the Philosophers* (New York: Routledge, 1995), 218.
89 Ibid., 218.
90 Stein, *Writings, 1932–1946*, 267.
91 Gertrude Stein, *Four Saints in Three Acts, Selected Writings of Gertrude Stein*, ed. Carl Van Vechten (New York: Vintage, 1945), 607.
92 Stein, *Doctor Faustus Lights the Lights*, 583. Further references will be cited in the text.
93 Gertrude Stein, *Ida: A Novel* (New York: Vintage Books, 1941), 7. Further references will be cited in the text.
94 Irigaray, "Fecundity," in *An Ethics of Sexual Difference*, 186.
95 Braidotti, *Nomadic Subjects*, 135
96 "Composition as Explanation," 517.
97 In this sense she also challenges Anthony Appiah's sense of "rooted cosmopolitanism" (see ch. 1).
98 Caren Kaplan, *Questions of Travel: Postmodern Discourses of Displacement* (Durham, N.C.: Duke University Press, 1996), 94
99 See *Wars I have Seen* (New York: Random House, 1945), and *Brewsie and Willie*, in Stein, *Writings, 1932–1946*.
100 Marc Robinson, ed., *Altogether Elsewhere: Writers on Exile* (Winchester, Mass.: Faber and Faber, 1994).
101 Here Beckett seems most *à propos*.

6 CONCLUSION

1 Hannah Arendt, *The Human Condition* (Chicago: University of Chicago Press, 1958).

2 For example, see Pamela Caughie, *Virginia Woolf and Post-Modernism* (Urbana: University of Illinois Press, 1991); Enda Duffy, *The Subaltern Ulysses* (Minneapolis: University of Minnesota Press, 1994); and Brian Richardson, "Remapping the Present: The Master Narrative of Modern Literary History and the Lost Forms of Twentieth-Century Fiction": *Twentieth-Century Literature* 43 (Fall, 1997), 291–309.

3 See Susan Stanford Friedman, *Mappings: Feminism and the Cultural Geographics of Encounter* (Princeton: Princeton University Press, 1998).

4 As readers of Wyndam Lewis or Drieu de la Rochelle will surely know, not all modernist fiction resists fascist authority. I make no claims that the models drawn here represent all possible versions of community in the period, but rather that the impulse to reconstruct community against simple nationalism, for example, is far more common and more powerful in high modernist fiction than is commonly supposed. For the authoritarian impulse, on both the left and the right, see Susan Rubin Suleiman, *Authoritarian Fictions: The Ideological Novel As a Literary Genre* (New York: Columbia University Press, 1983).

Index